The Puritan Origins of the American Self

The Puritan Origins of the American Self

Sacvan Bercovitch

New Haven and London   Yale University Press

For Gila and Eytan

Contents

Preface

Broadly considered, my subject is the development of a distinctive symbolic mode. In particular, I wish to demonstrate the richness of the seventeenth-century New England imagination through a study of what I take to be a central aspect of our Puritan legacy, the rhetoric of American identity. I have set the discussion in a comparative European-American context, so as to specify the unique qualities of the colonial outlook; I have emphasized certain rather technical Puritan terms, because I believe they can deepen our understanding of persistent forms of thought and expression; and I have centered my analysis on the interaction of language, myth, and society, in an effort to trace the sources of our obsessive concern with the meaning of America, the long foreground to the astonishingly comprehensive ideal of the representative American, with its proportionately comprehensive claims and anxieties.

As my scope is wide, I have chosen a narrow focus: Cotton Mather's title to his Life of John Winthrop—"Nehemias Americanus," "The American Nehemiah." I use it somewhat in the Puritan manner of "opening" a scriptural text. To unveil its full import is to reveal, I trust, the complexity, the intricacy, the coherence, and the abiding significance of the American Puritan vision. My argument follows the logic of Mather's phrase, which moves from the personal to the historical (Nehemiah to the New World) and, in doing so, links the biblical hero, the New England magistrate, and the enterprise at large in an emphatically American design. The first chapter deals with the Puritan view of the self, the second, a study in contexts and definitions, with the role of the individual in history, and the third with the idea of national election, which for the Massachusetts Bay settlers involved both personal and historical redemption. In the fourth chapter I examine the formal and conceptual implications of the approach that eventuates in Mather's *Magnalia Christi Americana*. The last chapter, which extends those implications into the nineteenth century, devolves upon Emerson as the major influence upon the American Renaissance. My intention here is neither to reinterpret the period nor to present a full-scale revaluation of Emerson (these are the subjects of a separate forthcoming study), but to outline the process by which Puritan themes, tensions, and literary strategies were assimilated into American Romanticism.

I would like to thank the American Council of Learned Societies and the Columbia University Humanities Council for grants that enabled me to complete this book, and the friends who improved it in various ways: H. M. Bercovitch, Leo Braudy, Ann Douglas, Lyndall Gordon, Peter Hawkes, Myra Jehlen, Karl Keller, James McIntosh, Richard Reinitz, Ormond Seavey, Peter Shaw, Kenneth Silverman, and Michael Wood. Materials from chapters 3, 4, and 5 appear as essays in *Early American Literature* (1974), *Canadian Review of American Studies* (1975), and the English Institute Essays for 1975.

As a rule, I have limited my notes to works directly cited, and to a minimal commentary on issues that most needed clarification. In several chapters I've allowed myself to interpret "minimal" somewhat freely—either to indicate the range of materials under consideration or to offer examples of the kind of detailed analysis American Puritan literature requires—but I have consistently (and severely) restricted myself to representative texts. An adequate list of "works consulted" would cover primary and secondary sources in literature, history, and theology since the Reformation. All references to Mather's Life of Winthrop are from the Appendix to this study.

1

Puritanism and the Self

Cotton Mather, who had something of a passion for epitome, found an especially apt title for his Life of John Winthrop. "Nehemias Americanus" pays tribute to the first governor of New England as a saint, as a model magistrate, and as the leader of a great enterprise. Nehemiah, we recall, led the Israelites back from Babylon to their promised land. As the first governor of their restored theocracy, he inspired them to take up once again the burden of their covenant. He revived their sense of destiny, ensured their protection against heathen neighbors, organized further migrations from Babylon to Judea, reformed civil and religious abuses, and directed the reconstruction of Jerusalem from a wasteland into a city on a hill. His successors ranked him with Jacob, Moses, and David. Surely, Mather could have chosen no parallel more fitting for the man who directed the settlement of New Canaan, no clearer way to indicate his hero's role in the epic venture celebrated in the *Magnalia Christi Americana*.

Mather's title is compelling in still another sense: it offers an epitome of his biographical technique. Winthrop as Nehemiah conveys the hagiographical "exemplar" of which the *Magnalia*'s readers have often complained; Winthrop as American, the magistrate in his specific time and place, indicates the kind of historical portrait that has made the *Magnalia* a source-book for the study of colonial New England. The conjunction of terms suggests Mather's eclectic method. It also suggests a far-reaching effort at synthesis. For in fact Mather's hybrid American Nehemiah conforms neither to the principles of hagiography nor to those of secular biography. He is not, like the medieval saint, a man whose divine call sets him apart from others; nor is he, like the Plutarchian hero, a man made great by worldly achievements. Moreover, Mather deliberately blurs the image of the Old Testament leader by comparing Winthrop to a wide range of exemplary figures, from the epic champion to the Reformation martyr. In effect, he transforms all of these parallels, and the biographical norms they imply, into a distinctive concept of the representative American saint.

Exemplum

The obvious connection between the terms of Mather's title lies in the hero's public role. "Nehemias" recalls Winthrop's function as magistrate; "Americanus" indicates his service to the New World state. This essentially historical view is what first strikes us about the biography. Mather's account of Winthrop tells of the man in his time with the homely detail of early colonial art. It describes the governor's plain style in dress and conversation, his aversion to drinking toasts (though he kept a bottle of good wine handy for visitors), his easy relations with his inferiors, even while he maintained a strict sense of class prerogatives. It records several instances of his quick wit and, at some length, a number of his most important speeches. Nor is the portrait entirely flattering. We learn that the clergy had to rebuke Winthrop for excessive leniency, that he incurred grave financial debts, that many eminent persons disliked him, that his controversial policies brought him to an "ignominious hearing" before a general assembly, and that near the end of his life he was wracked with self-doubt bordering on terror.

All this is obvious enough to any reader. It is necessary to point out the obvious because of the persisting belief that Mather's biographies are an exercise in filiopietism. This view ignores, first, the sheer bulk and diversity of information he provides. The best modern study of colonial medicine, for instance, draws upon his discussions, in Winthrop's Life and others, of tumors, circulatory ailments, hypochondria, and the effects of tobacco. Historians have also profited from Mather's critical observations. His comments on Winthrop's shortcomings have frequent parallels in other biographies of magistrates; and his descriptions of what might be called clerical melancholia—William Thompson's psychosomatic distempers, Nathanial Mather's suicidal depressions, Ezekiel Rogers's morbid sense of isolation from man and God—may well have influenced Hawthorne's portraits of the Puritan minister. Moreover, the charge of filiopietism overlooks the *Magnalia*'s occasional bantering tone. Winthrop's "cure" for wood-thieves, which Mather records at some length—the governor's decision to share his wood-supply with the poor so that they need not resort to stealing—is typical of the numerous anecdotes that enliven the work, the sometimes memorable repartee, and the tongue-in-cheek humor.[1] The "merry disposition" he attributes to Winthrop is not inapplicable to Mather himself. Furthermore, the critics' reduction of the biographies to pious *exempla* obscures Mather's concern with worldly accomplishments. Among his other qualities, Winthrop is a responsible businessman; he is commended for the fact that "his children all of them came to fair estates and lived in good fashion." For them as for many of the *Magnalia*'s heroes, Puritanism opened the way to material as well as spiritual prosperity; and in at least two Lives, those of Theophilus Eaton and Sir William Phips, Mather's delineation of the rise from rags to riches makes him worthy of the title of father of the American success story.

Finally, the current pejorative view of the biographies underrates their value as chronicle history. Mather amassed documents of all sorts in the *Magnalia*, published and unpublished. In particular, the Life of Winthrop surveys most of the major political issues of the time: the uneasy diplomatic negotiations between Old and New England, suggested in George Cleve's report to King Charles and in the accusations leveled by Thomas Morton of Merry Mount; the internal dissensions of the 1630s, as evidenced by the machinations of the Antinomians and the mutiny of the town of Hingham; the early problems between Plymouth and Massachusetts, exacerbated by the rigid separatism of Ralph Smith and Roger Williams; the dispute between the merchant Robert Keayne and the Boston widow Goody Sherman, which led to the formation of the bipartite General Court. Mather recurs to these conflicts in other Lives, as well as in the *Magnalia*'s narrative sections, thus linking his heroes sequentially, in the framework of an ongoing historical enterprise. Throughout the work, his selection of key events shows a marked sensitivity to the nature of New England's development.[2]

Mather's historicism reflects the temper of the age. Significantly, he was the first American to use the term "biography," associated from its appearance in the late Renaissance with the revolt against panegyric.[3] With his contemporaries, he advocated a direct, detailed investigation of personality and events, praised the methods of the classical biographers, and denounced hagiography for its gross partiality and neglect of evidence. "Whether I do myself commend," he assures us, "or whether I give my reader an opportunity to censure, I am careful above all things to do it with truth." His biographies abound in records of all kinds: speeches, judicial briefs, letters, and sermon extracts in the Life of Winthrop; in other Lives, selections from diaries, genealogical and financial accounts, inventories relating to private as well as public matters. How much should men "fear the judgment of posterity," he remarks, "if historians be not allowed to speak the truth after their death"! No danger of our finding hyperbole or fancy in *his* work—"what *should* have been, rather than what really *was*." His Lives are "impartial," "Truth from first to last," and report everything with an "exact veracity" which heeds no party but that of conscience.[4]

It need hardly be said that Mather protests too much. His Lives report mainly what serves, or can be made to serve, his didactic ends. But then the same reservation applies to biography through-out the eighteenth century. Exceptions may be found, but by and large the art of biography from Roper through Walton to Johnson forms a transitional mode between hagiography and modern biography. Though it insists on details, it forces them into the framework of the ideal. Its aim is to teach by use of examples. It rebels against medieval allegorization without really allowing for realism, in our empirical sense of the term.[5] This transitional mode—we might call it exemplary biography—suggests Mather's place in the main currents of English biography of his time. His concept of Winthrop as individual and as *exemplum* follows from his belief that the discrete fact and the moral generality could complement one another. This holds true for even his briefest, most impersonal biographies, those which lend themselves most plausibly to comparison with medieval hagiography. In fact, the proper comparison here is with the Character, the abstract rendering of a certain social or psychological type, which (as it became popular in Restoration England) reinforced the didactic trends in biography. Mather's brief Lives share many traits with those of the leading Character-writers, especially Thomas Fuller and Joseph Hall. So also do a number of his longer biographies, some of whose titles seem to designate Virtuous Characters: *"Scholasticus,"* "A Man of God," "Early Piety Exemplified," even "Nehemias Americanus."

We must return, therefore, to the divergent implications of Mather's title. Winthrop's American aspect, we might say—his association with a particular enterprise—emphasizes his position as governor in order to reveal the individual; his aspect as Nehemiah renders him, as an individual, the *exemplum* of statesmanship. In this sense, the parallel wrenches him out of time. Insofar as the New Englander *is* the Hebrew governor, his actions extend beyond any particular situation to demonstrate the principles of just government. Nehemiah serves here as archetype, an organizing metaphor which allows Mather to vaunt a host of similar parallels that universalize Winthrop's accomplishments. History is invoked to displace historicism. The temperance of Plato's guardian, the courage and diligence of Plutarch's Cleomenes, Cicero's eloquence and Cato's integrity, the fortitude, wisdom, and piety of King Asa and of Macarius the Great—what seems a baroque plethora of allusions is really an effort to blur the specific into a composite ideal of civic authority.

The process of shaping the ideal gives form and direction to the Life. As the biography moves forward, the generalities increase in proportion to the details. The more we learn about Winthrop the more inclusive the outline grows. Gradually, the actual magistrate expands into an abstraction. Winthrop is chosen governor of the infant colony: he is another Moses in the wilderness. Winthrop suppresses Anne Hutchinson and her Antinomian followers: quotations from Virgil link him to Aeneas battling the elements stirred up by vindictive Juno. Winthrop's courage shows him to be a lion in adversity: he is worthy of Solomon's robes and scepter. Winthrop is generous to the destitute, no less to his defeated opponents than to the poor and sick: his behavior follows the best tenets of Roman law, it issues in the kind of altruism that led William of Paris to oppose Catholic misrule, and it takes rise from the biblical precepts concerning the exemplary magistrate (Prov. 14 : 26–34) who protects the chosen people, ensures their place of refuge, and exalts them by his righteousness.

The passage from Proverbs calls attention to a broader meaning of Mather's concept of *exemplum*. "A true Nehemiah," Mather explains, turns the old heathen virtue of patriotism to the service of God. Like the biblical saint Winthrop is more than an ethical leader: he is one of the elect, in the tradition of Reformed biography "greatly imitable as a Christian." This tradition, we know, grows out of the medieval Saints' Lives; it also reflects certain basic premises of the Puritan outlook. Perhaps the most familiar of these is the twofold concept of calling, the inward call to redemption and the summons to a social vocation, imposed on man by God for the common good. In keeping with their militant this-worldliness, the Puritans laid special emphasis on vocation. Predictably, they drew their standards for the magistrate from the familiar Renaissance treatises; but they made one further, quintessentially Calvinist demand. Invoking various scriptural models, they distinguished the merely good ruler from the saintly ruler, and insisted that the saintly ruler reflect his inward calling in his social role. Faith, indeed, was crucial to the proper execution of his duties. As his vocation was a summons from God, so his belief led him to do well in public office.

In affirming this connection between legal and spiritual calling, the Puritans extended the *exemplum* perforce beyond the Good Magistrate to encompass the whole man. They found a biographical precedent in the early Christian funeral orations. Specifically, the Life of Winthrop alludes to Ambrose's orations for Valentinian and Theodosius, in which Ambrose praises each of these Roman emperors as the exemplar of all *Christian* rulers. Over and again Mather echoes Ambrose's phrases: the refuge of the poor and the erring, magnanimous towards his enemies, faithful to his friends, humble before his critics, the pattern of sainthood and secular authority alike. The influence of these eulogies upon Mather, and upon colonial literature in general, is considerable.[6] It extends even to matters of structure. The standard form established by Gregory Nazianzus (to whose orations Mather several times refers) leaves its impress upon the Life of Winthrop: an opening encomium, a description of endowments, a list of achievements, and a rendering of the death scene, followed by a public exhortation.

It would be misleading to single out this influence above others. What seems certain is that Mather makes use of the funeral oration to integrate the Puritan concept of calling with the Renaissance ideal of just government. We need read no further than the first page or two to learn that Winthrop was self-effacing and magnanimous, that he came from a family of means, that his decisions were "exquisitely" tempered by wisdom and guided by a code of moderation. As for his piety, he would have preferred, writes Mather, to have devoted himself to the study of Calvin. When heaven decided otherwise, summoning him to civic administration for the common good, he "so bound himself to the behavior as a Christian as to become exemplary for a conformity to the laws of Christianity"—a conformity that carried beyond the statehouse, beyond even church and home, to the privacy of his heart. Thus Mather recasts the good works of the administrator into the *visibilia* of the saint. In effect, he heightens the implications of Nehemiah as archetype so as to elevate the American into a Christian Everyman. New England's Winthrop, he would tell us, resembles Israel's Nehemiah as a believer seen temporally in the vocation of governor. We read that Winthrop's impartiality stems from his abhorrence of idolatry; that his humility shows him to be a suffering servant of the Lord; that he is another Job in his compassion, causing "the blessing of him that was ready to perish to come upon him, and the heart of the widow and orphan to sing for joy."

The allusion to Job is characteristic of Mather's technique in this regard. Appropriately, the passage he selects concerns Job's exemplary justness.[7] But since it is the suffering Job who speaks those words to the Comforters, the scriptural context invests the social action with the atemporal meanings of the psychomachia. Justice, patience, and humility are only virtues; justice, patience, and humility as Job practiced them are attributes of the redeemed soul. In these terms Mather traces New England's tribulations under Winthrop directly to Satan, whom God has permitted, now as in Job's time, to test His saints. In these terms, too, he imposes the image of saintly affliction upon each stage of his hero's career: the hardships Winthrop experienced (yet "with how much resignation") in leaving England, crossing the Atlantic, adjusting to a strange land, and there enduring the calumnies of various tempters. In these terms, finally, Mather sums up Winthrop's trials (near the end of the biography) by way of, successively, his estate, his family, and his personal condition (cf. Job 1)—adding that amidst all this the governor had to suffer the rebuke of false comforters. The cumulative effect is to render the American Job-Nehemiah, in one of Mather's recurrent epithets, a lesson of our Lord, teaching us that every believer must endure conflict and temptation, as Christ did. It is a lesson that not only transcends the ideal of the Good Governor but transmutes history itself into a drama of the soul.

To transmute history does not in this case mean to reject or submerge historical details. It does mean that the "real facts" become a means to a higher end, a vehicle for laying bare the soul—or more accurately, the essential landmarks in the soul's journey to God. And the journey of the soul thus abstracted provides a guide for every man—of any age, any culture, indifferently past, passing, or to come—in the choices he must face, the war he must engage in between the forces of evil and good in his heart. Hence the parallel between Nehemiah and the American. Secular realism tells us what is different, unique, about the individual; Mather uses detail to convert *historia* into *allegoria*. He makes the particular events of Winthrop's life an index to the hero's universality.

EXEMPLUM FIDEI

The concept of the soul's journey is a Christian commonplace, of course; but Mather's application of the concept suggests a sweeping distinction between Reformed and medieval Catholic thought. Whereas the Reformed biographies leap from the individual to the universal, the Catholic hagiographies begin and end with the extraordinary and the unique. To be sure, they offer practical instruction, and sometimes urge us to follow in the saints' way. But the saints' way cannot really be ours. Even when we acknowledge their occasionally vivid personal traits, they impress us not as models for emulation but as objects of veneration, intended (in the words of one medieval writer) as a means between God and man.[8] The difference between this kind of Life and Mather's appears most clearly in terms of their common source—the life of Jesus and, by extension, the *imitatio Christi*, through which believers made their sainthood manifest.[9] *The Golden Legend*, after 1200 the standard medieval collection of Saints' Lives, reveals the *imitatio* partly by way of the saints' virtues and acts of martyrdom. But above all it stresses the supernatural feats they perform: the miracles which demonstrate their sainthood, and which expressly recreate the biblical pattern. In the course of *The Golden Legend*, the *imitatio,* so considered, comes to repeat each of Jesus' miracles many times over—the healing of the sick, the blind, and the lame; the resurrection of the dead; the multiplying of the loaves of bread; the casting out of the devils; the epiphanic descent of the dove and of the angels.[10]

The Reformers' objections to all this may be simply stated. Setting aside the problem of credibility, it was both naive and pernicious to base the *imitatio* on Christ's miracles. In the first place, His miracles were *prima facie* what Luther called "external events"; that is, they affected the outward state of particular persons, in a certain time, in a specific place. To offer them as the substance of belief was to lower the Christ-event to secular history, rather than lifting men from secular concerns to Christ. Secondly, the true import of His miracles was spiritual, not literal, and as such they could be repeated by all believers. To raise the dead was in itself of no avail; the point was to preach the Resurrection to the spiritually dead, and *that* required no supernatural intervention. The *imitatio* should provide a framework for experience. Miracles by definition violate the nature of experience: they "conform to no laws but occur by a special divine inspiration wherein God breaks the law." [11] Finally, from all these perspectives, the emphasis on miracles (whether as *Acta Sanctorum, Passiones,* or *Martyria*) suggested that merit follows upon performance. Thus the Catholics were distorting the very essence of belief, barring mankind from even the prospect of hope; they were inducing Christians to expect salvation from works rather than faith.

The Reformed alternative was the *exemplum fidei.* Formulated by Luther in the course of his attack on the Catholic saints, it proposed a mode of *imitatio* that emphasized the spirit rather than the letter of the deed. In this view, the miraculous pattern of Christ's life unfolded in organic stages of spiritual growth. The anomaly did not matter, only the common truths which the anomaly signified in context: the process of calling, temptation, and salvation shared by all believers. What Christ performed "God hath done for the Soul of the Least Saint." Any Christian's life opened, as did the New Testament, into "a volume full of temptations: . . . A wonderful History, because a History of such experiences, each one whereof is more than a Wonder." Such wonders implied no merit on the performer's part. The power and the glory were God's; His kingdom belonged to those who did His will rather than their own. "I labored more abundantly than they all, yet not I," Paul said (1 Cor. 15 : 10). So it was with Christ also; in these terms His experiences lighted the way to the kingdom for all believers. There were "no greater acts than their obedience, both Active and Passive," in accordance with the spiritual pattern of His life.[12]

Luther's formulation rests on one of the furthest-reaching tenets of the Reformation: the principle of *sola fides,* which removes the center of authority from ecclesiastical institutions and relocates it in the elect soul. Of course, the Reformers never questioned the inviolability of the church per se. They pointed out, following Augustine, that the church could be understood either as the temporal hierarchy, represented by the pope, or else as the eternal invisible church, the sum total of those predestined, for reasons and by means no man could fully determine, to life everlasting. Augustine seems to have wavered between the two in defining the true church. The Reformers had no doubts. They identified the temporal hierarchy as the seat of Antichrist and turned instead to the relationship between the believer, *exemplum fidei,* and the community of the elect, the universal society of *exempla fidei,* from Abel through Nehemiah to the present, whose members, perceptible by faith alone, were all one in Christ. In this view, the norms of the good life were eschatological, not institutional. Behind every experience of the saint stood Jesus Himself, *exemplum exemplorum* for both the believer and the organic body of believers. The way to salvation lay in an internalized, experiential reliving of His life.

This eschatological consciousness shapes much of Reformed thought, and of Puritan thought in particular. No doubt it tended to fragment the movement, to encourage the chaotic proliferation of sect upon sect. The concept of *exemplum fidei* may best be seen as a counter-reaction to that fragmentation. It was a giant effort at cohesion and control, expressly opposed to the outburst of individualism that marks most of the other intellectual movements of the Renaissance. For as the Reformers condemned the institutional Catholic *imitatio,* so also, and just as virulently, they condemned the humanist doctrine of *imitatio hominis,* with its flaunted freedom of the intellect, its pagan tributes to the splendor of the human body, and its extravagant claims for self-determination. Those tributes and claims rested on the vision of man as microcosm; the Reformers required a higher authority, an external absolute. "Every man, individually, is an epitome," they agreed; but they proceeded to distinguish between the natural and divine meanings of the term: "every natural man (who in a natural consideration is called *microcosmus,* an epitome of the world), in whose conscience God hath his throne . . . may be called *microchristus,* the epitome of Christ mystical." [13]

The distinction is a crucial one. Both humanism and Protestantism shift the grounds of private identity from the institution to the individual; and it has been said of each movement that its concept of *imitatio* makes every man his own church. But the humanists considered the true church to be a macrocosm of the self-fulfilled individual. The Reformers demanded that every individual reconstitute himself by grace a reflection of the church. That "every man is a *world* in himself," they argued, simply proved mankind to be Adam's progeny. The world was "all of red earth . . . a rednesse that amounts to a shamefastnesse, to a blushing at our . . . sinnes, as red as scarlet." The notion of microchristus, on the contrary, according to which every believer "hath *a Church* in himself," required Christians to surmount their bloodstained commonality with mankind.[14] Erasmus, Luther's great humanist antagonist, exulted in man's "natural gifts." Luther's reply was that the only gifts of value, the only identity worth aspiring to, lay utterly beyond man's powers.[15]

The humanists differed from the Reformers neither in their worldliness nor in their optimism, but in their individualism. Whether they saw man as the quintessence of dust or as the paragon of creation, a very god in action and apprehension, it was the microcosm that held their attention. Indeed, one major strain in their thought excludes the divine altogether from the ideal of self-fulfillment. The tradition of humanist personal literature, extending from the fourteenth through the seventeenth centuries— from Petrarch's *Letter to Posterity* to Cellini's ebullient autobiography, Jerome Cardan's melancholy *Book of My Own Life,* and, most fully, Montaigne's *Essays*—is concerned exclusively with the autonomous secular self. Leaving the question of sainthood to theologians, each of these writers declares the primacy of the single separate person, and justifies his self-study on its intrinsic merits, without pretense at religious or even moral instruction. He assumes that what he has thought and done will interest others because it is authentically *his*, the product of his own personality in all its rich uniqueness. The model of identity he offers posits that no two selves are alike. "We seek other conditions," writes Montaigne,

> because we do not understand the use of our own, and go out of ourselves because we do not know what it is like within. So it is no use for us to mount on stilts, for on stilts we must still walk on our own legs. And on the loftiest throne in the world we are still sitting on our own behind.
>
> The most beautiful lives, in my opinion, are those which conform to the common and human model, with order, but without miracle and without extravagant behavior.[16]

The familiar Puritan terms are there—"common model," "order without miracle or extravagance"—but directed *against* the concept of microchristus. Wedding ironic self-consciousness to self-acceptance, Montaigne would deprive us of the stilts of christic identity so that we might better use our own fallible limbs.

Another major strain of humanist thought, opposite but equal to that of Montaigne, exulted in the Christ-event as an emblem of human magnificence. Replacing the skeptic's appreciation with the mystic's fervor, the leading figures of the Italian Renaissance proclaimed Jesus to be the epitome of "our undeniable glorification," a cosmic *ecce homo* that consecrated our "unconstrained and limitless freedom." In the pattern of His life they found the proof-text that each of us, by nature, is potentially "a certain God." Mankind has "so great an image and similitude of the divine that it has been rendered a participant of immortality and beatitude." More than that: our palpable *improvement* upon the works of God—the fact that the world is "much more beautiful" now than it was at its "rude creation"—constitutes a visible sign of our immortality. The Incarnation was nothing more or less than a divine confirmation of man's achievements. Christ descended from heaven to earth, explained Giannozzo Manetti, in order that He might glorify human nature, which God

> had made so beautiful, so ingenious, so wise and so opulent, so worthy and so potent, finally so happy and so blessed for its total and absolute perfection in every respect, that through

admixture with divinity itself it should not only be conjoined in
that person of Christ with the divine person but also rendered
one and the same with the divine nature. And this seems to
have been uniquely done for man, . . . for the admirable
certain dignity of his nature and also for his own incredible
excellence.[17]

Absolute perfection! Incredible excellence! As Montaigne's views
would have seemed to Reformers the counsel of despair, so
Manetti's could be nothing else for them than the cloying eloquence
of Flesh, the wilderness mirage of Satan's last temptation. Their
preachers had warned them of it often enough. The High Calvinist
Arthur Dent instructed them about the nature of man: "a gulf of
grief, a sty of filthiness." "Preach much about the misery of the state
of nature," Charles Chauncy urged the seventeenth-century Congregationalists; that misery teaches us to adhere to Christ. The
silver-tongued Presbyterian, Henry Smith, described the effects of
opulence and power: "honey in thy mouth and poison in thy
stomach"; "*Rejoice, O young man, in thy youth:* . . . if there were no
judgment day, that were a merry world." [18] We have been told that
the Puritans' personal literature is a major "manifestation of a
growing self-consciousness," that every one of them "had to speak
honestly of his own experience." [19] Their writings yield a different
conclusion: there, self-examination serves not to liberate but to
constrict; selfhood appears as a state to be overcome, obliterated;
and identity is asserted through an act of submission to a
transcendent absolute.

The origins of this mode of regimentation lie in the devotional
imitatio as it develops from the Church Fathers down through the
late-medieval mystics. But the devotional exercise centered upon
the contemplative life.[20] The process it outlined—of purgation,
illumination, and union—offered at most an interior meditational
dimension to the forms of sacramental worship. The Puritans
stressed activism and experience. They held that *"Union with Christ
is not the end but the beginning of Christian life."* And Christian life, in
any form, was an *"application* of Christ," not a contemplative retreat
in contemptus mundi. The terms of application varied in accidentals
from one preacher to another, but in substance they carried a single
message: that all Christians shared the same plight, all had the

same calling, and all undertook the same wayfaring and warfaring pilgrimage. The Puritans schematized the "art of living" accordingly. "God's dealings are much the same with all his Servants," wrote the leading Puritan conservative Richard Baxter. *"Christ leads me through no darker rooms / Than He went through before."* The revolutionary William Dell argued that "Nature of one makes many, but Grace, of many makes one; for the Holy Spirit, which is as fire, melts all the Faithful into one mass or lump." According to New England's Richard Mather, "by much *beholding the glory of the Lord in the glass of the Gospel"*—and acting out our perceptions—*"wee are changed into the same Image."* [21]

It has become fashionable to link the production of mirrors during the Renaissance with the growth of modern individualism. This may hold true for the humanist Renaissance. For Baxter, Dell, and Richard Mather, the mirror radiated the divine image. They never sought their own reflection in it, as did Montaigne and his literary descendants through Rousseau. They sought Christ, "the mirror of election," and "Prospective-Glass for Saints"—or rather mirror, prospective glass, and image all in one: communion meant *"a putting on of Christ,"* transforming oneself completely into His image. Manetti, Ficino, and Pico held up the christic mirror to show man his own splendor. The Puritans felt that the less one saw of oneself in that mirror, the better; and best of all was to cast no reflection at all, to disappear. Their mirror was scriptural: "We all with open face beholding, as in a glass, the glory of the Lord, are changed into the same image" (2 Cor. 3 : 18). Their concept of change was an exegetical cliché: "we begin to feel towards God, in a measure, as he does towards himself; . . . we begin to love him with the same kind of love, and from the same motives, as he himself does." Their view of the nature of that reflection was closer to the Church Fathers than to the Renaissance. The soul is like a mirror turned towards the sun, wrote Gregory of Nyssa; it images not itself but the Son's rays; and it does so most brilliantly on a surface "pure and shining," cleared of all "stains of dirt." [22]

For the Puritans, the dirt necessarily disfigured the reflection, and they spoke not of stains but of "dung-hills," "bogs of Filth," "Lumps of Lewdeness," "Slough and Slime." Furthermore, they described the cleansing process not, with Gregory, as an ascetic inward retreat, but as a commitment to this world. God *wanted* them to experience the slime: "he will have our hands actively in it"—and in it not for "one instant but [for] the whole course of a mans life." We must "be soaked and boiled in affliction," as Job was, or Nehemiah, if we would "have some relish acceptable unto God"; we "must goe under the Flaile, the Fan, the Milstone, and the Oven, before [we] can be Gods Bread." Would you wash your face clean? asks John Bunyan—well, "first take a glass and see where it is durty": "labour" to discern your every crime, "experimentally" persuade yourself that you are "the biggest sinner in the world," "plunge" yourself into the foul waters of your heart till you know there is "none worse than thyself." "You must be empty, if ever Christ fill you," went the pulpit refrain: "you must be nothing, if you would have Christ." The Puritan's humanity was fulfilled, as Nehemiah's was, insofar as it was plunged and purged, washed clean of the "Vomit in [its] Cheeks," its sullied flesh "destroyed," its "whole body of Sin" transformed, emptied, melted—rendered a pure and shining surface on which the individual in his daily thoughts and actions would reflect back the unstained image of his redeemer, and so dissolve into the timeless pattern of spiritual biography.[23]

AUTO-MACHIA

There were many ways to make that revelation public. Fox and Lilburne in their polemics compare their sufferings with Christ's, Milton insinuates his own temptations into the drama of *Paradise Regained.* More explicit, of course, are the personal writings of the period, the countless testimonies, declarations, relations, even broadside manifestos, whose authors fit their most intimate experiences to the contours of christology, subsuming anything unique about themselves into a few standard structural and verbal forms. The standards themselves are expounded in equally numerous case-books, treatises, and sermons: John White's *Way to the Tree of Life,* John Downame's *Christian Warfare,* Louis Bayly's *Practice of Piety,* Thomas Shepard's *Sincere Convert,* Arthur Dent's *Plaine Mans Pathway to Heaven: Wherein Every Man May Clearly See Whether He Shall Be Saved Or Damned.* The message of these manuals, repeated to the point of tedium, is that saints' Lives are valuable not for themselves, but because they make the true norms of identity accessible to all good men. The humanists, in this view, together with the idolatrous fabricators of *The Golden Legend*, would substitute man for God, intercessor for Mediator; Protestants held nothing to be exemplary just "because such and such men have done it." [24] Rather, they emulated the man insofar as he emulated Christ. Thus the story of Nehemiah reminded them that every servant of the Lord must endure great affliction; and although they acknowledged this to be their just punishment, nonetheless they felt obliged to look deeper, as Nehemiah did, and rejoice that the affliction might indicate His love.

The dialectic between justice and mercy would seem to offer a safe guide through the paradox of christic identity, with its double focus on fact and ideal, activism and self-denial. Given the tenets of Calvinism, however, the dialectic only served to heighten the paradox. The Protestants went further than the humanists in divesting the individual of all external resources. Their call for self-examination had an urgency that far exceeded the classical-humanist demand for self-knowledge. Yet they also, and in the same breath, outdid the medieval preachers in denouncing innate depravity. The thing itself was not merely for them a poor, bare, forked animal; it was a sink of iniquity. With an uncompromising analytical ferocity that scandalized humanist and Catholic alike, they diagnosed mankind as "accursed, poisonous, ruinating, dismall, Woefull, Miserable, and forlorn, Execrable beyond the relief of all Created help whatsoever." The trouble with the Catholics, explained the Anglican Richard Hooker, is that they claim righteousness for *themselves*. They pretend to an "inherent grace . . . the augmentation whereof is merited by good workes"—whereas, of course, the slightest introspection proves otherwise. It remained for the Puritans to develop the anatomy of the inherent state. Because they were the most activist of the Reformers, they became the most expert and eloquent analysts of man's implacable evil. Edward Taylor's self-scrutiny takes the form of a descent into "A varnisht pot of putrid excrements," a labyrinth of illusion haunted by "Fears, Heart-Achs, Grief." His imagery seems restrained by comparison with other Calvinists, before and after him, convulsed with the nausea of their sins. The solution he proposes is a commonplace of the literature: "Then Lord, my tumberill / Unload of all its Dung, and make it cleane." [25]

Modern historians of the Reformation claim that "self from now on stands for man," as though this meant an increased sense of personal worth. The Puritans' understanding of that phrase begins with Augustine: "Two loves have given origin to these two cities, self-love in contempt of God unto the earthly . . . [and] love of God in contempt of one's self to the heavenly." As the Puritans developed and amplified the conflict, self-versus-God became the motivating force of their activism. So it appears in their definitions of the soul's pilgrimage: as we "travaile towards *grace*" the "terme from which we travaile is . . . *Sathan*, and ourselves." Most amply, it appears in the *self*-compounds which they added to the language. Those that define the damned include *self-affection, self-confident, self-credit, self-fullness, self-honor, self-intended, self-practice, self-safety, self-sufficiency*; the few that mark the redeemed include *self-emptiness, self-revenging*, and (what Thomas Hooker called the Christian's two chief lessons), *self-trial* and *self-denial*. Richard Baxter's treatise on *The Benefits of Self-Acquaintance* contrasts the godliness of *self-abasing* and *self-abhorring* with the illicit acts of *self-determination*. His authoritative *Christian Directory* presents the contrast in full perspective:

> Man's fall was his turning from God to himself; and his regeneration consisteth in the turning of him from himself to God. . . . [Hence,] self-denial and the love of God are all [one]. . . . Understand this and you will understand what original and actual sin is, and what grace and duty are. . . . It is self that the Scripture principally speaks against. . . . The very names of Self and Own, should sound in the watchful Christian's ears as very terrible, wakening words, that are next to the names of sin and satan.[26]

The basis of Puritan psychology lies in this contrast between personal responsibility and individualism. We can say, with William Haller, that they believed "man's chief concern should be with the welfare of his own soul," only if we bear in mind their horror at the "very name of Own," their determination "to *Hate* our *selves* and *ours*," their opposing views of *soul* and *self*. The way of the soul, they maintained, starts "with a holy despair in ourselves" and proceeds "with a holy kind of violence" back to Christ; it means acknowledging the primacy of that which is Another's, and *receiving* the ability to respond. Hence the advantage of self-knowledge: the terror it brings may exorcise our individuality. It may drive us to "desire to be found, not in ourselves." It may teach us that to love our neighbors as ourselves is to realize how drastically "self is against the good of our neighbours"; that at best the saint has "no more feeling or relishing . . . himself, then if he were not at all"; and that what Augustine meant by our two opposing wills was the conflict between "our own proper Will" and "the Divine Will": that is, between a private, inherent, discrete identity, and an imposed, Christ-centered exemplariness that results in "self-nothingnesse." [27]

Polonius states a humanist commonplace when he speaks of being true to oneself. Calvin sets out the Reformed position when he requires us to "rid our selves of all selfe-trust," and his words resound throughout Puritan literature. "Not what Selfe will, but what the Lord will," thundered Thomas Hooker. The self was "the great snare," "the false Christ," a spider's "webbe [spun] out of our bowels," the very "figure or type of Hell." To "lay downe God-self," to root out "the Devils poison and venome or infection of Self," was at once "to kill the old Adam" in us, to defeat the infernal "rebels against the commone good, all [of them] private respects of mens selves," and to strike a blow against "Antichrist, that is, the SELFE in all." Lord, pleaded the German pietist Jacob Boehme, "cast me down I pray thee to the ground in my received self, (. . . I, that which is called I, or myself), and kill this self of mine through thy death"; "do thou overcome in me self (. . . Or I, or ihood, or iness, that which we mean when we say 'tis I) . . . cast my whole self . . . down to the ground in thy death." [28]

The language in these passages conveys the dilemma of Puritan identity. The vehemence of the metaphors, the obsessiveness of the theme, the staccato syntax, the sense of clauses recoiling rather than progressing (since every gesture against I-ness contains its own counter-gesture), the interminable-because-unresolved incantations of the "I" over itself—every aspect of style betrays a consuming involvement with "me" and "mine" that resists disintegration. We cannot help but feel that the Puritans' urge for self-denial stems from the very subjectivism of their outlook, that their humility is coextensive with personal assertion. Necessarily, the militancy they hoped would abase the self released all the energies of the self, both constructive and destructive. Never was form more expressive of content than in their pervasive use of the personal mode, whether as confession (self-display as the chief of sinners), or as eulogy (fascination with famous men, from Nehemiah to Winthrop, who had presumably overcome their humanity), or as exhortation (appeals to the will to acknowledge its own impotence). All these works attest to the same impasse. All record the "Self Civil War"—as they repeatedly describe the struggle—of a Puritan Sisyphus, driven by self-loathing to Christ and forced back to himself by the recognition that his labors are an assertion of what he loathes. "Unto myself my Selfe my Selfe betray," wrote George Goodwin in a popular early seventeenth-century poem; "I cannot live, with nor without my Selfe." [29]

Goodwin's poem is part of a genre devoted (in effect) to the exploration of the profound Puritan ambivalence towards selfhood. "Self Civil War" is a fair term for it; a better one, I think, is the term Goodwin chose, "Auto-Machia," since it evokes both modern autonomy and medieval psychomachia. In any case, the poem itself is highly representative:

> I sing my SELF; my *Civil Warrs* within;
> The *Victories* I howrely lose and win;
> The dayly *Duel*, the continuall Strife,
> The *Warr* that ends not, till I end my life.
> And yet, not Mine alone, not onely Mine,
> But every-One's that under th' honor'd Signe
> Of Christ his Standard, shal his Name enroule,
> With holy Vowes of Body and of Soule.

The civil war here suggests an entire culture in transition. On one side, like an emblem in the old morality plays, Christ's standard waves over the triumphant microchristus (the I-become-Everyone); on the other side, foreshadowing the romantic's isolation (and the post-romantic's alienation), stands the I-in-process, whose daily, hourly losses threaten what ought to be a foregone resolution. At the center, the archetypal Puritan protagonist-antagonist, "my SELF," tries to make sense of its own nature by proving that the terms of the conflict are predetermined, certified and sealed from eternity under the signature of Another. "*I* sing," Goodwin exults, "*I* win the victories," "*I* end *my* life"—and then abruptly, "Not mine

alone, not onely mine." But the double negative also calls attention
to the double "mine"; and the resonance of "onely," "alone,"
continues into the uneasy counterpoint between "*his* Standard" and
"*his* Name," with its ambiguous identification of the self either with
Christ or with other selves in "continual strife." The last line
ostensibly pays tribute to the soul's "holy vowes"; in fact, the sense
it conveys of ongoing battle simply brings us back to the problematic opening epic invocation.

In spite of himself, we realize, Goodwin expresses the spirit of an
age that was to be decisive in the development of Western
individualism. It is an involuted manifestation of that spirit, to be
sure, a sort of narcissistic *Liebestod*, constantly reenacted because
incapable of fulfillment: the individual affirming his identity by
turning against his power of self-affirmation. But to affirm and to
turn against are both aspects of self-involvement. We can see in
retrospect how the very intensity of that self-involvement—mobilizing as it did all the resources of the ego in what amounted to an
internal Armageddon—had to break loose into the world at large.
The metaphor of "civil war" suggests this, as do the haunting
arguments of Max Weber, and the tremendous vitality of the
colonial church-state, from Winthrop's political achievements to
Cotton Mather's gargantuan literary productiveness.

It is also true that, in the course of inner civil war, certain
Protestants seem to make a temporary truce with themselves. Louis
Martz has argued persuasively that some of their poems of
meditation succeed in reaching "a moment of illumination, where
the speaker's self has, for a time, found the answer to its conflicts."
But such moments are rare, sudden respites amidst an otherwise
constant barrage of images of violence and struggle. Edward
Taylor, one of the poets Professor Martz discusses—and whom
other critics have called a Puritan mystic, even a secret Catholic or
Anglican Platonist—is broadly representative in this respect. His
verses build on the tension between the need to write and the
futility of writing:

> I fain would praise thee, Lord, but when I would,
> I finde my Sin my Praise dispraises bring;

the futility exacerbates the need:

> [Shall] The little Bee present her thankful Hum?
> But I who see thy shining Glory fall
> Before mine Eyes, stand Blockish, Dull and Dumb? . . .

the writing itself dwells on the discrepancy between words and truth, metaphor and reality, so that

> Whether I speake, or speechless stand . . .
> I faile thy Glory;

and the poet uses that discrepancy as a rationale for talking forever about *himself*. As Karl Keller notes, Taylor's poetry finally devolves upon Taylor *in the process* of preparation, simultaneously demanding meaning and confessing his own meaninglessness, in an endless (because interminable) ritual celebration-exorcism of the Puritan self.[30]

The ritual was sustained by various doctrinal developments geared specifically (it would seem) towards the problems inherent in the auto-machia. One of these was the Puritans' pietistic voluntarism, which raised personal choice to the central position it held in humanist theology—without, however, losing sight of man's inability to choose correctly. A parallel development was their emphasis on practical divinity. For all their scholasticism, the Puritans exalted will above intellect, experience above theory, precept, and tradition. They defined conscience as "a mans judgment of himselfe, according to the judgment of God ["krisis"] of him,"[31] but their very insistence on God called attention to the inescapable I-ness in performance and self-judgment—and as their own words imply, in the "krisis" itself:

> One morning, as I was sitting by the fire, a temptation beset me; but I sat still. And as I sat still under it and let it alone, a living hope arose in me, and my heart was glad, and I saw it shine through all. This I saw [but] I then [did not] know where to find it in the Scriptures; though afterwards, searching the Scriptures, I found it.
>
> I feared it would shame my self that such an eminent professour as I was accounted, should discover such corruptions

as I found in my selfe. I grew very sad, and melancholy. I thought I had received some power to apply Christ unto my soule; but I thought I was not holy enough. I was worthy of nothing for I knew I could doe nothing. Now could my soule close with Christ. Hee would oft tell mee he loved mee, I did not doubt to believe him; If I went abroad hee went with mee, when I returned hee came home with mee. I talked with him upon the way, hee lay down with mee and usually I did awake with him.

I have been before God, and have given myself, all that I am, and have, to God; so that I am not, in any respect, my own. I can challenge no right to this understanding, this will, this body, or any of its members—no right to this tongue, these hands, these feet, these eyes, these ears, this smell. I gave them to God, and I have been this morning to him, and told him, that I gave myself *wholly* to him. I hope, I truly find in my heart a willingness to comply as long as I live.[32]

These quotations represent Calvinists of different sects, eras, personality, and intellectual capacity (the second is from Winthrop). My purpose is not to minimize the differences—all of them significant, and many of them the subject of recent specialized studies—but on the contrary to recall them, however obliquely, in order to suggest the central, sustained, and tension-fraught impact of christic identity. In all its forms, the auto-machia presents the same clash of means and ends. For the humanist, whether he was a Manetti or a Montaigne, man was both means and ends. The Puritans went further than Montaigne in separating man from God, and further than Manetti in their homage to the divine absolute. The medieval and Counter-Reformation Catholic similarly polarized man and God, but he filled the gap, as it were, with the Church Militant. For the Puritan, faith alone could fill the gap. The "krisis," though God's, was the sinner's responsibility. The same "I" that once could not believe was the sole reliable witness—witness, judge, and historian—of the Lord's victory. That "I" had learned that self-denial was complete when "the soule knoweth it hath nothing." [33] But was it not, after all, the "I" that *knew* and *had*, even if nothing? And could the "I," having nothing, consider itself pure soul rather than a sinner in "krisis," freighted with the burden of self-identity? Such questions are implicit throughout the literature. By the rule of *sola fides* the Puritan had to come to terms with himself; by the terms of that confrontation he could not but admit his impotence; and through that shock of self-recognition he had somehow to reconstitute himself, still relying on the resources of the internal will, an *exemplum fidei*. He tried to explain away the contradictions by claiming that in this case the will was not his own but the action of the Holy Spirit in him. The printed results of his efforts belie his claim. The state of mind they reveal might be described as a schizophrenic single-mindedness. With few exceptions, the myriad auto-machiae demonstrate that private insecurity is proportionate to public affirmation, just as, conversely, the force of I-ness is transparent in the violent vocabulary of self-abhorrence.[34]

The struggle entailed a relentless psychic strain; and in New England, where the theocracy insisted upon it with unusual vigor—where anxiety about election was not only normal but mandatory—hysteria, breakdowns, and suicides were not uncommon. Nonetheless, the Puritans continued with increased energy to regiment selfhood by recourse to the *exemplum fidei*. The applications are manifold. They appear in the sudden ascendancy during this period of Augustine's *Confessions* as a model of self-portraiture. They appear in the parallels between private and doctrinal literature (Thomas Taylor's journal and his *Christ's Victory Over the Dragon*, for example, or Bunyan's *Grace Abounding* and his *Pilgrim's Progress*),[35] and in the stereotyped language, transferable episodes, and redundant signs of regeneration in Puritan confessions. Most readily, perhaps, they appear in the didactic uses of the auto-machia: as a prop, as a refuge from the terrors of self-doubt, and (to cite the very titles of these writings) as a self-conscious *Declaration of the Witness of God* or *Legacy for Saints*—which is to say, *An Invitation of Love* addressed *To All the Inhabitants of the Earth*, directing them *To the Life of God in All*, and demonstrating *The Righteousness of God to Man, Satan His Methods and Malice Baffled*, and *God's Mighty Power Magnified*, all by means of an *Experimental Knowledge of Jesus Christ* through *The Witness of God, Manifested in the Inward Parts*.

In the massive effort at control which these soul-searchings represent, spiritual biography played a crucial part. Granted the

link between the exemplary Life and the *exemplum fidei*, we could
hardly expect otherwise. It seems well-nigh inevitable in retrospect
that the genre of Puritan spiritual autobiography should have
developed out of the genre of biography. The earliest of the
Reformed saints' Lives portrayed the leading divines, and gave
choice extracts from conversation and private papers. The Lives
were intended to show the ideal type of minister, the extracts to
offer direct examples of the Protestant equivalents for the miracles
of Catholic hagiography: calling, conversion, temptation resisted,
and regenerate living. The examples became in turn a do-it-your-
self guide for the reader, especially if he belonged to one of the
congregations, like those of New England, which required personal
testimony for admission. More than any other form of personal
writing, the exemplary Lives provided a reliable model of christic
identity. Each of them was by definition auto-machia "justified" (in
the momentous Calvinist sense of the word). As the record of a
fallible woman or man, it documented the anguish of process. As
the commemoration of a glorified saint, it showed the *imitatio*
victoriously applied. The combination made for a paradigmatic
blend of *historia* and *allegoria*. "The greatest object out of Heaven,"
wrote New England's first biographer, John Norton, "is the life and
death of such upon Earth, who are now in Heaven." Other
ministers on both sides of the Atlantic repeated his claims. Why else
had God "raised up in all ages such excellent persons" but to
provide us with "worthy patterns to imitate"? Paul himself had
called the great men of the past our "ensamples" and their lives
"our admonition" (1 Cor. 10 : 10). Clearly, "if we will not
ingratefully frustrate the intentions of divine Providence for our
good, we must dispose ourselves to imitate those illustrious patterns
of virtue and piety." [36]

The call for spiritual biography reflected a wide variety of needs
in the entire seventeenth-century Protestant community. For ecclesiastical historians, the exemplary Life was an effective way of
authenticating the antiquity and sustained vitality of the Reformed
churches. For the clergy, it was an effective vehicle for bringing
dogma down to life. For every Puritan individually, it was an
effective guide for living up to the demands of dogma (the *ne plus
ultra* "art of living to God"), reducing as it did the tension in the
means (experience, process) even as it minimized the remoteness of

the end (the example of Christ). And from all these perspectives, the exemplary Life expresses the powerful counter-subjectivist thrust of the Reformation: the Puritans' recourse to the *imitatio* as a stabilizing human-divine center of authority—parallel if antithetical to Catholic Rome—mediating between the needs of personal religion and the claims of a transcendent ideal.

SOLA SCRIPTURA

Mather's use of Nehemiah as *exemplum fidei* is particularly significant in this context. Significant, at first, as a problem, for although we can readily see that the parallel supports the image of Winthrop, it is less obvious why Mather should need to make the Old Testament figure so prominent, or for that matter why he should need the support at all. The question extends, of course, to the *Magnalia* at large, and beyond. Seventeenth-century Protestant spiritual biographies repeatedly and insistently invoke the *imitatio* through parallels with "humane" precedents, rather than with Jesus Himself. The term "Nehemias Americanus" implies that the American is like Christ because he is like Nehemiah; the same formula applies to most of Mather's biographical allusions, and to those of virtually all Puritans' Lives. It is as though the biographers, conscious of their enormous charge, felt that they could not trust the *imitatio Christi* alone, the direct correlation between the individual's experiences and Christ's, to carry its own message. It would seem, indeed, that they intuited the inner contradictions of the automachia. The self (even when it denoted a *de facto* saint) clung too tenaciously to its own nature to yield a model of christic identity; and yet precisely because Christ's life *was* the model—an "Exact Coppy, written by the Deity of the Son of God, with the Pen of the Humanity, on the milk white Sheet of an Holy Life" [37]—His example could not serve of itself to order the processes of the self.

The impression of a deliberate strategy of evasion is not far from the truth. All evidence suggests a reluctance to equate the elect directly with Christ. In part, this may be traced to a reaction against those extremists who took advantage of the principle of *sola fides*—or who broke under the strains of continual striving—and declared themselves above authority, in some cases actually arrogating Christ's perfection to themselves. Winthrop attributed Anne

Hutchinson's heresies to such misconceptions; there were many more instances in England. Abiezer Coppe announced that *he* was "universal love"; William Erbery claimed possession of "the fullness of the Godhead"; James Naylor rode into Bristol *as* Christ entering Jerusalem; Ranters, Seekers, Shakers, and Muggletonians toured the countryside with similar doctrines and antics, in a crusade, as they termed it, to turn the world upside down. "They preached not Jesus Christ but Themselves," said Roger Williams of the Quakers; "yea, they preached the Lord Jesus to be Themselves." [38] No doubt he was exaggerating, but the fact remains that both George Fox and William Penn found it difficult to keep the movement under control. It was a short step from Geneva to Münster, from imitation to identification. If the tirade against the self sufficed to prevent most Puritans from taking that step, it seems certain that the emphasis on self-involvement encouraged an alarming number of would-be messiahs.

To strengthen the barriers around their flocks, the orthodoxy reiterated the fundamental distinction between the human and the divine. Unquestionably, they began, Christ is our supreme example; but a tremendous gulf separates exemplar from imitator. When we aspire to become an image of Christ, we must remember that ours is "the Image of the Seal in the Wax." We cannot follow His pattern unless we concede that it is ultimately beyond our grasp. "Our Lord's most imitable practice did proceed from an immense virtue of divine grace, which we cannot arrive to; it in itself is so perfect and high that we may not even reach it." Hence the very process of self-denial is also a provocation of the self. Christ's perfection may dazzle us by association into longing to be as God. Or conversely, it may so strikingly reveal our imperfections that we will abandon all hope, and fall prey to those "great uncertainties . . . of perishing and losing all," that terrible spiritual "heaviness, unquiet, . . . doubt and dullness, without comfort" which drove Judas to suicide.[39]

The divines expounded on each of these dangers at length, in treatises like *The Passions of the Mind* and *The Diseases of the Soule*. So long as you see yourself in terms of Christ, they cried, even as they demanded precisely that form of self-inspection, "you have cause to feare." Milton portrays Satan in *Paradise Lost* as caught in a vise of pride and despair. Every Christian who gazed long enough into the mirror of election stood in danger from one extreme or the other. The quandary reflected his dilemma of identity; and here again exemplary or spiritual biography offered a solution. "Other good men," the clergy explained, "had assistances in measure, such as we may hope to approach unto." Therefore, their lives provided a fit standard, an absolute "in measure," for our experiences—an authority which was beyond doubt, but not, like Jesus, beyond self. To some degree this authority was available in the tradition of spiritual biography itself: tales of the apostles, of the primitive Christians, of the martyrs from Nero's time to Queen Mary's. We have seen that Mather draws on all these sources; but, as the governing parallel of his Life of Winthrop suggests, the biographers found the authority they sought in the Old Testament. By that authority they could reiterate the premises of the microchristus ("the Fathers before Christ had as truly the same *Spiritual Life* in Christ as we"), even while they stressed the difference between man and Christ: although "the Life of his Divine Nature neither of us have," we are equal with the Israelites in "proportion and resemblance of his life." [40]

So considered, the Old Testament could be read as a collection of exemplary Lives, diverse enough in action, personality, and vocation to apply to any saint in any age. They were

> recorded unto succeeding Generations . . . as so many practical demonstrations of the Faithfulness of God: as so many full and glorious triumphs over the World, Sin and Satan, obtained by persons in like temptations, and subject to like passions with our selves.

Such demonstrations had a unique practical advantage. Not only did they apply to the ego in progress rather than to the perfected soul; they also bound the subject to the fixed pattern of scripture. Unlike all other exemplary Lives they constituted "a *divine* testimony of what the Faithful have done and suffered." [41] By correlating the contemporary life with that of the faithful Israelites, the biographer could trap the self, so to speak—diseased mind, unwieldy passions and all—between the Old Testament on one side and the New on the other. His *exempla* were thus simultaneously human and divine, and incontrovertibly authoritative in either respect.

Strictly speaking, of course, nothing was incontrovertible to the Reformed mentality. As it happened, the subjectivism unleashed by the Reformation not only failed to stop short at scriptural interpretation but probably accelerated under the influence of the Lutheran principle of *sola scriptura*. As every man was his own church, so too, now that the Bible was made universally available and declared to be sole authority, every man became his own exegete. There is eloquent testimony to this outcome in the Puritans' savage intrasectarian polemics, and generally in the widespread alarm over "Dark minds diving into the Scripture" and reemerging with "lies enough out of it to set whole countries on fire." The Reformers, determined at all costs to prevent that anarchy of the spirit, insisted on a christological reading of scripture. That is, they demanded a precise spiritual correspondence between the history of the Hebrews and the life of the believer. Like Christ, the Bible could be rightly perceived only by one who had transformed himself in His image. And like the process of that transformation, the story of Israel had its *telos* in the Christ-event. Interpreter and text confirmed one another in their mutual *imitatio*. For the Puritan, the crucial aspect of this correspondence was the palpable inequality of its constituent parts. The interpreter represented the self under probation; the text was definitive. The calculated result was a one-sided mode of confirmation: "Let *Israel* be . . . our glass to view our faces in." [42] Here as before, the mirror image expresses a sweeping rejection of individuality, and the Puritans pressed it as far as it would go. It was not enough, they cried, for the saintly exegete to submit to the Word, as Catholics pretended to. He must also ratify his every experience, all his thoughts and feelings, by the infallible standard of holy scripture.

Nothing more clearly attests to the Puritans' subjectivism than does this conjunction of *sola fides* and *sola scriptura;* and nothing more clearly demonstrates their regimentation of selfhood. Richard Baxter counsels his readers that "The great means to conquer this Uncertainty is Self-Examination," and then, as though realizing the open-endedness of his advice, he adds: "or the serious and Diligent trying of a mans heart and state by the Rule of Scripture." The sequence of thought speaks for itself. The formula it advances for transforming "Uncertainty" into "conquer," for circumscribing "trying" by "Rule," is a staple of pulpit oratory, and the basis for the most successful renderings of the auto-machia. For example, the poems of meditation mentioned earlier reach their moments of illumination through intricate correlations between personal and scriptural events, culminating in the fusion of self and subject. The same method dominates the writing of those most individualistic of Puritans, the early Quakers. Precisely because of their antiauthoritarian bent, it would seem, they found it crucial to root experience in sacred precedent, and they recorded the workings of their Inner Light in journals entitled *Jacob Found in a Desert Land, Babylon the Great, A Long Travel to Bethel, Asking the Way to Zion, Passing Through the Red Sea, Jacob Wrestling with God, Journey out of Aegypt into Canaan*. To make the purpose of the convention explicit, they described these parallels as the artillery of the spirit directed against the self, the "cement whereby we are joined as to the Lord so to one another." [43]

Their description is identical with that of the moderate and conservative clergy. Even as the latter warned their flocks that Christ was never got by a wet finger, by the mere reading of scripture, they insisted that the Bible was the comprehensive "sole norm." On this basis, the Puritans formulated their theory of the plain style. To speak plainly was not primarily to speak simply, and not at all to speak artlessly. It meant speaking the Word—making language itself, as self-expression, an *imitatio Christi* because it conformed to scripture. The too well-known admonition that introduces the *Bay Psalm Book*, "God's altar needs not our polishings," far from curbing the use of image and metaphor, opens the full linguistic richness of the Old Testament to preacher and layman alike. Read the Bible, rhapsodized John Donne, and you will see that ours is "a *figurative*, a *metaphoricall* God . . . ; A *God* in whose words there is such a height of *figures*, such *voyages*, such *peregrinations* to fetch remote and precious *metaphors*, such *extensions*, such *spreadings*, . . . such *third Heavens* of *Hyperboles*, so harmonious *eloqutions* . . . as all *prophane Authors*, seeme of the seed of the *Serpent*, that *creepes*," whereas the inspired authors of scripture are as "the *dove*, that flies." This is no invitation to metaphysical flights of wit and conceit. Insofar as Donne is advocating a certain style, he is advocating the style of the Bible, and in this sense his exhortation has many counterparts in the writings of Puritans throughout the century, from Thomas Adams's praise of metaphor (1614) to Cotton Mather's defense of his ornate "massy style" in the *Magnalia*.[44]

The plain stylist condemned eloquence for its own sake. He imitated the Bible's dovelike flights of language as he imitated Christ, in order to efface the self, to sacrifice the polishings of "I" and "our" on the christic altar of scripture. "Words must be judged acceptable, not by the . . . humors of men, but from the warrant they have from the scripture," and therefore "our safest way," wrote Milton in *De Doctrina Christiana*,

> is to form in our minds such a conception of God, as shall correspond with his own delineation and representation of himself in the sacred writings, . . . lest in our flights above the reach of human understanding, and beyond the writings of Scripture, we should be tempted to indulge in vague cogitations and subtleties.[45]

The nature of temptation here makes the act of literary creation inseparable from the act of self-denial. The safe way to which Milton summons us is at once stylistic and theological, and in either sense it depends on the christic correspondence between the believer and the sacred writings.

I need hardly say that Milton's stress upon *safety* indicates the force of the recalcitrant self. Few Puritan works exceed *De Doctrina* in flights of doctrinal or stylistic self-assertion. (*The Bay Psalm Book*, be it noted, expresses a similar case of doctrinal assertion on the part of a minority sect.) Yet the disparity itself between theory and practice indicates the Puritans' *need* for an infallible correlative to the self. To this end, they turned to scripture as the safest way also to regulate conscience. To this end, further, Ames's colleagues in England, Holland, and America outlined the character of the good magistrate (in such treatises as *Christ's Combat* and *The Soules Conflict*) through precedents in the careers of men like Nehemiah. And to this end, every Puritan biographer wrote, in one degree or another, as though he were bringing the scriptures up to date through his subject's life.

The result is a conventionalized rhetoric that blurs the difference between metaphor and experience, between one sect and another, even between traditionally distinct genres. The exodus from Egypt, christologically understood, links the poetry of George Herbert and of Edward Taylor, the Quaker Thomas Forster's diary and John Partridge's secular saint's legend of *Valiant Knight Plasidas*. "*Moses . . . writ of the Journeyings of the children of Israel*," says Bunyan in *Grace Abounding*. "*Wherefore* this I [also] *have endeavored to do*," so that "others may *be put in remembrance of what he hath done for their Souls*." This is a highly metaphorical way of examining oneself, he concedes—but were not "Gods Lawes, / His Gospel-laws in olden time, held forth / By Types, Shadows and Metaphors?" We feel, rightly, that Bunyan's use of types and metaphors constitutes a singular achievement. For Bunyan they are a means of making his signature interchangeable with that of all believers. "Woulds't read thyself"? he asks in *Pilgrim's Progress*; "O then come hither / And lay my book, thy head and heart together." [46] What we discover when we lay his book and our heads together is that personal pronouns are superfluous. To read oneself in *Pilgrim's Progress*, or in *Grace Abounding*, is to read the *imitatio* through the figures of speech of the Old Testament.

This synchronizing of author, reader, and scripture is made explicit by New England's finest first-generation stylist, Thomas Hooker. According to the *Magnalia*, Hooker was intent on "imitating the example and character of our blessed Saviour, of whom 'tis noted that, according to the prophesie of Isaiah, by him, 'The poor had the gospel preached unto them.' " He succeeded, in the opinion of his contemporaries, by making vivid for them the parallels between the way of Israel's salvation and their own:

> There must be Contrition and Humiliation before the Lord comes to take possession. . . . This was typified in the passage of the Children of Israel towards the promised Land. They must come into and go through a vast and roaring Wilderness, where they must be bruised with many pressures, humbled under many overbearing difficulties, before they could possess that good land which abounded with all prosperity, flowed with Milk and Honey. . . . The Truth of this Type [i.e., this foreshadowing of Christ], the Prophet *Hosea* explains, and expresseth at large in the Lords dealing with his People in regard of their Spiritual Condition, Hos. 2. 14, 15. *I will lead her*

into the wilderness and break her heart . . . [thereby furnishing] the soul with ability to fasten upon Christ.[47]

Hooker's method may serve to clarify the logic by which Mather integrates Winthrop's difficulties with Nehemiah's in the framework of sacred history. By reference to this framework we are to understand the American Moses' wilderness afflictions, his Job-like perseverance, his Solomonic wisdom as magistrate, and, climactically, his troubled moments before his Jacobean-Davidic "departure." Then, after we have set the New Englander firmly inside this configuration, we are to correlate the latter with the spiritual biography of Jesus. At either end of the configuration stand saint and Savior, the historical man and the *exemplum exemplorum*. The bridge between them is Nehemiah and the line of *exempla fidei*, from Jacob to Solomon, which Nehemiah evokes.

Again, it may be helpful to illustrate the process through a specific passage. I have mentioned the deathbed scene as a gesture towards realism, and so it is, to judge by other accounts of the event. Yet equally it is the deathbed scene of many other saints whom God leaves for a time directly before "they leave the world; plunging them on their death-beds in deep temptations, and casting their souls down to hell, to rebound the higher to heaven." This well-worn stereotype ultimately refers us to Christ, but for Mather the intermediary parallels come from the Old Testament and thence from the tradition of ecclesiastical biography. In particular he cites Theodore Beza's influential Life of Calvin ("pour servir d'example à ceux qui se revoltent de Jésus-Christ"), which records the master's last troubled appearance at the Friday-night-before-Pentecost supper of his disciples.[48] In general, Mather's rendering of the scene evokes the full sweep of sacred history:

> there was allowed unto the serpent the bruising of the heel [after Adam's fall, Gen. 3 : 15] and accordingly at the heel or close of our lives the Old Serpent will be nibbling more than ever in our lives before, and when the Devil sees that we shall shortly be where the wicked cease from troubling [Job 3 : 17], that wicked one will trouble us more than ever—so this eminent saint now underwent sharp conflicts with the tempter [as did Israel and Christ in the wilderness], whose wrath grew

as the time to exert it grew short [Rev. 12 : 12, with reference
to the "spiritual Israel," the church of the elect]; and he was
buffeted with the disconsolate thoughts of black and sore
desertions . . . .

But it was not long before those clouds were dispelled, and
he enjoyed in his holy soul the great consolation of God! . . .
[Then,] having like Jacob first left his council and blessing with
his children gathered about his bedside [Gen. 49 : 33], and like
David served his generation by the will of God [Acts 13 : 36],
he gave up the ghost [Matt. 27 : 50, Acts 5 : 10, with regard to
the crucifixion; cf. Job 10 : 18, 11 : 20, 14 : 10].

The interaction between the literal event, scriptural parallel, and
christic referent offers strong evidence of Mather's artistry. Even
while he details Winthrop's descent into near-despair, he controls
the movement within the pattern of redemption, as that pattern
applies, like the life of Christ, both to the individual and to the
church at large. Mather starts with the Fall, but in such a way as to
remind us of its affirmative value: "the bruising of the heel" comes
from the text of the *protevangelium,* the immutable promise of grace
to Adam's heirs ("thou shalt bruise his heel," Gen. 3 : 15). He
proceeds to the trials of Job, and the triumph of the true church;
and having identified both these events with his hero's *agon,* he
crowns Winthrop's victory over the tempter with references to the
father of Israel and to Israel's exemplary ruler. Then, summarily,
he links Winthrop to Christ Himself, the Second Adam at the
moment when He fulfills the covenant of grace and so reverses the
effects of man's disobedience. The process of association illuminates
the intricate threefold rhetorical pattern which unites all the
narrative elements of the biography, the personal and biblical levels
entwined in the christological. In that pattern, the auto-machia is
so situated as to call forth, from experience itself, the image of the
exemplum fidei in the final act of self-effacement.

The same pattern recurs in virtually all of Mather's Lives. In
October, 1719, taking stock of his hundred and thirty-four biogra-
phies ("whereof more than Fourscore *stand in the Church History*"), he
thanked God for "using me thus, to discover unto the World, the
Glory of my SAVIOR." Some five years later, in his Preface to
Parentator, his biography of his father, he explained that he recorded

"the *Vertuous* tempers and Actions of . . . Men" as "*Epistles of Christ unto the rest of Mankind.*" As epistles of Christ, too, he advertised his other writings—sermons, treatises, funeral orations, and homilies on the *ars moriendi*—that draw upon scriptural parallels repeatedly to urge our "Assiduous *Endeavor*, to *Imitate* our Saviour," to "Be EXEMPLARY" by being "able to say . . . *Follow me, as you have seen me follow Christ*," and, in short, to realize that "Without the *Imitation of Christ*, all thy *Christianity* is a mere *Nonentity*." His diaries invoke a host of Old Testament heroes (including Nehemiah) so as to proclaim his own "Conformity to the Lord" in "*all the Circumstances of* [His] Crucifixion." Not accidentally, the only "Popish" work he approved and valued, and the only one published by the seventeenth-century colonial press, was Thomas à Kempis's *Imitation of Christ*. "It may be of some good Consequence for me," Mather confided in his diary, "to read a Chapter in that Book, the last Thing I do, every Night." [49]

2

The Vision of History

Christology provided Cotton Mather with a superb rhetoric for biography, and he made effective use of it both formally and conceptually. His Life of Winthrop blends the disparate biographical methods of his time and conveys an imposing image of the hero as man, governor, and saint. The parallel with Nehemiah expands from civic to moral *exemplum* and thence to *exemplum fidei;* the facts of Winthrop's American career combine in the pattern of the scriptural microchristus. It is a remarkably coherent synthesis, except in one respect: it fails to account for the biography as part of a historical venture. Winthrop's christic identity defines his stature as another Nehemiah; but this has no apparent bearing on what his American-ness implies, that he is one of a *series* of magistrates and divines who contributed to a particular New World enterprise. Christologically, "Nehemias" absorbs "Americanus" as a definition of Winthrop. Yet we can hardly avoid recognizing that it is Winthrop's role in history which really places the biography in context. What unites the Life of Winthrop with the corporate action of the *Magnalia Christi Americana* is not, to all appearances, the exemplariness of Nehemiah, but the idea of the exemplary American.

FIGURA

The problem would seem to have a ready solution in exegetical tradition. For the seventeenth-century Puritan, *exemplum fidei* denoted a type of Christ; and what he meant by type pertained equally to biography and to history. In its original form, typology was a hermeneutical mode connecting the Old Testament to the New in terms of the life of Jesus. It interpreted the Israelite saints, individually, and the progress of Israel, collectively, as a foreshadowing of the gospel revelation. Thus Nehemiah was a "personal type" of Jesus, and the Israelites' exodus from Babylon a "national type" of His triumphant *agon*. With the development of hermeneutics, the Church Fathers extended typology to postscriptural persons and events. Sacred history did not end, after all, with the Bible; it became the task of typology to define the course of the church ("spiritual Israel") and of the exemplary Christian life. In this view Christ, the "antitype," stood at the center of history, casting His shadow forward to the end of time as well as backward across the Old Testament. Every believer was a *typus* or *figura Christi*, and the church's peregrination, like that of old Israel, was at once recapitulative and adumbrative. In temporal terms, the perspective changed from anticipation to hindsight. But in the eye of eternity, the Incarnation enclosed everything that preceded and followed it in an everlasting present. Hence Mather's parallel between Winthrop and Nehemiah: biographically, the New Englander and the Israelites were correlative types of Christ; historically, the struggles of the New England saints at that time, in this place—the deeds Christ was now performing through them in America—were "chronicled before they happened, in the figures and types of the ancient story." [1]

So understood, typology contributes much the same elements as does christology to the Life of Winthrop. It emphasizes the *imitatio*, it translates secular history, whether of individuals or of communities, into spiritual biography, and it recalls the tradition of the Saints' Lives. Patristic hagiography, for instance, resonates with the figuralism of church liturgy (e.g., the flight from Egypt in the Holy Saturday sacrament of baptism). Later developments tended to reinforce the method. When after Constantine the call to martyrdom lost its practical value, writers turned increasingly to the passion as *figura:* St. Christopher, they explained, was not literally crucified, but "we call him a martyr" anyway because, on his miracle-working way to the heaven, he "carried the cross of Christ continually in his heart." [2] This tendency grew rapidly after the Reformation. Typology recommended itself to the Reformers as an ideal method for regulating spiritualization, since it stressed the literal-historical (as opposed to a purely allegorical) level of exegesis, and then proceeded to impose the scriptural pattern upon the self, in accordance with the concept of *exemplum fidei*. For these and similar reasons, typology became a staple of Protestant writings, including even the Character genre. In particular it seems to have been a family speciality with the Cottons and Mathers, to judge by the procession of great figural studies, from John Cotton's *Exposition of Canticles* (1655) through Samuel Mather's monumental *Figures or Types of the Old Testament* (1683), a work almost as impressive in its range of figural applications as Cotton Mather's unpublished "Biblia Americana" and almost as detailed in its analysis of types as Increase Mather's *Mystery of Christ Opened and Applyed* (1686).

Christology equated the saint with the heroes of scripture; typology merged the saint's life with scripture history. It taught the believer that the process by which he fastened to Jesus "was *typified*"—to recall Hooker's discourse—"in the passage of the Children of Israel towards the promised land." "Draw the [whole] Scripture to thine own heart, and to thine actions," went the standard pulpit injunction. "All the promises of the Old Testament [are] made, and all accomplished in the New Testament, for the salvation of *thy* soule hereafter, and for thy consolation in the *present* application of them." The argument behind this emphasis on the present was simple and comprehensive. Since Christ as antitype encompassed all of history, there was no reality outside of the human-divine paradigm. To deny Christ was also to be a type—in the manner of Cain, Judas, or Corah. The man who never read the scriptures had the Bible without the book, as John Donne put it: Genesis, Exodus, Job, Nehemiah—"he hath all in his memory, even to the *Revelation*." Donne's concept of memory derives from Augustine's figural *Confessions*; its meaning for seventeenth-century spiritual biography and autobiography is made vivid in Thomas Browne's *Religio Medici*:

> That which is the cause of my election, I hold to be the cause of my salvation, which was the mercy and beneplacit of God, before I was, or the foundation of the world. *Before Abraham was, I am,* is the saying of Christ, yet is it true in some sense if I say it of my selfe, for I was not onely before my selfe, but *Adam,* that is, in the Idea of God, and the decree of that Synod held from all Eternity. And in this sense, I say, the world was before the Creation, and at an end before it had a beginning; and thus was I dead before I was alive; though my grave be *England,* my

dying place was *Paradise;* and *Eve* miscarried of mee before she conceiv'd of *Cain.*[3]

In this context, Winthrop as *figura* is virtually indistinguishable from Winthrop as microchristus. Nonetheless, it is important to examine Mather's figuralism in its own right. To begin with, the use of types is central to his imagery. When in the deathbed scene he calls Winthrop another David (citing Acts 13), and alludes to the bereaved children as the tribes of Israel, he unmistakably associates the twelve tribes with the twelve apostles, and Winthrop with Jesus, as He was foreshadowed by David (Acts 13 : 22–36). In effect, Mather forges the link between past and present through Christ's omnipresence as antitype. Or again, when he describes the governor's Job-like benevolence, he enhances that christic image within a sort of figural kaleidoscope of good works:

> It was oftentimes no small trial unto his faith to think "how a table for the people should be furnished when they first came into the wilderness!" [Ps. 78]. And for very many of the people his own good works were needful, and accordingly employed for the answering of his faith. Indeed, for a while the governor was the Joseph unto whom the whole body of the people repaired when their corn failed them. And he continued relieving of them with his open-handed bounties as long as he had any stock to do it with; and a lively faith to see the return of the "bread after many days," and not starve in the days that were to pass till that return should be seen [Gen. 49, 50], carried him cheerfully through those expenses.

Winthrop appears here in several guises: as an open-handed, devoted, and beleaguered public official, as the Good Magistrate, and as a Reformed Christian. But it is the *figura* that dominates. Mather announces this, as it were, in his opening statement, which summarizes Winthrop's actions as a trial of faith (see Heb. 10, 11). It finds ample expression in the references to David and Joseph which thread his account. In Psalm 78, which Mather quotes, David denounces the Israelites who during the exodus blasphemed God, although He preserved them with water from the rock and manna from heaven. We need not enter into the typological intricacies of the text (rock/Christ/church, water/baptism/redemption, etc.)—as Mather does in his *Psalterium Americanum*—in order to grasp the basic connections: the exodus with Jesus' wilderness temptations; the manna with His triumph over evil as well as with His feeding of the people; the ungrateful Israelites with the stiff-necked Pharisees and Sadducees. The same pattern extends to Joseph, who foreshadowed Christ, Mather notes, both as provider and, earlier, as God's injured and insulted servant. As the configuration comes to bear upon the New England magistrate—in *his* wilderness, providentially overcoming *his* trials, providing for *his* often ungrateful people—the *figura* that emerges bespeaks the furthest moral, spiritual, and eschatological reach of Winthrop as *exemplum fidei*.

And yet as *figura* Winthrop remains rooted in history. Since typology, to repeat, is quintessentially concerned with *littera-historia*, the same hermeneutic which raises Winthrop beyond time locates him in time and place, as "Americanus"; the same technique which broadens our sense of Nehemiah as archetype deepens our sense of him as precedent, as a distinctive individual engaged in certain historical events that occurred some two millennia before the settlement of Massachusetts Bay. This is the second, larger reason for recognizing Mather's use of typology: it turns our attention to ordinary, temporal, geographical facts. It is precisely to underscore Nehemiah's figural significance that Mather refers to him always from a *historical* angle. In detailing Winthrop's notions of civic discipline, he comments that "he thus did the part of a ruler in managing the public affairs of our American Jerusalem, when there were Tobijahs and Sanballats enough to vex him," alluding to the Persian and Samarian officials who opposed Nehemiah. Later, he writes that in his personal behavior Winthrop "made himself still an exacter parallel unto that governor of Israel by doing the part of a neighbour among the distressed people of the new plantation." Finally, Mather's epitaph versifies Josephus's eulogy to Nehemiah as the glory of his countrymen. Throughout the biography, he insistently reminds us of Nehemiah's specific institutional and organizational accomplishments, impresses us with the Hebrew less in his abstract grandeur than in his political reality, as a national leader, "bonus ac justus," whose relevance to the colony abides in certain social acts. The one line from Josephus that Mather alters, the last line in the epitaph, states that Winthrop's legacy is the wall of defense he built, the "Novanglorum moenia," substituting "New England" for the original "Jerusalem."

The substitution attests to Mather's overriding emphasis on history. But his context, we must remember, is sacred rather than secular history. Jerusalem, Babylon, and Israel are the landmarks of the scheme of salvation. So, too, are New England and America, insofar as they represent (as Mather says they do) ecclesiastical matters and the mighty works of Christ. In short, the central purpose of his figural technique is to refer the *littera-historia* in Winthrop's career, and in the *Magnalia* at large, to the history of redemption. The point warrants elaboration because scholars have misread Mather as a *providential* historian. Certainly, he believed in providence; but with all Christians of his time he distinguished sharply between kinds of providence. The distinctions are conveniently summarized by one of Winthrop's English contemporaries, John Beadle, in a work acknowledged to be a characteristic expression of seventeenth-century Puritanism:

> Some acts of God, are acts of common providence, and so he feeds us, and cloaths us, he doth as much for the creatures; so he feeds the Ravens. . . . Some acts of God are acts of speciall priviledge; and thus he gave *Abraham* a child in his old age, and made *David* of a Shepherd a King. Some acts of God, are acts of pattern; and thus he shewed mercy to *Menasse*. . . .
>
> Some acts of God are acts of wonder: it is a wonder that any soul is saved.[4]

God's acts of wonder stand apart from the rest in that they govern the *soul's* progress. They constitute providential signs of grace which chart the believer's embattled course to an otherworldly perfection, thus equalizing him with every regenerate Israelite against the background of eternity. All the other forms of providence pertain to history. They tell us about the self (rather than the soul) in progress—its mundane needs, its political involvements (Menasseh), its social guises, from paterfamilias (Abraham) to *pater patriae* (David). Conceptually, however, these historical providences divide into mutually opposed outlooks. Feeding and clothing are affairs of the *civitas terrena*, encompassing saint and sinner alike, heathens and "creatures" as well as Christians. They form the substance of providential history. God's acts of mercy and privilege extend to the elect alone, the subjects of ecclesiastical history from Abraham through David and Nehemiah to Winthrop. Grounded as these providences are in prophecy and promise, they form the substance of the work of redemption. They are figural providences, we might say, as distinct from secular providences.

The distinction implies a twofold approach to history. As Augustine conceived it, providential history concerns the political, cultural, economic, and moral life of individuals, societies, civilizations—everything, in short, that makes up the story of the City of Man. The Greeks and Romans had read that story as a series of recurrent actions, cycles of growth and decline as predictable as they were futile; and Augustine agreed. He rejected only the pagan notions of the underlying cause (fate, chance, fortune). Whatever happens, he contended, is controlled by God, Who leaves "nothing unordained," through particular providences. Despite their divine source, the meaning of these providences is always immediate, specific, and temporal. God speaks to us through them of "the good things of this life and its ills," the blessings and punishments common to all mankind. Historically interpreted, they provide a framework for human activity, a running commentary on our earthly endeavors; and for Augustine, the interpretation invariably confirmed the nature of our fallen world. God granted the Romans a splendid empire in reward for their good works; but their virtue, and therefore their splendor, soon faded. "Prosperity never fails to turn to adversity." [5]

Of course, historiography did not necessarily entail homiletics. The providential approach could serve simply to illuminate man's achievements. Thus the humanists used it to justify their rejection of any theological or supernatural explanations in historical research. Beginning with the separation of earthly from sacred affairs, *Historie* from *Heilsgeschichte*, they gradually introduced what we now term historical realism. But the Reformers retained the Augustinian *significatio*. All secular events, they insisted, "beeing captived to the trueth of a foolish world," taught the immemorial lesson of Ecclesiastes. "God has collected a fine, splendid, and strong deck of cards," Luther snarled, in a review of the past, "representing mighty, great men, such as emperors, kings, princes, etc.; and he defeats the one with the other." The acts of heaven, echoed Ralegh in his *History of the World*, "giue victorie, courage, and discourage, raise, and throw downe Kinges, Estates, Cities, and Nations." [6] Through all its manifestations—in drama, epic, handbooks on government, histories proper—Renaissance Protestant historiography is shaped by the cyclical *vanitas vanitatum* that characterizes Augustine's view of providence.

Augustine himself, however, had little interest in providential history; primarily, he devoted his thought to the story of the City of God. From this perspective, he recast the pagan notion of recurrence into that of an expanding spiral. Christianizing the Old Testament eschatology in terms of the covenant of grace, he emphasized the developmental scheme which Paul outlines—in the same passage that defines *figura* as *exemplum* (Heb. 10, 11)—as leading "by degrees" from Ararat, Sinai, and Golgotha forever upward toward the Holy Mount of New Jerusalem. The covenant pertained in this context not to the individual but to the entire spiritual house of Israel. The one was seen as analogue to the other, each of them a mirror image of Christ as antitype. "Israel are often called collectively God's son . . . and his first-born, as if the whole multitude of them were one person." And collectively, as the true church, the progress of Israel was as firmly assured as was the saint's stage-by-stage progress towards heaven. Milton describes this as "the Race of time / Till time stand fixt" [7]—a sort of relay race toward eternity, whose participants were essentially identical (all one in Christ), while temporally they represented ascending steps in the work of redemption. Although the substance was the same, the manner of dispensation altered. Thus the exodus out of Babylon was greater than that out of Egypt, a brighter manifestation of things to come. The image in the christological mirror gradually wiped out the varieties of self and circumstance. The image in the mirror of providence revealed the cyclical pattern which linked all selves and circumstances despite their apparent variety. The image in the mirror of redemption was dynamic, progressive, and variegated, reflecting the different stages of the evolution of the church.

Renaissance Protestants contrasted redemptive and providential history under many headings: revealed and natural knowledge, holy and temporal affairs, ecclesiastical and political history. William Ames distinguished between God's primary and subordinate "Gubernation," Bacon between the history of prophecy and the history of providence. For my purpose, the most convenient terms are those now in use: soteriology and secular history, where secular history designates the providential view (not the humanists' a-religious, empirical realism) and soteriology the mode of identifying the individual, the community, or the event in question within the scheme of salvation. The dualism, by any name, confirms—as it were beyond providence—God's overarching, inviolable plan, "the *summum* and *ultimum* of all the divine operations and decrees," as Jonathan Edwards called it, or in the words of an earlier New Englander, Samuel Torrey, "the Sum of all Gospel Prophesie . . . in every Age and Generation . . . until all the whole Mystery of God be finished, and Time shall be no longer." None but the elect were concerned in the happy outcome. Those among them, like Cotton Mather, who felt called to calculate the progress of the church, did so figurally, by correlating the prophecies with contemporary affairs. Their speculations pertained to corporate rather than personal matters, and as such they were neither moral, primarily, nor christological, but (in the framework of scriptural or sacred time) historical. However dismal the repetitive course of human, subordinate affairs, no matter how ominous the signs of secular time, the elect might rejoice as members of the *communio praedestinarum,* in an age closer than any before to the "utmost Prophetical Period." [8]

In that framework Mather places Nehemiah and Winthrop. He invites us to discriminate between the two rulers according to their chronological positions in the apocalyptic timetable. In that framework, too, he would have us understand the providences that guide Winthrop's life. But when we do so, we find ourselves unavoidably conflating God's acts of wonder with the events of secular history. As Mather describes them, the common providences by which Winthrop survives the wilderness, and helps others survive, are indistinguishable from the figural providences by which he becomes governor, defeats his enemies, and brings blessings upon his children. To extol Winthrop as "Americanus," then, would seem to deny the very basis both of spiritual biography and of church history. Figural providences are unique, as Augustine was careful to explain. In personal terms, they separate saints from sinners: "even in the likeness of the sufferings, there remains an unlikeness in the sufferers," for "the same violence of affliction proves, purges, clarifies the good, but damns, ruins, exterminates the wicked." Historically, they separate the holy from the secular communities:

> it was not only for the sake of recompensing the citizens of Rome that her empire and glory had been so signally extended, but also that the citizens of that eternal city, during their pilgrimage here, might diligently and soberly contemplate these examples, and see what a love they owe to the supernal country on account of life eternal, if the terrestrial country was so much beloved by its citizens on account of human glory.[9]

The problem with "Americanus" is that it connects Winthrop with a terrestrial *and* a supernal country. As the representative American, he stands at once for citizen and saint, state and church, New England and ecclesiastical history, *res Americana* and *res Christi*. In sum, his exemplary status yokes together two historiographical modes—one providential, the other figural—apparently as different from each other as (in another framework) *historia* is different from *allegoria*.

PROVIDENTIA

One way of approaching Mather's effort at synthesis is by contrast with the colonial classic in providential history, William Bradford's narrative of Plymouth Plantation. A Separatist on the saint's course to heaven, Bradford assumes the traditional dichotomy between secular and sacred, and he sees the plantation itself, accordingly, in terms of common providence. To be sure, with all Protestants of his time he rejoices in the progress of the church: the expanding Reformation, the approaching Parousia, and briefly, during the early 1640s, the Puritan victories in England. But as a Separatist he expects no more from his own congregation than that it should hold fast to the principles of the spiritual Israel; and as historian (not church historian) of Plymouth, he chronicles the fate of a wholly temporal venture. The Pilgrims have come to America as they had earlier gone to Holland, in order to worship God in peace. Inevitably, they find themselves, in America as elsewhere, enmeshed in what Bradford calls "the mutable things of this unstable world." Indeed, he deliberately uses the New World background to accent their plight. As he describes it, the country's "weatherbeaten face" and "savage hue," reminiscent of the "barbarous shores that the Apostles reached," become an emblem of our fallen state—

> sharp and violent, and subject to cruel and fierce storms, dangerous to travel [even] to known places, . . . full of wild beasts and wild men. . . . Neither could they [the immigrants], as it were, go to the top of Pisgah to view from this wilderness a more goodly country to feed their hopes; for which way soever they turned their eyes (save upward to the heavens) they could find little solace or content in respect of any outward objects.[10]

This is the landscape of providential history. Somewhere beyond lies the balm of Gilead; the story itself concerns the beasts and storms of secular time, and appropriately it is a story of gradual decline. Bradford's style reflects his subject. As David Levin and others have shown, his organization is cyclical, his tone melancholy, his vision tentative, alert for irony and ambiguity. We read of reversals that lead to unhoped-for success, of successes that pervert the very purpose of colonization. Throughout, the settlers struggle to make sense of a perplexing variety of circumstance and character; and all too often the acts of their enemies are just as bewildering as those of apparent saints, even so exemplary a saint as the zealous (but sometimes strangely infirm) Robert Cushman. The patriarch William Brewster is an exception that proves the rule. Bradford portrays him as another Jacob: not the Jacob of "Nehemias Americanus," father of a new Israel, but the Jacob microchristus of spiritual biography, wandering "from one nation to another . . . through famine, fears, and many afflictions," until at last, at the age of eighty and weary of this world, he "died sweetly and rested in the Lord, as infinite others . . . have done, and still shall do." The Life shines with a sort of lonely, transcendent glow amid the shadows of contradictory motives, of intertwined good and evil, which have darkened Plymouth's past and which bode still bleaker days to come. For if Bradford knew all along that the emigrants' course was probable at best, he learns a grimmer truth

from his experience: "men set their hearts . . . though they daily
see the vanity thereof." His last image of Plymouth is that of "an
ancient mother . . . foresaken of her children." His last comment
concerns a colonial agent who decided to remain in England,
unexpectedly and "much to the weakening of this government";
then, "*Anno* 1647. *And Anno* 1648," and silence.[11] The abrupt silence
resonates with the essential lesson of providential history, that this
world is a house built on sand.

The difference between Bradford and Mather as historians lies in
their different concepts of "Americanus." For Bradford, the Plymouth settlement was part of a secular experience from which he
tried to infer the meaning of providence. For Mather, the New
World errand was part of church history; he deduced its providential meanings from the preordained scheme of redemption. Thus
Winthrop's experiences signified not the common providences of a
governor but the figural providences of an *"Ecclesiarum Clypeus,"* a
"shield" of a theocracy. Every good Christian combined his
evangelical with his social calling, and every Good Magistrate
represented his society at its best. Winthrop, like Nehemiah, stood
for an extraordinary society, a church-state fashioned after the
pattern of Moses, David, and Solomon, and like the early Christian
congregations a place of refuge for God's persecuted people. Our
rulers, explained Jonathan Mitchel in a sermon on Nehemiah,
differ from those of other nations in that they seek the welfare of the
saints, and they claim that extraordinary honor because of the
community they serve: "we in these places are eminently . . .
advantaged to be an holy people." According to Increase Mather,
"God of his free Grace, hath seen meet to dignifie an handful of his
People . . . [and has] promised as an high favour . . . [that] *their
Governours shall proceed from the midst of them."* [12] Brewster's heroism lay
in his ability to transcend his circumstances, Winthrop's in his
capacity to lead the communal enterprise.

Mather accents Winthrop's representativeness in these terms at
many points in the biography, from his introductory remarks about
New England's "father" to his closing description of the dying
patriarch. The description is figural, we have seen, as well as
christic, and as *figura* emphatically historical. The children surrounding Winthrop are the tribes of God's *American* Israel; the
passage in Acts which Mather cites (13 : 17–36)—describing as it

does the *magnalia*, or *miracula*, wrought by Christ ("Israel's Savior") in Egypt, the wilderness, and Canaan—designates the New World of the new chosen people. Mather's allusions do not always depend on scripture. Often he suggests what may be called the governor's soteriological exemplariness through personal detail. He does so when he discusses Winthrop's legal views and practice, simply by presenting these as a revival of the Hebrew and early Christian principles of government. He does so more subtly in discussing Winthrop's private life. When, for example, he recounts the "stock of heroes" from whom *his* hero descended, he barely mentions the parents. Instead, he concentrates on the family's renown in the days of Henry VIII and Bloody Queen Mary—the grandfather who served England's first Protestant king, the grand-uncle who aided the Marian martyrs—intending us to understand that the Massachusetts leader, like the enterprise he sired, is child and heir of the English Reformation, and hence of the Reformation generally, the highest dispensation to date in the progress of the church.

As soteriological *exemplum*, then, Winthrop's heroism derives wholly from his involvement in history. To appreciate the extent and depth of that involvement, we might consider a comparable idea of the magistrate, comparable at least in its reliance on typology. I refer to the idea of the divinely appointed ruler, which reaches down from the Middle Ages to the Restoration. As Ernst Kantorowicz has shown, the basic premise of this tradition is that the ruler has two selves, corresponding to the "two bodies" of Christ, personal and "super-individual." Personally, the ruler is a natural man, and like the man Jesus susceptible to the natural order of things. Super-individually, as Vicar of Christ, he is divine, a "christomimētēs—literally the 'actor' or 'impersonator' of Christ" [13] —descended from the anointed Hebrews who foreshadowed the true King of Israel. In this function the ruler stands above the body politic, absolute and immutable, a God-man impervious to the vicissitudes of secular time. Thus his very right to govern distinguishes the ruler individually from himself (in the Puritan sense of "self"), and historically from the community he governs. His magisterial office makes him part of the history of salvation; their role as subjects keeps the members of the community within providential history.

This distinction between ruler and people recalls medieval hagiography, with its implicit separation of the miracle-working saint from the mass of mankind. More pointedly, it indicates the scope of Winthrop's exemplariness as governor. Mather's soteriology is directed towards the *integration* of the ruler as a type of Christ with his community. As, christologically, the personal and the divine harmonize in the *exemplum fidei*, so, historically, governor and colony are one in the work of redemption. Moreover, the source of integration lies not with the christomimētēs but with those he serves. For Mather, the community vindicates the ruler. The figural providences that demonstrate Winthrop's election are one aspect of New England's development. The parallels that *exalt* the man— Jacob, Moses, Macarius, David, Solomon, even Job, and above all Nehemiah—*define* the church-state. His similarity to the Old Testament heroes makes Winthrop unique as an individual, but representative as "Americanus."

This representative quality simultaneously identifies Winthrop in history and sets him beyond the scope of common providence. For other Christians, nationality was a secular designation. Brewster was a saint, but his English traits, or his Dutch habits of dress, or his New English diet, identify him within secular history. In Winthrop's case, as in Nehemiah's, communal identity situates the individual in sacred history. *Because* he is "Americanus," his day-by-day experiences constitute "the gleamings forth of Truth / Laid in Prophetic Lines." [14] They form a wheel within a wheel, to use a favorite Puritan image (borrowed from Ezekiel's apocalyptic vision); or better perhaps, remembering the different movements of providential and prophetic time, a circle within a spiral. What would elsewhere be a common providence becomes an act of wonder. What for other saints might be a sign of grace—the birth of a son, the rise to greatness—become for Winthrop (as for Nehemiah) historical facts which join the hero's spiritual growth with the temporal movement of a holy commonwealth.

Virtually every step in Winthrop's journey enforces the congruence of private and public salvation. At the start, his genealogy establishes New England's ties to the Reformation; at the end, his death predicates the glories in store for New Israel; the experiences which bring him from one point to the other, from sacred past to promised future, illuminate the progress of the colony. Providence

calls Winthrop to America because a "Moses . . . must be the
leader of so great an undertaking." Providence directs him to the
bar so that he may better serve "a famous plantation founded and
formed for the seat of the most reformed Christianity." The
evildoers who vex him reveal themselves as providential obstacles to
the purposes of the divine plan. If the settlers themselves sometimes
rise up against him, "the victories of this great man over himself
. . . also at last proved victories over other men"; providentially,
his afflictions ensure "an even exacter parallel" between Nehemiah's church-state and New England's. Summarily, it is his fate and
fortune, as the pagans would have phrased it, to have been a
zealous patriot. His "eternal memorial" is an action in time that
issues in a communal legacy. The walls of the New World
Jerusalem bespeak the merging of history and spiritual biography
in the flow of the work of redemption.

In this figural context, Mather integrates the exemplary Life and
the Church History. Like the biography, the *Magnalia* is "an
history," Mather tells us, "to anticipate the state of New-Jerusalem." Like the biography, the *Magnalia* begins by exploring New
England's ties to the Reformation and ends by projecting the
theocracy into the future. And as in the biography, the *littera-historia*
Mather records in his narrative sections, from the discovery of
America (book 1) to the colonists' final conflict with the Tempter
(the Indian wars, in book 7) express the movement of sacred time.
John Higginson's preface to the *Magnalia* describes at once Mather's
historiography and the controlling theme of "Nehemias Americanus":

> It hath been deservedly esteemed one of the great and
> wonderful works of God in this *last age*, that the Lord stirred up
> the spirits of so many thousands of his servants . . . to
> transport themselves . . . into a *desert land* in America . . . in
> the way of *seeking first the kingdom of God.* . . . Surely of this *work*,
> and of this *time*, it shall be said, *what hath God wrought?* And, *this
> is the Lord's doings, it is marvellous in our eyes!* . . . And therefore
> he has taken care, that his own *dealings* with his people in the
> course of his *providence* . . . should be recorded . . . as (Exodus
> xvii. 14,) "The Lord said unto Moses, *write this for a memorial in a
> book*" [Higginson then cites similar directions from Exod.

17 : 14, Deut. 31 : 19, and Ps. 102 : 18, 44 : 1, 78 : 3–5, and 45 : 17]; . . . and this is one reason why the Lord commanded so great a part of the *Holy Scriptures* to be written in an *historical way*, that the wonderful works of God towards his church and people . . . might be known *unto all generations:* and after the *scripture-time* . . . he hath stirred up some or other to write the *acts and monuments* of the church of God in all ages; especially since the *reformation of religion* from anti-christian darkness. . . .

And therefore surely it hath been a duty incumbent upon the people of God, in this our New-England, that there should be extant, a true *history* of the wonderful works of God in . . . America: which . . . may stand as a *monument*, in relation to future times, of a fuller and better *reformation* of the Church of God, than it hath yet appeared in the world. For by this *Essay* it may be seen, that a *farther practical reformation* than that which began at the first coming out of the darkness of *Popery*, was aimed at . . . . [We] came out into a *wilderness* for that very end . . . . How far we have attained this design, may be judged by this *Book*.[15]

This is an unusually astute account of Mather's aims both as chronicler and as biographer—because Higginson understands, as most later readers have not, that those aims are at bottom soteriological. When Higginson speaks of providence, it is to make plain the figural nature of providence in this instance. The people in question are unique—God's chosen; the time they live in is portentous—"this *last age*"; the events that characterize it are *"marvellous in our eyes!";* they signal nothing less than the establishment of God's kingdom on earth; and the *"historical way"* towards that consummation leads forward through "all ages" with an ever-enlarging sense of fulfillment: Israel, the church of Christ, the Reformation, and now *("what hath the Lord wrought"!)* this *"desert land* of America." Providence is a function of promise here, and the hero primarily an agent of history, himself a providential *figura* in the spiral of preordained correspondences—in Higginson's thrice-repeated phrase, one of "the wonderful works of God" that have culminated in the ecclesiastical history of New England.

MIRACULA APOCALYPSIS

The phrase is not Higginson's, of course. It comes from Isaiah's millennial vision (25 : 1 ff.), which exegetical tradition joined to the description of Christ's *miracula* or *magnalia* upon His entry into Jerusalem (Matt. 21). So considered, the phrase vividly evokes the Second Coming, and as such it recurs throughout colonial literature. The old Salem minister may have recalled some of Richard Mather's "Seventy Lectures" to the emigrants, virtually all of them glowing with the expectation of eschatological wonders, and Edward Johnson's *Wonder-Working Providence of Sion's Savior in New-England*, which hails the colony as "the wonder of the world," created to demonstrate "to all Nations, the neere approach of the most wonderful workes that ever the Sonnes of men saw." Probably he had read New England's official response, in 1648, to European critics, where Thomas Shepard and others sought to "recount the singular workings of divine providence" in America in order to "stop the mouths of all that . . . blaspheme the goodness of God in His glorious works." Almost certainly he had heard of John Cotton's sermons on Canticles and Revelation, which proved that the settling of Massachusetts Bay was the climactic wonder of the Reformation, and which conveyed the proof with such authority that one settler, at least, felt inspired to inscribe his response in poetry:

> From the beginning to this Day
> Were ever seen such works I say,
> . . . .
> Now shall Jehova Reign for Aye.[16]

In any case, Higginson knew the numerous second- and third-generation accounts of these wonder-working providences: how they had revealed New England as "a type and Embleme of New Jerusalem," a manifestation of "glorious issues" at hand, "a *First Fruits* of that which shall in due time be accomplished in the whole world throughout." "Consider," cried Increase Mather in 1675, "That there are no persons in all the world unto whom God speaketh by [His] Providence as he doth to us"; "Mention, if you can," he challenged Christendom in 1686, "a People in the world so priviledged as we are!" He kept repeating the challenge through the first decades of the eighteenth century in such works as *A Sermon Shewing That the Present Dispensations of Providence Declare That Wonderful Revolutions Are Near* (1710). Higginson himself had joined in this view long before, in an impassioned election-day address on

The Cause of God and His People in New-England (1663). From the same platform ten years later, his colleague and Increase's predecessor as Harvard's president, Urian Oakes, summed up what "in sober sense of many of our Divines" was the meaning of two generations of the New England Way:

> if we . . . lay all things together, this our Commonwealth seems to exhibit to us a *specimen,* or a *little model of the Kingdome of Christ upon Earth,* . . . wherein it is generally acknowledged and expected. This work of God set on foot and advanced to a good Degree here, being spread over the face of the Earth, and perfected as to a greater Degrees of Light and Grace and Gospel-glory will be (as I conceive) *the Kingdome of Jesus Christ so much spoken of.*[17]

From Cotton through Oakes, the emphasis on figural providence has a single purpose: to impose a sacred *telos* upon secular events. The miracles of grace that John Beadle attributed to the justified saint, the orthodoxy extended to the destiny of their church-state. *Here,* with respect *to us,* insofar as they are *our* mercies, God's temporal judgments are previews of last things. It is a wonder that Winthrop should be saved, and that in his last moments he should receive assurances of glorification. It is no less a wonder that the colony he represents should persevere through its wilderness trials to become a specimen of the imminent kingdom. For the saint, such *miracula* crown the privileges that mark the journey of his soul. For the church, they crown the figural providences that ensure its warfaring progress towards Armageddon. In Winthrop's case, both kinds of *miracula* blend in the "acts of pattern" that prove the colony's role in the salvation of mankind. Urian Oakes argues this conjunction in *The Soveraign Efficacy of Divine Providence.* His most famous Harvard student set out its implications at large, a decade later, in *The Wonderful Works of God* (1690). "An *Age of Miracles,*" announced Cotton Mather, "is now Dawning upon us," one in which we of "this *New-English Israel* . . . are more involved than any men Living." It were well, therefore, if some "good historian" among us in these ends of the earth would memorialize the men and events that shaped our past: "O Lord God, Thou hast begun to shew thy Servants thy Greatness . . . ; we shall . . . very quickly see those, glorious Things which are spoken of *thee, O thou City of God!*" With that wonderful prospect before his eyes, as Higginson understood, he wrote his church-history of New England. Predictably, he began with a vision of "the WONDERS of the CHRISTIAN RELIGION"—the *magnalia Christi* of the drama of redemption—reaching their climax in the "wonderful displays . . . [of] His Divine Providence" on the American strand.[18]

This eschatological application of providence to a colonial venture required explanation to the world at large, and the clergy readily responded. In a secular view, they began, the ways of God are mysterious. Providences "interfere with one another sometimes; one providence seems to look this way, another providence seems to look that way, quite contrary to one another." Sometimes, indeed, they "seem to run counter with His word." Small wonder that even the best of men—even saints like Bradford, who holds a place of honor in the *Magnalia*—have "been put to a non-plus here." But we, the colonists continued, we New England saints, *"the Apple of God's eye,"* need not resign ourselves to those "dark and amazing intricacies." For us, "The Works of Divine Providence are great and wonderful." By and large, we have been "dandled in the lap of his providence." God has "prospered his people here beyond ordinary ways of providence," showered a "singular" and "almost unexampled, unparall[el]ed mercy" upon our efforts; in fact, "the matchless favors of God unto New England" show that He has from the start been "so dealing with New England as not with any nation." And even when His judgments have gone hard against us, and deservedly so, they confirm our place in the grand design. Elsewhere, His retribution may be ambiguous or incomprehensible or a sign of utter disaster. Here we may feel secure that though "the Lord may afflict us . . . he will not destroy us." More accurately, He will afflict us because He would save us. As Increase Mather argued in his *Doctrine of Divine Providence* (1684), echoing John Winthrop's words of over half a century before, the "way of gods kingdome is accompanied with most difficulties." [19]

The notion of gracious affliction is commonplace enough in the saint's Life, but startling as a framework for interpreting the secular, terrestrial course of a community. We might well see it, indeed, as the epitome of the colonial clergy's attempt to elevate the mundane into the realm of sotoriology—of redemptive history and last things. They prepared the saint for heaven by making visible the prospect of hell; they prodded the colony forward by stressing God's untoward providences. In both cases, they were telling their listeners that His wrath twined with His love in "the Golden Checker work of the Draw net of [figural] Providence." *"There is a great difference,"* they observed, *"in those temporal judgments, which the wicked and the righteous are subject to in this world.* For when such judgments fall on the wicked, they are Paenal, they are part of the Curse . . . . Whereas it is otherwise with the Righteous; the afflictions that befall them are . . . fatherly ones . . . ; the Lord chasteneth [them] . . . as a father doth his son in whom he delights." The image is christological, but its purpose in these sermons is unmistakably historical and communal. "Have you not observed that there have been more . . . awfull tremendous dispensations of divine Providence in New-England then in any place [else] . . . ?" Rejoice, therefore, in the venture you have espoused. *"God is terrible out of his holy Places,"* [20] and blessed are the New Englanders whom He chastens: their hardships are an earnest of the dawning Age of Miracles—like Winthrop's afflictions, the cornerstone of the holy city to come.

A striking third-generation example of this dialectic is Cotton Mather's *Wonders of the Invisible World* (1693), which restructures the Salem witchcraft episode into a preview of Armageddon, and New England in general into an emblem of the church triumphant. The second-generation view is represented by Increase Mather's *The Day of Trouble Is Near* (1674), one of the fiercest of colonial jeremiads, delivered at the onset of King Philip's War, the most ominous event the settlers had yet encountered. Why, Increase thundered, has God so scourged His people? Why has He set the Indians upon us to pillage and destroy? Why, because we *are* His people: the pattern, the privilege, is prescribed in scripture. Our "most dismall *Providence* . . . was decreed before the world began"—and decreed to this end, that whereas other communities His providence destroys, ours it corrects, sanctifies, and so girds for further accomplishments. When God exposed Christ to sufferings, He laid bare the figural ways of providence with respect to the church in all ages. David was sorely troubled, as was Jacob, Job, Moses, Solomon, and Nehemiah; and the reason is not far to seek:

> God hath Covenanted with his people that sanctified afflictions shall be their portion. . . . *When glorious Promises are near unto*

their birth we may conclude also that a day of trouble is near. . . . This
is the usual method of divine Providence, . . . by the greatest
Miseries to prepare for the greatest Mercies. . . . *Without doubt,
the Lord Jesus hath a peculiar respect unto this place, and for this people.*
This is *Immanuels Land.* Christ by a wonderful Providence hath
. . . caused as it were *New Jerusalem* to come down from
Heaven; He dwells in this place: therefore we may conclude
that he will scourge us. . . . [In the words of] a Jewish Writer
. . . who lived in the dayes of the Second Temple [i.e., after
Nehemiah's return from Babylon]; "the dealings of God with
our Nation . . . and with the Nations of the World is very
different: for other Nations . . . God doth not punish . . .
until they have filled up the Measure of their sins, and then he
utterly destroyeth them; but if our Nation forsake the God of
their Fathers never so little, God presently cometh up on us
with one Judgement or other, that so he may prevent our
destruction." So . . . he'll reckon with them [other communi-
ties] for all at last; but if *New-England* shall forsake the Lord,
Judgement shall quickly overtake us, because God . . . will be
gracious to the remnant of Joseph.[21]

The difference, Increase Mather is saying, between the providences
visited upon New England and those visited upon "the Nations of
the World" is like the difference in meaning between scriptural
precedents applied to the damned and to the elect. Nehemiah can
serve at most as a model of morality for the unregenerate; but he
illuminates the saint's way to heaven. Similarly, God's judgments
elevate or destroy "other Nations"; whereas in "our Nation" they
signify His concern with the community's salvation.

The transformation of local providences into *miracula apocalypsis*
speaks directly to the meaning of "Americanus" in the Life of
Winthrop. Significantly, Cotton Mather applies the same figures to
the governor that his father does to the colony at large—Jacob, Job,
Solomon, Moses, Joseph, Nehemiah—and with much the same
intention. Like Immanuel's Land in Increase's sermon, "Nehemias
Americanus" proclaims the forward movement of redemptive
history. As the representative of theocracy, the Hebrew stands not
with but behind the Puritan. The restored Jerusalem under
Nehemiah forms the background, as it were, for the greater New

World Jerusalem. That background includes all the other Old Testament and early Christian parallels which Mather summons to convey Winthrop's figural meaning. And that figural meaning, we have seen, renders Winthrop *unus inter pares,* one among many other heroes of redemptive history, reincarnate as Americans. Urian Oakes, writes Mather, our "Drusius Nov-Anglicanus," was "a Moses among his people, . . . the Jerom of our Bethlehem! . . . Had Austin [i.e., Augustine] been here, he might now have seen 'Paul in the pulpit'." As we read from one Life in the *Magnalia* to the next it comes to seem as though all the great men of history—including Augustine, *redivivus* in Richard Mather—had converged on the American Bethlehem, as witness to the birth of the kingdom. Hooker and Cotton were our Luther and Melancthon, Thomas Parker our Homer, Edward Hopkins our Solomon, John Fiske our Calvin, Francis Higginson (father of Salem's pastor) our Noah, Thomas Cobbet our Eusebius, Thomas Prince our Mecaenas, John Davenport our Jethro, Thomas Shepard our Seneca and Aristotle in one, Charles Chauncy our "Cadmus Americanus." The colony has its equivalent of the heroines of the past in Anne Bradstreet; Sir William Phips conjures up a constellation of civic and military notables; the Mathers provide abundantly in most other fields of endeavor.[22]

To delineate the colony's ancestry thus is to predicate its future. Mather's biographical parallels function as a substitute for local secular history, a sort of *Heilsgeschichte* antiquarianism informing us of New England's true descent. By definition they also open out into a *Heilsgeschichte* teleology. Attesting as they do to sequence and gradation, Mather's parallels demonstrate New England's superiority to the communities that foreshadow it. If they link the American with some Greek or Roman epigone, the American usually has "greater things to be affirmed of him than could ever be reported concerning any of the famous men which have been celebrated by . . . Plutarch." Mather searches the archives of Europe for an equal to Phips only to abandon "that hemisphere of the world" for "the regions of America." *His* famous men are "better qualified," better educated and "better skilled" than their forebears (and more modest). Winthrop is not simply like Aeneas but, by virtue of his beliefs (i.e., those of the theocracy) a more heroic Aeneas. He resembles but supersedes Caesar in the communal laws he espouses,

Alexander and Hannibal in the Puritan precepts he follows. "Let Greece boast of her patient Lycurgus"—so Mather begins the biography—"let Rome tell of her devout Numa . . . . Our New England shall tell and boast of her Winthrop, a lawgiver as patient as Lycurgus, but not admitting any of his criminal disorders; as devout as Numa but not liable to any of his heathenish madnesses." Most of the biographies open with a similar comparativist survey. All the glories of Greece cannot equal Thomas Hooker, in whom the reader may "behold at once the *wonders* of *New-England.*" Tales of the early church usher in the *"golden men"* of the "primitive times of New-England." If a perpetual flame lit the tabernacle of old, "the tabernacle . . . in this wilderness had *many* such 'burning and shining lights.' " Curious pagan customs adumbrate our "more worthy" practices. The American saints rather than the "pretended successors to Saint Peter," body forth the apostolic succession. "*Fires* of martyrdom" [23] from Nero to Queen Mary illuminate the voyage of the *Arbella*.

In sum, like the figural providences he records, Mather's biographical parallels demonstrate that all roads to New Jerusalem lead through the Great Migration. On this premise, each Life in the *Magnalia* establishes the colony's place in the grand design, while the preface to each group of Lives affirms the individual's place in the colonial mission. Mather introduces the divines by proclaiming New England the holiest country in the world, the magistrates by announcing that the church-state surpasses all other regions this side of heaven in civic virtue. "I know very well," he adds, that historians like "to throw an air of grandeur around the origin of States," and to inflate their records with "mythic traditions." But not he. His are "the real facts," agreeable to an enlightened age. If, as he tells us, he embeds them in "multiplied references to other and former concerns, closely couched, for the observation of the attentive, in almost every paragraph," he does so in order to make the facts bloom like "choice flowers" in the garden of God. To this end, in his narrative sections, he marshals a host of providential *magnalia*, every one an emblem of the entire community. And to this end he parades before us the heroes who made "the *beginnings* of this country . . . illustrious," and its subsequent growth "a *specimen* of many good things" to come.[24]

Hence the commingling of teleology and spiritual biography in

the Life of Winthrop: Lycurgus, Numa, and Moses look forward to
the New World governor; the cultures of Greece, Rome, and Israel
point towards the Puritan church-state—"this little *nation*," Mather
calls it, "yet a nation of heroes!" [25] As the two kinds of exemplariness, individual and cultural, coalesce—as New England makes
good her boast by telling of her Winthrop—the multiplied references surrounding New England's father become a corporate
genealogy, a stock of heroes culled from the entire family of man to
illustrate the colonial cause. They create a historical context which,
like Winthrop himself, does honor to a national cause without
becoming part of secular history, and to the cause of Christ without
becoming a generalized allegory. It incorporates *exempla* from every
corner of Christian and pagan antiquity, and it extends from the
ancient to the modern world. Mather is careful to make these
"embellishments" conform to the theme of government; and if at
times they seem to run to an indiscriminate catalogue of *memorabilia*,
that is precisely his intent: the random, sweeping effect conveys the
density required by his soteriological concept of Winthrop, the
model both of sainthood and of theocracy, Nehemiah's counterpart
as microchristus and, simultaneously, the greater Nehemiah because he is the governor of the American Israel.

PROPHETICA

Mather's teleology has its basis in Reformed thought. One of the
central motifs in early Protestant sermons is the flight from Babylon
under Nehemiah. Spiritually, it signifies Christ's deliverance of His
beloved from the bondage of sin. Historically, it signifies His Second
Coming, when He will complete His combat with Satan, and reveal
in full glory what He accomplished in the flesh. The emphasis, that
is, on the actual past accents the timeless, selfless *imitatio*. The
perspective on the supernatural future reveals the actual movement
of history. Of course, the Reformers did not invent this prophetic
sense of the Christ-event—this sense of time as a predetermined
exfoliation of the meaning of certain men and events, so that we
may know everything at any given moment provided we recognize
our relative position in a developmental scheme. Long before
Luther, the medieval scholastics had codified Augustine's seven-
stage scheme of *Heilsgeschichte*, giving due stress to the Babylonian

captivity (the fifth stage), the present Christian millennium (the sixth stage, dated from the Incarnation), and the heavenly paradise (the seventh and last period), generally referred to, in order to intimate the organic development from Creation to Judgment Day, as the Great Sabbatism. But the scholastics discouraged prophetic speculation. Wisely fearing the disruptive enthusiasm such speculation could provoke, they insisted instead on the private and institutional aspects of typology, in effect opposing the christological use of the *figura* to the soteriological. Augustine, they pointed out, had centered his doctrine of last things on the individual experience. For that purpose, the sacramental life of the church sufficed; there, the believer could find both form and means of deliverance. In all other respects, he should attend to common providence.

It was precisely by recourse to prophecy that the first Reformers sought to justify their break with Rome. In 1522, the same year he denounced the Saints' Lives, Luther concluded from a study of Daniel that the sixth stage represented not the Christian era but just the reverse—the reign of Antichrist. He did not flinch from following through the stupendous import of his discovery. The sixth stage of history, he declared, was not postmillennial, as Augustine had believed, not a constant efflorescence of Christ's influence until the Second Coming. The millennial period was yet to come; the church still languished in premillennial darkness, awaiting its deliverance, as during the fifth period the Hebrews had languished in Babylon. Upon this premise, he announced the summary challenge of his new-found Protestantism. As the Hebrews had been called by Nehemiah from captivity, so now the Reformers were being called to liberate the new chosen people, the remnant of Joseph heralded by Revelation, from its thousand-year bondage to the Romish Whore. Luther's identification of Catholicism with Antichrist led him to encourage a fresh, literalist study of the past, mainly to prove papal corruption. His prophetic summons was sounded from Protestant pulpits for the next two centuries. It unleashed an avalanche of histories—of the Reformation, the world, particular nations, towns, and counties—all of them guided by the belief in the approaching Judgment Day:

> Although that which is foretold . . . was in part fulfilled when
> the people of God returned from Captivitie in Babylon at the

end of seventie yeares: yet we must not limit the place to that
time onely. . . . For as some passages in this Scripture were
never fully accomplished . . . so many things that literally
concerned the Jewes were types and figures, signifying the like
things concerning the people of God in these latter dayes.[26]

That time, these latter dayes, never fully accomplished: in such figural
formulations soteriology displaced christology, or more precisely,
christology became a function of the work of redemption. The
imitatio was the absolute means to a temporal end, giving the
individual the right to declare himself part of an ongoing corporate
journey towards a glory that was present but still inchoate,
evolving, its full prophetic sense yet to be made manifest. And as the
eschatological focus thus shifted from memory to anticipation, the
correspondence between the believer and the Bible narrative took
on a radically historical significance. The *process* now, not the fact of
fulfillment demanded elucidation. The source of personal identity
was not the Jesus of the gospels but the ongoing works of Christ
leading towards the Messiah of the apocalypse. For historically
considered, Jesus too was a *typus Christi*, a scriptural figure signifying
greater things to come. He had completed the *spiritual* drama of
redemption, but the literal conquest of Satan, the actual transformation of the wilderness, remained still to be accomplished. The
kingdom He regained in the Arabian desert adumbrated New
Jerusalem. The deeds that together formed the perfect *exemplum fidei*
were partial signs of the miracles He would perform at Gog and
Magog; and not He alone, but all the "people of God in these latter
dayes."

This process of fulfillment was no less rooted in sacred history
than was the typology that linked the Old and New Testaments,
and no less centered on the concept of Christ as antitype. But in one
case, history culminated in the New Testament narrative: all types
met in the Incarnation; the believer's christic identity was absolute
and comprehensive. In the other case, history continued *through* the
prophecies of the Old and New Testaments: the meaning of the
antitype was developmental; christic identification devolved upon
postscriptural events in the progress of the church. Soteriologically,
then, an intricate hierarchy of types and antitypes unfolded,
denoting *relative* perfections in different moments of time—"centu-

ries," as for the first time they came to be termed, and "periods."
This sense of progression was sometimes applied to scriptural events
(e.g., Nehemiah's release from Babylon as a partial fulfillment of
Moses' exodus from Egypt). In the main, however, it concerned
promises which had "never been fully accomplished." Thus Israel's
salvation, though spiritually fulfilled in Christ, also foreshadowed
the Conversion of the Jews, an event "more eminent and wonderful,
for the TYPE must needs come short of the ANTITYPE." So, too,
Eden foreshadowed both Canaan and, more wonderfully, the reign
of the saints. As a prophetic type, the conquering armies of Joshua
adumbrated the children of light at Armageddon, and Joshua
himself (with Nehemiah and other Israelite leaders) heralded not
only Jesus but the conquering Son of Man. In these terms, Luther
pronounced himself the New Moses of the Reformation, Bale and
Foxe pronounced England the elect nation, and the New England
settlers, as we have seen, discovered in their migration God's call to
His redeemed, and world-redeeming, remnant. Our undertaking,
wrote Winthrop in 1629, "appears to be a worke of God. . . . He
hath some great worke in hand wch he hath revealed to his prophets
among us." As antitype of the Hebrews under Nehemiah, they were
to found a specimen of New Jerusalem, "a preface to the New
Heavens," [27] in the New World.

It would probably overestimate Mather's artistry to read a
deliberate framing device in the word reversals that begin and end
the biography: Nehemiah for Winthrop, New England for Jerusalem. Unquestionably, though, Mather meant the title to suggest
(and the biography to dramatize) what these substitutions intimate.
Ten years earlier, Samuel Wakeman declared in an election-day
sermon that "*Jerusalem* was, *New England* is, they were, you are God's
own, God's covenant People; . . . put but in *New-England*'s name
instead of that of *Jerusalem*," and you shall see the meaning of our
errand. To amplify that comparison Mather reports in the *Magnalia*'s General Introduction his study of the "Figures variously
Embossed" in the Bible's "*Prophetical* as well as *Historical Calender*." He
has succeeded, he tells us, in having "all the *typical* men and things
. . . accommodated with their Antitypes" and "the *histories* of all
ages, coming in with punctual . . . *fulfilments* of the divine Prophecies." Such calculations were especially pertinent to biography: in a
proto-Hegelian dialectic, they defined the individual against the

entire spectrum of history, sacred and secular. When New England ministers insisted, as they repeatedly did, that *"Prophecie* is Historie *antedated*, and Historie is *Postdated Prophecie,"* they were typologically accommodating the spiritual state of each of their listeners to the providential *magnalia* of the community, and hence to the direction of redemptive history:

> Prophecies in the Old Testament . . . help in the belief of New-Testament prophecies, many of them being already accomplisht, others also of them agreeing with Those in Revelation [i.e., they remain yet to be accomplished]. . . . *Prophecie* is Historie *antedated* and Historie is *Postdated Prophecie:* the same thing is told in both. . . . Therefore the Historie of the Old Testament is Example to us. . . . Such accommodations will be easy to New England; seeing there is such considerable similitude and agreement in the circumstances.[28]

This local emphasis, they continued, was by no means parochial. The destiny of Christ's people in America was the destiny of mankind. What they had "advanced to a good Degree here" had its fuller meaning in Christ's end-time kingdom. Conversely, the holy men and institutions of times past, though inscribed in Scripture *sub specie aeternitatis*, served now to illuminate the settler's place in what Mather called the "long line of *Inter-Sabbatical Time."* In this prophetic light, three generations of New England orthodoxy hailed the colonists as the heirs of the ages, warning the world that they were shortly to raise an earthquake which would shake all Christendom. John Eliot exulted in those prospects with every Indian conversion he obtained, and Anne Bradstreet, predicting the imminency of Christ's Fifth Monarchy through the *persona* of "New England," called for a holy war against Rome and Turkey. The second-generation echoes and amplifications include sermons, treatises, and poems by virtually every ministerial luminary. The major third generation voice was Cotton Mather's, but he found ample support from such diverse figures as Samuel Willard, whose *Fountain Opened*, a variation on Increase Mather's millennial *Mystery of Israel's Salvation* (1669), went through three editions by 1697, and Samuel Sewall, who organized a debating club on the fine points of Revelation and carried on an enthusiastic correspondence with Edward Taylor on the precise time and place of the Parousia.[29]

With all the authority of that tradition, John Higginson, by 1697 the colonial Nestor, wrote his "Attestation" to Mather's Church History. By that authority he acclaimed the *Magnalia*'s exemplars as prefigurations of a "better *reformation* of the Church of God, than it hath yet appeared in the world." Men like Winthrop, he explained, were worthy of imitation as saints, and as saints worthy bearers of the title "Americanus." But he had to admit that as Americans— that is, as men in history, bearing a specific relation to the future—they fell short of the ideal. "They did as much as could be expected from learned and godly men in their circumstances," but the circumstances themselves were limiting. They pointed to, but did not constitute, the *"perfect reformation."* And that heuristic quality, he concluded triumphantly, gave those men the right to serve as our guides—to *"refresh our souls"* in our proleptic participation in the "times of greater light and holiness that are to come . . . when the Lord shall make Jerusalem . . . a praise in the earth." [30]

It was not by chance, then, that Nehemiah became the favorite ministerial as well as magisterial *exemplum* of the colonial clergy. He stood for the succession of exoduses, at once repetitive and developmental, that would culminate in the exodus from history itself: Noah abandoning a doomed world, Abraham setting forth from idolatrous Ur, the Hebrews fleeing their Egyptian persecutors, the primitive Christians leaving heathen Rome, and, in modern times, the emergence of the true church from the dungeons of Rome. Within this framework, the flight from Babylon applied with special force to their own departure, in due time, from the deprivations of Europe. Mather begins the *Magnalia* by imaging that departure as the last and greatest of premillennial migrations. His image is a commonplace in the literature. During the preceding half-century the orthodoxy turned to the Jerusalem of Nehemiah more persistently than to any other single Old Testament episode. They invoked it through the *figura* of the second temple, comparing their leaders almost as a matter of habit to the temple foundations, stones, and pillars. They evoked it within other, larger metaphors, as in their recurrent references to "the wall and the garden." They explicated it by a variety of hermeneutic approaches, including those of the cabalists. They enacted the correspondences in their convenant-renewal ceremonies—one of their main devices for rallying their congregations to the Good Old Way—which they modeled proudly on Nehemiah's practice upon his return to Jerusalem. And they repeatedly defined the Good Old Way as the inspiriting-reprimanding voice of Nehemiah upon their walls, a ghostly ancestral presence trying to *"encourage the hearts and strengthen the hands of the* [present] *Builders of our Jerusalems wall."* [31]

In all cases, the message was the same. Nehemiah's undertaking foreshadowed the final deliverance of the church, whose bright pattern now shone from these ends of the earth more radiantly than ever before. The Life of Winthrop sustains the pattern with other parallels, including those drawn from classical antiquity. I indicated that Aeneas functions as precedent and moral *exemplum,* but here again figural exegesis is the key to Mather's full meaning. Almost from the start typology extended perforce to pagan literature. Since, doctrinally, all truth emanates from one center, which is Christ, it follows that heathen myths, insofar as they contain *some* truth, refer to Him. To be sure, particular mythical forms (names, places, incidents) obscure and at times distort the essence. But once the essence stands revealed in the light of the New Testament, it necessarily partakes of the basic pattern, thus paving the way, in the words of Clement of Alexandria (one of Mather's favorite expositors among the early Fathers), for the march of the elect. Samuel Mather notes that the gods Iao, Jove, Euios, and Adonis adumbrate Jehovah and Jesus. Correctly interpreted, the legends that describe their deeds exemplify God's plan of redemption. Mather's use of Apollo in his Life of Sir William Phips is representative:

> The story of Og, the king of the woody Bashan, encountered and conquered by Joshua, the Lord General of Israel, with his armies passing into Canaan, was the very thing which the Gentiles, in after ages, did celebrate under the notion of the serpent Python (which is the same with Typhon) destroyed by Apollo. . . . 'Tis as clear that Apollo, who was anciently called Paean, or *healer,* is the same with Joshua. . . . They by whom Typhon was combated, came out of Egypt, and so did the armies of Joshua. . . .
>
> Reader, 'twas not unto a Delphos, but unto a Shiloh, that the planters of New-England have been making their progress, and [the Indian] King Philip is not the only Python that has

been giving them obstruction in their passage and progress thereunto. But . . . all the *serpents,* yea, or giants, that formerly molested that religious plantation, found themselves engaged in a fatal enterprize. We have by a plain and true history secured the story of our successes from falling under the disguises of mythology. . . . And we will not conceal the *name* of the God our Saviour. . . . No, 'tis our Lord Jesus Christ, worshipped according to the rules of his blessed gospel, who is the great Phoebus, that "SUN of righteousness," who hath so saved his churches from the designs of the "generations of the dragon." [32]

The passage demonstrates how easily figuralism lends itself either to a biographical or a historiographical approach, and how naturally, for an American Puritan, it comes to embrace scriptural model and local providence. For the Plymouth Separatists, Joshua was a *typus Christi* leading us through "the remaining part of our pilgrimage," and the story of Og simply one more lesson in grace: the Israelites' "bloody victory" shadows forth the spiritual blessings awaiting all who have been washed in the blood of the lamb.[33] Mather subsumes that view within a soteriological application which brings all of time to bear upon the meaning of King Philip's War. The Bible story is "the very thing" celebrated by the pagan poets Homer, Ovid, and Virgil; the legendary Python, that old serpent, "is the same with" Og and Satan; and Apollo "is the same with" Joshua who "is" Jesus who in turn "is the great Phoebus." As he strips away the "disguises of mythology," Mather transforms the timeless present into a sweeping temporal revelation. In *his* "plain history," Christ antitypes Joshua-Apollo, and the victorious New England army antitypes the Israelites entering Canaan. That is to say, both Jesus the Nazarene and the New Englanders foreshadow the Son/Sun of Righteousness. (The christic reference comes from the vision that closes the Old Testament: Malachi's paean [4 : 1–5] to the great and dreadful Day when God's redeemed people, protected by His healing Apollonian wings, will destroy the wicked). The entire configuration is geared toward the colonial errand; but Mather invokes it, we must remember, for the purposes of biography. From Delphos to Bashan to New Canaan, the progress of history serves to define Sir William Phips as the American Joshua.

At several points, Mather hints at a similar configuration in the parallel between Aeneas and America's Winthrop. But in general he does not explicate the parallel as precisely as he does that of Apollo or Python. There was no need. He had every reason to assume the reader's familiarity with the long exegetical tradition that christianized Aeneas in his role as leader, saint, and father of the people. Besides, Mather makes it plain that he conceived the *Magnalia* as a greater *Aeneid*. He alludes to the Roman epic more frequently, more consistently, than to any other work (except for the Bible), from his opening invocation, a direct paraphrase of Virgil's, to the last section, concerning the wars against Og-Philip, which he entitles "Arma Virosque Cano." His purpose here pertains equally to the colony and to its first governor. New England's plantation excels the founding of Rome as its heroes resemble and outshine the Trojan remnant, and as the Shiloh they approach supersedes the Augustan *Pax Romana*.[34] In this context, it would be excessive to apply the heaped-up commentaries on Virgil as prophet of Christ, on the *Aeneid* as allegory, on Aeneas as *typus Christi*, to the Life of Winthrop. We can see readily enough what Mather intended: to reinforce the structure of the biography by making Winthrop's *magnalia* intrinsic to the pattern of Christ's mighty deeds in America. More clearly than any other pagan hero, pious Aeneas, the Good Magistrate destined by Jove/Jehova to harrow hell, to rebuild the walls of Latium and change the course of civilization, enacts the design of exodus and restoration that unveils the prophetic sense of New England's Nehemiah.

Mather supports the design by way of many other classical and Christian figures: Lycurgus and Numa Pompilius, the fabled restorers of Greek and Roman law (as Winthrop, adumbrating Christ in His kingly office, helped restore the forms of theocracy); the emperors Valentinian and Theodosius, who transformed Rome from a heathen to a Christian state (as Winthrop helped transform the American wilderness); Calvin and Luther, the Nehemiahs of the Reformation, who prepared the way for the exodus to New England. But as we might expect, he draws most heavily on scriptural parallels, particularly those which carried traditional associations with Nehemiah in American Puritan rhetoric. Several of these I have already mentioned. Winthrop resembles David insofar as David was "a cleare Prophet . . . of every particular

Christian," insofar as the Davidic kingdom foreshadowed the church-state, and insofar as that church-state (Mather notes elsewhere) was a "praesage" of New Jerusalem. The parallel with Job culminates, we recall, in Winthrop's deathbed "conflicts from the tempter, whose wrath grew as the time to exert it grew short." As such, it evokes a historical stereotype which had become almost as familiar as the christic saint to colonial audiences: "Sorrowful *Job*, the type of this *Immanuels Land*." A few years before, Mather himself had enlarged this into a central theme of an election-day address on Nehemiah (1690). His father had made it a leitmotif of his sermons throughout King Philip's War, similarly connecting magistrate with suffering servant in the context of colonial eschatology. In the first place, the clergy explained, God's concern for Job, as for Nehemiah, pointed to His wonderful latter-day figural providences: had He not "set an hedge about [us] as about *Job*, . . . *walled us about as his peculiar garden of pleasure*"? More importantly, Job's reward, like Nehemiah's, forecast "the End of the Lord with New-England": "His called and Faithful, and Chosen shall *more than overcome at last*"; in the colony's anguish lay "a certain Prognostick that happy times are near, even at the Doors." [35]

Undoubtedly, Cotton Mather meant to reinforce this prognosis by identifying Job-Winthrop's tempter as the Antichrist, whose wrath would grow "great as the time to exert it grew short" (Rev. 12 : 12). Undoubtedly, too, he hoped his readers would recognize his reference to John the Baptist when he wrote that Winthrop eschewed the " 'soft raiment' which would have been disagreeable to a wilderness." The passage from Matthew (11 : 7–15) was one of the most popular subjects of discourse in seventeenth-century New England—partly as an apostrophe to the "wilderness-condition" (in clothes, thought, morals, style, and so on), more broadly as a figural text. Observing that John is referred to here as the Elijah heralded by all the prophets—and that Christ first explains His miracles here as messianic signs (cf. Matt. 11 : 5 and Isa. 35, 61)—the ministers applied the Baptist's errand to that of the theocracy at large. Thus Danforth defines *New-England's Errand into the Wilderness* (1670): "John was greater than any of the prophets that were before him, not in respect of his personal graces" (for so understood he was one in Christ with every saint) "but in respect of the manner of his dispensation"—of his relative place, that is, in the work of redemption. Before him, foreshadowing the Baptist, were "the children of the captivity" who left Babylon to rebuild the walls of Jerusalem. After him, antityping the Baptist, were those who crossed the Atlantic to enjoy "the signal and unparallel[ed] experiences of the blessing of God" in "this wilderness." [36] Through them, the forerunner of the Incarnation stood revealed as witness to the Second Coming.

Other ministers before and after Danforth announced the good news with the same visionary enthusiasm. "The Ministry of *John Baptist* . . . may be looked upon as a Type of the last and great day." When the Baptist "arose like a bright and shining light," Jesus appeared to him "at the end of the Jewish world *in the end of the world*" (i.e., the wilderness) as a "partial fulfilment" of His promise to the church, that "all the ends of the World shall . . . turn unto the Lord." To bring that light to its full brilliancy was the colony's cause and end; and now, considering their accomplishments—considering also their afflictions, comparable to those in the Baptist's days—they could "conclude that the Sun [of Righteousness] will quickly arise upon the world": "John come thou forth, behold what Christ hath wrought / In these thy dayes." According to Edward Johnson, this particular image of corporate destiny begins with the first migration. "I am now prest for the service of our Lord Christ," he reports a departing Puritan telling a friend, "to re-build the most glorious Edifice of Mount Sion in a Wildernesse, and as John the Baptist I must cry, Prepare yee the way of the Lord, make his paths straight, for behold, hee is comming againe, hee is comming to destroy Antichrist, and give the whore double to drink the very dregs of his wrath." [37]

Johnson may have been thinking of Richard Mather, who had made that image familiar in the previous decade. But of course his emigrant is more largely a dramatic device, a *persona* for the entire enterprise. That representative emigrant comes to life towards the end of the century in the person of Richard's grandson. From the pulpit, in his diaries, through his published work, Cotton Mather reaffirms time and again that God has summoned him, the rightful heir to the theocratic dynasty, "as a John, to bee an Herald of the Lord's Kingdome now approaching." "I went to the Lord," he tells us, shortly before he began his Life of Winthrop, "and cried unto Him that the Ministry of His holy ANGELS might be allowed unto me, that the holy ANGELS may make their Descent, and the Kingdome of the Heavens come on." Soon after completing the biography he had another epiphany: "I feel the Lord Jesus Christ most sensibly carrying on, the Interests of His Kingdom, in my soul, continually," and so directing me to "become a *Remembrancer* unto the Lord, for no less than whole *Peoples*, Nations and Kingdomes." The grand type of all the Lord's remembrancers, he continues, was Moses, and like the Israelite he has commemorated the providential wonders of the past, and memorialized his people's exemplary heroes. That obligation fuses in his mind with his role as prophet and witness. To celebrate the founding fathers was *ipso facto* to predict the millennium, as Ezekiel had, and, like John the Baptist, to be "eminently *serviceable* in the *mighty Changes*." [38]

Mather's self-vaunting seems almost hysterical—until we recognize that, here as in his would-be *imitatio*, the self he vaunts is suprapersonal, the embodiment of what Ezekiel promised, Nehemiah undertook, and John witnessed. Speaking for himself, he speaks also for the remnant that Winthrop, as a second Moses, led into this wilderness. That parallel had first been advanced by the governor himself, in his vision of the city on a hill whose inhabitants have miraculously sprung into new life, "bone come to bone" (Ezek. 37 : 7). Winthrop modeled the famous exhortation that closes the *Arbella* sermon on Moses' farewell discourse at Pisgah, and that discourse, as every passenger knew, was "the Prophetical Song" of the church. What Moses had seen then, "in a true Glass" and "by the Spirit of Prophecy," was the return of God's people once and for all from captivity. Moses had not really spoken, that is, to the Israelites before him, who were to conquer Canaan only to fall from greatness. Rather, as a *figura* of Nehemiah and John the Baptist, he had addressed himself to the spiritual remnant that would be the wonder of the world in the ends of the world. Ezekiel, who was granted the same vision, "said of the Church in Babylon, *Shall these dry bones live?*"; for him, as for Moses and Nehemiah, "This Prophecy . . . [was] yet to be fulfilled." For Winthrop, the migration marked the beginning of "the accomplishment of that Prophesie concerning *the . . . coming together of those dry bones*," when the Holy City would descend upon the hill of Zion.[39]

"The eyes of the world are upon us," Winthrop had said. His biographer announces that "what is prophecied and promised" has been "fulfilled in us." The light of the city on a hill has become the light of the world. "Behold, ye European Churches, there are golden Candlesticks (more than twice times seven!) in the midst of this 'outer darkness': unto the upright children of Abraham, here hath arisen *light in darkness*." The image, from the *Magnalia*'s General Introduction, brings together many aspects of Mather's heraldic role: the seven books of his own Mosaic history, the movement from Ezekiel's valley of dry bones to the American wilderness, and the final stage of that movement, emblematized by the more than doubled golden candelabra (cf. Rev. 11), whose light arose in the darkness of John the Baptist's day. Then the darkness comprehended it not. Now its meaning was unmistakable. The greatest of the prophetic visions, Mather commented, "go successively by Sevens." As the *summum* and *ultimum* of those visions, his sevenfold proclamation to the upright children of Abraham looks forward to the time when the seven trumpets of the apocalypse would begin to sound—"Which, that it is near, even at the door, I may say, through grace I doubt not. . . . For the New Jerusalem there will be a *seat* be found in wide America." [40]

The proclamation also refers us back to those "Abrahams," led by Winthrop, who were "more than Abrahams," for "there never was a Generation that did so perfectly shake off the dust of Babylon, . . . [nor] a place so like unto New Jerusalem as New England." Increase Mather made this comparison on May 23, 1677, as the watchman of an errand undertaken on behalf of all nations and peoples. His father, Richard, and his father-in-law, John Cotton, had similarly spoken for the Great Migration as heralds of the Lord's kingdom. His son could hardly escape feeling that Christ was carrying on the same interests through him. How should he not "be touched with an Ambition, to be a Servant of . . . this now famous Countrey, which my two Grand-fathers Cotton and Mather had so considerable a stroke in the first planting of; and for the preservation whereof my Father, hath been so far Exposed"? [41] Surely Cotton Mather felt the race of sacred time most sensibly in his soul as he identified John Winthrop with the succession of prophets leading towards himself: Jacob (Abraham's grandson and patriarch of the tribes of Israel), Moses, David, Nehemiah, and John the Baptist, the namesake of New England's first governor. Surely also he heard the flutter of angels' wings as his biography drew to a close, and he recalled how the prophet for whom *he* had been named had conducted the deathbed fast for Winthrop—directly after those momentous "conflicts from the tempter"—and how "the venerable Cotton" had then proceeded to remind "the whole church" of the governor's Davidic greatness, parental beneficence, and Christ-like sorrows, in what was in effect a type of Mather's Life of Winthrop. Cotton Mather, we might say, brings both his own family line and his grandfather's funeral sermon to fulfillment by showing us the comprehensive historical design implicit in "Nehemias Americanus." As the public and private meanings of his biographical parallels converge, they form a soteriological *exemplum* of astonishing breadth and coherence. Mather's Winthrop is a man representative of his profession, of his society, of sainthood, of his biographer, and, as "Americanus," of the conjunction of all of these with the providential wonders, the *miracula apocalypsis,* that demarcate the forward sweep of redemptive history.

3

The Elect Nation in New England

Mather's synthesis of rhetorical and exegetical conventions is particularly remarkable in an age struggling with disparate theories of history and of the self; but the very effort at synthesis would seem to contradict the most salient implication of "Nehemias Americanus"—the implication, in fact, with which I began my inquiry—that Mather considers Winthrop's heroism to be not only representative but in some basic sense unique. Like "Americana" in the title of the church-history, "Americanus" enhances the sacred referent (Christ, Nehemiah) within a special historical context. Just what that specialness entails, however, cannot be accounted for by Mather's traditional techniques. Soteriology and christology are intrinsic to all Reformed thought, and perhaps inherently interrelated. The attempt to combine them in hagiography antedates the funeral orations of Ambrose and Gregory Nazanzian. The same belief that directed the Protestant (of whatever persuasion) towards communion with God often directed him to seek the prophetic key to the future. He employed the same scriptural imagery to discuss auto-machia and apocalypse. The analogy between the growth of the soul and the progress of the church appears throughout Protestant literature, including the commentaries on Revelation. And all these factors enter into the general Calvinist effort to combine religious with political ideals.

Against this background, the Life of Winthrop seems just one more variation on a central theme of English Puritanism. We know, for example, that the emigrants derived their concept of errand from the Elizabethan premises for national election, and that those premises are most amply set forth in John Foxe's great church history, which Mather acknowledges as precedent for the *Magnalia*. We know further that Mather and Foxe have much in common as biographers: the long heritage of ecclesiastical hagiography; the pronounced influence of Eusebius, who fathered the typological approach to history; an obsession with the millennial calendar ("full seventy years of Babylonish captivity," Foxe announces in the preface to his *Book of Martyrs*, "draweth now well to an end");[1] and the idea of the hero as representing a corporate mission. By defying the tempter, Foxe's English saints embrace the cause of England. By attending to their social vocations, his English magistrates contribute to the victory of the church. In sum, Mather's figuralism appears in every substantive way—intellectual, stylistic, exegetical —to follow the techniques of Foxe and his successors. Except for the accidental variant of locale, what, we may ask, is unusual about Mather's Winthrop? What is *American* about the rhetorical and conceptual design of "Nehemias Americanus"?

BRITANNIA REDIVIVA

The question requires us to turn to English Reformed soteriology, and especially to the norms of national election established by Foxe's generation and sustained through the Puritan Revolution. Like Mather, Foxe dramatizes those norms biographically, by identifying the English martyr within the scheme of redemption. "No man," he admits,

> liveth in that commonwealth where nothing is amiss. But yet because God hath so placed us Englishmen here in one commonwealth, also in one Church, as in one ship together, let us not mangle or divide the ship, which being divided perisheth, but every man serve in his order with diligence, wherein he is called.[2]

If we could overlook the problematic use of "church," we might attribute the exhortation to Winthrop himself. Its sense of destiny recalls the *Arbella* sermon; its demand for unity resembles the great speech Mather records, in which Winthrop outlines the foundations of theocratic liberty. But Foxe's use of "church" suggests a basic discrepancy in outlook from the Bay Puritans. For Winthrop and Mather, the progress of the American theocracy, church and commonwealth together, is part of ecclesiastical history. Foxe is less clear in his identification of the English church. Since he fears its destruction, he would seem to be referring to the "indiscriminate" Anglican establishment: surely, as a Calvinist he knew that the true church would persevere and that membership in it did not ultimately depend on diligence.

In another sense, however, he may well have intended to implicate the imperishable community of the elect. For Foxe the English patriot knew that his country had been singled out for an extraordinary purpose. The delicate balance he suggests between "amiss" and "But yet" hinges on what he considered to be a stupendous coincidence; in this last age England was to lead the nations of the world in the destruction of Rome. We might therefore call his reference to the church an ambiguity—provided we recognize that to be ambiguous here was not to confound terms: *ecclesia* with commonwealth, the glory of sainthood with the grandeur of patriotism. Just this sort of confusion, Foxe argued elsewhere, had sustained the Catholic heresy. National election denoted for him the coalition of separate historic movements, secular and redemptive, at a climactic point of inter-Sabbatical time. Over half a century before Foxe, Luther had similarly urged his "Dear Germans [to] take advantage because our moment has come." Like him, Foxe stressed that the spiritual realm and the earthly each had its separate duties, each separately its punishments and rewards. Only now, as never before, in England above all other countries, the two realms stood in conjunction, like planets revolving "about each other in orbits complementary but independent," [3] attracted by the force of the approaching apocalypse.

Following the logic of this view, *The Acts and Monuments of These Latter and Perillous Dayes, Touching Matters of the Church . . . Speciallye in this Realme of England* is a hybrid work. It is a martyrology of God's people and a chronicle of English kings, the two genres held together by the pervasive import (at once national and universal) of "these latter days." Foxe shows how the true church is always and everywhere persecuted. He also teaches his compatriots the precepts of civic loyalty. And if his national focus makes us feel at times that he identifies sainthood with British citizenship—makes us forget, that is, as he never does, about the eternal conflict between the world and the kingdom—we are brought back to his meaning by his dual concept of heroism. This may be illustrated by his Lives of John Wycliffe and Edward III, whose careers (according to Foxe's interpretation of Revelation 20) introduce the final period of redemptive history. Edward III was the first great "bridler of the pope's usurped power"; Wycliffe more fully than anyone before diagnosed "the poison of the pope's doctrine." [4] Each plays a key role in launching the attack against Antichrist—one in the area of power, the other in the area of doctrine.

The difference in role leads to a difference in biographical approach. Wycliffe appears as one of the redeemed, engaged in theological polemic in a wasteland darkened by Catholic malice. Significantly, his grievances center on the distortion of ecclesiastical into worldly policy. The pope insists on confining the church within certain borders and limits. Wycliffe demands: "What doth it make matter *where* Peter served the Lord? . . . The works of the Holy Ghost [are] . . . not of the place." Foxe is proud to call him his countryman, but he makes it clear that Wycliffe's life demonstrates the supranational tenets of Christian belief. Heaven's grace sustains the martyr in his anguish, his deliverances are *exempla* of God's help to all saints, his hardships and triumphs the story in brief of the entire church. The imitable pattern he leaves behind is that of the microchristus, as set forth, for instance, in Foxe's *Sermon of Christ Crucified*, or in a letter Foxe records by the Marian martyr John Bradford:

> consider that this world is the place of trial of God's people. . . . Consider where you be, not at home but in a strange country [Heb. 11 : 9]. . . . Now am I climbing up the hill; it will cause me to puff and blow before I come to the cliff. The hill is steep and high, my breath is short, and my strength is feeble. Pray therefore to the Lord for me, that as I have now through his goodness even almost come to the top, I may by his grace be strengthened not to rest till I come where I should be.[5]

Bradford's allusion to Paul applies to all men who journey towards spiritual ripeness, from the apostle himself through Shakespeare's Duke of Gloucester.

The portrait of Edward III shows little or nothing of this allegorical ascent. In Foxe's words, it deals with "matters pertaining to the public regiment"—Luther's *weltliches,* as distinct from *geistliches, Regiment.* Here the narrative is vivid in *res gestae:* political intrigue, documents of diplomatic negotiations, mob riots, and events and persons at court, not excluding Alice Perrice, "the wicked harlot" who "bewitched the king's heart" and for a time "governed all." It is a tale told by a providential historian, signifying the Good Magistrate. The model differs somewhat from the earlier manuals on government in that it integrates the Calvinist concept of godly instrument with the usual aristocratic and royal ideals. But in either form the magistrate's duty extends no further than to help the nation "go along with God's Providence." Principally, Foxe tells us, Edward is commendable for his meekness and clemency. By these and similar standards he judges even the saintly kings, like Alfred, whose government he holds up to Elizabeth for imitation. Indeed, he adjusts his moral advice throughout to support Elizabeth's secular authority, her role as leader of the *weltliche Regiment* in Christ's Reformed army. "Such princes," he observes, "as have most defended the Church . . . have not lacked at God's hand great blessing and felicity." [6] By which he means not the felicity of heaven, as he does in Wycliffe's case, but the terrestrial blessing of national election.

For all this, the structure of his work testifies that national election confers the blessings of power and doctrine alike. Foxe's dual approach calls attention to the difference between the two types of representative men in order to stress the portentous (because startling) fact of their conjunction: Wycliffe with Edward III no less than with the Marian saints, and all of them with Elizabeth. His strategy, that is, relies upon our acceptance of the traditional dichotomy between chronicle biography and hagiography, so that we may recognize the significance of their confluence at this time, in this special realm of England. He had every reason to anticipate that reaction from his readers. The traditional dichotomy continues virtually uninterrupted from the Middle Ages through the seventeenth century. Thomas Fuller, for instance (to select another prominent influence upon Mather), uses entirely different criteria for secular and ecclesiastical figures. When he characterizes the Gentleman, he considers birth, breeding, and behavior; his sketch of the Statesman, like Bacon's *Life of Henry VII*, is a lesson in the ways of this world: "though God causeth sometimes the sunne of successe to shine as well on bad as good projects, yet commonly wicked actions end in shame." As for the uncommon instances, the evil schemes that sometimes thrive, "what shall I say [?] . . . I'le look no longer on these whirlpools of State, lest my pen turn giddy." He feels on surer footing in the realm of spiritual biography—as when he extols William Whitaker, a saint much like Walton's George Herbert, who counted his "earthly employments avocations." Basically, Fuller confides, his "cue of entrance is to come in where the state writer doth go out." Observing that the study of history best becomes a gentleman, church history a Christian, and British history an Englishman, he prefaces his own *Church-History of England* with the old pious *significatio:* "it is not fit that good men should live long on earth. . . . Wicked men think this world too good, God knows it is too bad, for his servants to live in." [7]

Nonetheless, the very title of the work, juxtaposing as it does church and nation, shows the influence of Foxe; and in the course of the narrative Fuller comes to invest "Englishman," metaphorically, with at least something of the status of "Christian," in accordance with Foxe's dual approach, and with that of Protestant historiography in general. For of course Foxe did not invent the approach *ex nihilo.* He himself refers us to Eusebius; to some extent, too, his outlook may reflect the late medieval *encomia* to Catholic saints who died for a national cause. In the main it derives from Reformed church historians, such as the Magdeburg centuriators, the martyrologist Jean Crespin, the apocalypticist Heinrich Bullinger. In theory, their concerns are wholly soteriological. But responding as they did to Luther's call for a literalist revaluation of the past, they turned perforce to secular affairs (economic, political, even domestic) in order to demonstrate the unrelieved horrors of Catholicism. William Haller has shown that John Bale, Foxe's contemporary and immediate inspiration, altered this pattern to focus on the providential matter of Britain. But Bale did so within established forms. If anything, his specialized antiquarianism reinforced the distinction between saint and magistrate.

Bale's motive bespeaks his method. Convinced that he was living at the end of time, awaiting in exile a wholesale transformation of England, besides other nations, he felt it his duty to redirect his country to its rightful place at the vanguard of the Reformation. On one level, this required conscientious research. He had to rescue the actual past, "all affections set apart," from the distortions of Catholic chroniclers. On another level, one which deeply engaged his affections, his calling led him to celebrate the English martyrs.

He portrays them as a haloed company of pilgrims forsaking earthly prosperity and fleeing the seven deadly sins as they travel towards the bliss of heaven. Under persecution they provide "examples of Christ . . . unto all those that the Lord shall after like manner put forward." In death they relive the crucifixion. Bale's chronicles are meant to change national policy, "now," "in this life," "here on earth." His exemplary Lives confirm John Bradford's Pauline epistle; finally, England is not home but a place of trial, a country as strange as any other to God's chosen. From his spiritual hilltop, high above the issues of policy and change, Bale trumpets the atemporal summons of Nehemias microchristus: "Either we are citizens in the New Jerusalem or in the old superstitious Babylon." [8]

This method he passed on to later English church historians: for example to John Knox, whose *History of the Reformation in Scotland* reshapes the national past into a polemic against the "bloody wolves" of Rome.[9] Foxe went beyond Bale and Knox in only one respect, though that proved decisive in making his work the central statement of Elizabethan chauvinism. Instead of treating his local concern as one aspect of a larger conflict, he used the traditional approach to buttress the national theme. He brought spiritual and chronicle biography together in the framework of English history. By implication, he endowed English identity with a unique twofold significance, and rendered "England" a metaphor for the confluence of redemptive and providential history. What makes it metaphor, rather than either fact or conceit, is the ambiguity I spoke of before. Church is *not* nation, in the last analysis, nor is country religion, nor God English.[10] That is Foxe's point, the basis for his protestant patriotism, when he affirms that, nonetheless, these opposites do meet and touch, however provisionally, however transiently, at this latter-day intersection of sacred and secular time. He found precisely the right form for his argument in a chronicle church history that holds up a mirror for magistrates within a book of martyrs.

Foxe's rhetorical formula became the staple of the entire literature of national election. When subsequently the Puritans announced England's destiny in the language of covenant, it was to assert the confluence, in Britain alone, of the national union and the covenant of grace. Historians have long recognized the links between Foxe and the Puritan movement: between the *Book of*

Martyrs and anti-Episcopal, even antimonarchical, sentiment; between the struggle against Marian apostasy and the flight from Anglican Babylon; between the ideals of godly prince and godly rule; between the Elizabethan Settlement and the "divine politics" of regicide, which brought together, again metaphorically, redemptive and national history. Most striking, perhaps, was the similar fate of the metaphor in both periods. As the disparity between the constituent providential and christic parts of national election became increasingly evident, what before had been a vehicle for political success turned *sui generis* into a motive for rebellion. The Puritans charged that the Anglicans had violated the communal cause by raising national institutions above the rights of the nation's elect. They rallied—Quakers, Baptists, Seekers, Shakers, Levellers, Diggers, and Fifth Monarchists with the moderate and conservative factions—to restore the proper balance, on behalf of their common vision of England. They learned once more that New Presbyter was but Old Priest writ large—that reality had betrayed the rhetoric, or given it the lie.

It may be that they exacerbated the problem of translating metaphor to practice by expressing national election in terms just as ambiguous ("Army of Saints," "Holy Commonwealth"). In any case, their deuteronomic outlook—their identification of England with Israel—tended to mock their own effort. They first advanced that outlook as a middle way between providential and sacred history. Recognizing that England belonged to the City of Man, yet insisting on the country's divine call, they distinguished themselves from other nations by "resurrecting" (as Edmund Calamy boasted) the Hebrews' national or federal covenant. In retrospect, it seems clear that Calamy's term is misleading. The federal covenant was not a revival of biblical practice, but the product of a long effort to adapt Calvinism to English political life. Calvin had sundered the covenants of grace and works, declaring the latter obsolete as a means of salvation, and demanding obedience to the law purely as a matter of form, because God willed it so. But obedience for its own sake served poorly as a premise for civic authority, especially where the saints were concerned, and in part the story of English Puritanism, from Tyndale through Ames and Baxter, is the story of the realignment of the two covenants. Calvin had written as a rebel, in reaction against what he considered the corrupt legalism of

Catholic Rome. The Puritans were concerned with mobilizing society in support of an established creed. Gradually, they rewelded the sundered bonds of grace and works, through the notion of mutual obligation. The elect must repay God in time, they argued, for what He had granted them from eternity, by making palpable the fruits of their calling: "where wee looke for the like mercie, wee must performe the like dutie"; God, Who "never left mankind to guess at the way of salvation," has seen fit "to propose conditions to men, and [to] give them assurance of the benefit in that way"; although He offers grace as "a singular and absolute Promise," yet we must "enter into a Covenant state with him" and comply with "the Condition required on our part." [11]

As these phrases suggest, the Puritans never consciously abandoned the principal tenets of Calvinism. So far as they were concerned, they were merely defining man's role within the orthodox predestinarian framework. One part of the definition, developed by the Zurich theologians and adapted by Tyndale, pertained to christology and the duties of the covenanted saint. Another part, most broadly formulated by Johann Cocceius, a student of William Ames in Holland, pertained to soteriology. Cocceius restricted himself to the evolution of the church, but the terms of his analysis—process, gradation, "human occurances" [12] —made the *foedus gratiae* amenable to secular as well as sacred purposes. In any case, that was what many English Puritans believed in the mid-seventeenth century. Literalistically, they argued, Israel's covenant provided a providential model that was connected *by implication and analogy* with the work of redemption. When Nehemiah led the Hebrews back from captivity, God preserved them by temporal means and rewarded them with material goods. And yet by virtue of their role in sacred history, the entire event—return, rededication, restoration—had a larger figural import. It differed not only in spirit but *as fact* from the ordinary events of (say) Lycurgus's Greece or Numa's Rome. To Cromwell and his followers, that difference in fact precisely defined their own "peculiar" situation. Since England was not the church of Christ, its inhabitants could not identify *en masse* with Israel as *figura*. But since England had a role to play, albeit a worldly one, in the work of redemption, they could apply Israel's story to their own deuteronomically: as analogy, precedent, and moral *exemplum*.

On these grounds Edmund Calamy declared the resurrection of Israel's federal covenant. That pact between God and His people, he explained in a popular parliamentary address, *England's Looking Glass*, concerned "earthly affairs" only. It was "carnal," "natural," and "corporate"—and in those terms a mirror of the country's recent history.[13] Now as then, God's national judgments, bringing temporal, material blessings or disasters, followed from certain contractual agreements. Were not the English, like the biblical Hebrews, summoned by God to a terrestrial goal, under conditions of legal, outward behavior? And did not that correspondence convey England's special role, without trespassing on the rights of the elect? The spiritual Israel *would* inherit the kingdom; the English Israel *could* clear away obstacles to Christ's return. It was true that the Israelites had failed in their contract; with Nehemiah's death, piety had given way to hypocrisy, and in time God had justly revenged Himself for their broken promises. But that was no reason to suppose that the perishable ship of England would follow the Hebrews' course to shipwreck. On the contrary, the precedent girded them doubly for success: as a reminder of the benefits of obedience, and as a warning against falling short of their commitment. If Englishmen lived up to their part of the bargain—reforming their church and state in accordance with scripture and Calvin—God would grant them the worldly protection, power, and privilege He had once granted the Hebrews. More than that, He would make them His two-edged sword against the dragon of Rome, His instrument of political and ecclesiastical progress towards the millennium.

It was a persuasive argument, and it gave rise to hundreds of exhortations on national destiny. Only that destiny was admittedly in and of this world. When the spirit of rebellion hardened into the forms of another *status quo*, the distance between precedent and *figura* became more conspicuous, more ominous. It seemed increasingly obvious that the Hebrews' experience, understood as moral *exemplum*, not only resembled that of other nations, but provided the model of providential history—the cycle of rise, decline, and fall—that doomed heathen and Christian societies alike. Various dissenters had warned the establishment of this prospect long before:

> in the times of the Old Testament, God punished the wicked Jews by the *Chaldeans* or *Assyrians*. . . . Afterward he punished

the *Chaldeans* or *Assyrians,* by the *Persians*; the *Persians,* by the
Grecians; the *Grecians,* by the *Romans,* . . . the *Romans* by other
Nations, as by the *goths* and *Vandalls.* . . . And of later times,
how God hath scourged one Nation by another for their sins,
and doth at this day, is well known unto all.[14]

After 1650, the pattern seemed increasingly applicable to the
English Israelites. The scriptural parallels that the revolutionaries
had used to vaunt their mission were turned mercilessly against
them—on the one hand, by non-Puritans who scorned the claims of
deuteronomism as being excessive or self-serving; on the other
hand, by disillusioned saints who came to see in deuteronomism a
parodic desecration of the design of redemption.

A similar problem arose out of the ambiguous relation of local
history to the apocalypse. That international Reformation demanded a national revolution, and that each movement involved a
historical design, few Puritans doubted in 1640. But all of them
knew the difference between federal progress and sacred teleology.
With time, the difference expanded into a debate on means and
ends which all but paralyzed the Puritan regime. Both sides in the
debate made use of apocalyptic texts, and both invoked the
authority of Mede, Twisse, and Brightman, the leading nationalist
expositors of Revelation. They diverged in one point only, but that,
as John Wilson has shown, proved to be fundamental: the relation
of human willing to divine will.[15] One side of the debate, led by the
Independents, maintained that the divine agency was all-sufficient.
Focusing on the imminent millennium, they placed their hope
entirely upon God's promise, revealed to the elite alone. England
would be carried into the glorious future on the crest of prophecies
fulfilled, whether their countrymen liked it or not, irrespective of
human initiative. The other side of the debate, led by the
Presbyterians, insisted on man's participation in the process of
fulfillment. What mattered to them was the present and the
possible, rather than the inevitable. Stressing God's current signs of
favor or displeasure, they advocated concrete improvements, discipline in church and state, an adequate sense of responsibility—the
duties, in sum, required by providence rather than the enthusiasm
inspired by expectations of the Second Coming.

For a period, these two camps of national election found it

expedient to cooperate. Their antagonism revived after the revolution all the more fiercely for its brief repression. The Puritan victories in battle rapidly brought to the fore a series of irreconcilable antitheses in program and belief: magistrate *versus* saint, ideological conformity *versus* the demands of the Holy Spirit, layman *versus* Christian, nation *versus* congregation, general suffrage *versus* the rule of the elect, pragmatism *versus* chiliasm. As always, the radicals disagreed among themselves, but as always they united in their identity as saints. Even in England, they realized, it was impossible to mingle the kingdom and the world. The enemy was ubiquitous, equally in Rome, Canterbury, and Westminster, and they fled from his temptations, as from the treacheries of the self, to the inviolable sanctuary of the soul. They reached their haven by different paths. John Lilburne, the self-proclaimed emblem of trueborn Englishmen, ended his life a Quaker, convinced of mankind's intractable evil. Sir Henry Vane began his career as governor of Massachusetts, where he sided with the Antinomians against Winthrop; back in England, he found he could support the revolution without compromising his beliefs; he imaged himself after his political disappointments as a solitary and desolate Christ. Andrew Marvell's portraits of Cromwell shift from the prophetic tones of *The First Anniversary* to the ambivalent figuralism of *An Horation Ode*. In *Appleton House* he offers what is clearly a private hail and farewell to the Revolution, by invoking the exodus as a metaphor of the providential drama of the absurd, in contrast to the christic *figura* of the enclosed garden. Milton's changing views of reformation and the poet's vocation have often been studied from this perspective. In each area he tried hard to harmonize his conflicting allegiances. He acknowledged his failure—which is to say, the failure for him of the metaphor of national election—by singing the paradise within and, in his *History of Britain*, by moralizing over the futility of providential affairs. "One's country," he wrote to a European correspondent in 1666, "is wherever it is well with one." [16]

The failure of the metaphor resulted in the definitive separation of nation from election. Politically this meant the separation of state from church, the process of redemption from the law of nature. As Christians must be free to find their way heavenward, so too, wrote

Richard Overton, echoing many other dissenters, from Milton to the Levellers,

> by natural birth all men are . . . born to like propriety, liberty and freedom, and as we are delivered of God by the hand of nature into this world everyone with a natural innate freedom and propriety, . . . even so we are to live, everyone equally . . . to enjoy his birthright and priviledge, even all whereof God by nature hath made him free. . . . Every man by nature being a king, a priest, a prophet, in his own natural circuit and compass, whereof no second may partake but by deputation, commission, and free consent from whose right and freedom it is.[17]

The pointed substitutions here, of *nature* for *grace* and *man* for *believer*, constitute a sweeping denial of Foxe's dual vision. Overton titled his pamphlet *An Arrow Against All Tyrants*, aiming it specifically at the visionary militants who would join civic and Christian goals. Broadly considered, it is an arrow directed against the factitious bond of citizen and *exemplum fidei*, intended to sever once and for all the dichotomies inherent in national election—"army" and "saints," "commonwealth" and "holy," selfhood and Christhood, the history of England and the history of redemption. Michael Walzer has argued that the Puritan uprising—led by professional revolutionaries who made politics the instrument of a metaphysical *Weltanschauung*—marks the beginning of modern radical ideology. This may be so; but the collapse of the revolution, as A. S. P. Woodhouse has observed, resulted in a clear-cut distinction between the spiritual and the secular which was to become a mainstay of democratic capitalism. The momentous metaphor of "Englishman" which had unified the *Book of Martyrs* yielded to the division of "man by nature" from "saint by grace." Henceforth, their only common ground would be the right of each to his own freedom and propriety.

To some extent, of course, the honorific national association remained, as did the use of figuralism. Charles II returned to an accolade of "poems of state" comparing the Protectorate with the Egyptian bondage and the king with Moses and Nehemiah. But these panegyrics, and the *laudatio regiae* that later welcomed William and Mary, have little of the earlier dynamic. Fundamentally, they invoke the medieval concept of the king as *typus Christi,* and in all social matters, therefore, their outlook is deuteronomic *as distinct from* redemptive. Like the Puritans before them, the Restoration and neoclassic eulogists speak of Englishmen as Israelites. Unlike the Puritans, they deal exclusively in the area of providence, often using the scriptural parallels as irony, or as poetic artifice, or as a mock-heroic device that parodies the apocalyptic tone of an age which by present consensus had been nothing short of barbaric. Dependent as it was, finally, upon secular affairs, the belief in England's national election could not withstand the reversals of history. Its demise is celebrated after the Restoration in such works as Edward Stillingfleet's *Origines Britannicae,* which opens by thanking "Divine Providence" for having left

> men contented with the places of their habitations: for if all mankind should love and admire one and the same country, there would be nothing but destroying one another in hopes to enjoy it; whereas now, since the true Paradise is lost, it seems to be most convenient for the world, that every nation should believe they have it at home. . . . From hence I look on all national quarrels as very foolish and mischievous, it being reasonable that all persons should love their own country, as they do their parents. . . .
>
> But is it not possible for learned and ingenious men to inquire into and debate the several antiquities of their nations without making a national quarrel about them? . . . He that takes upon him to do that ought . . . to compare histories and annals . . . and then with great impartiality to deliver his judgment.[18]

Stillingfleet's attitude characterizes the mood of the Restoration. There are Puritan guides to *The Young Man's Calling,* instructing the reader how to behave "in that Station and Imployment in which Providence hath placed [him]." And there is many a Puritan *Young Man's Guide through the Wilderness of This World to the Heavenly Canaan.* The directions sometimes overlap, but the unifying national ideal is absent. Absent too are references to the hastening millennium, except in Anglican satires (like Butler's *Hudibras*), or in denunciations of the chimeras of an ignorant, strife-torn generation, or in lamentations over the lost cause—that wretchedly mistaken quest for temporal glory, as the great apocalypticist John Owen now judged it. Edmund Calamy, the son of Cromwell's leading covenant theorist, acclaimed the royal succession and England's return to established legal forms.[19] Dryden's political career moves rapidly from the patriotic euphoria of *Annus Mirabilis* to the clouded vision of *Absalom and Achitophel,* and eventuates, after his conversion to Catholicism, in *Britannia Rediviva,* which depicts England as a backsliding Israel threatening its divinely anointed christom-imētēs.[20] More rapidly still, Pope's youthful celebration of a British golden age gives way to his vision of the private estate and rural piety. What remains of the old outburst of national pride takes the shape of research into the common past: the country's origins, customs, achievements in peace and war, and in these terms its outstanding or exemplary men. The characteristic Reformed church history of the period is Samuel Clarke's *General Martyrologie.* Its Lives set *"before us what hath been . . . [and] what will be again: Sith the self same Fable is acted over and again in the world, the persons only are changed that act it."* [21] Insofar as England figures in this drama, it is wholly within the history of providence.

NOVANGLORUM MOENIA

Historians tell us that America experienced a similar development. They have called the *Magnalia* the last work of its kind, a monumental elegy to a defunct corporate ideal. Within a month after he preached the funeral sermon for Cotton Mather (1728), Thomas Prince undertook to correct his predecessor's "vain imaginings" of the colonial past. We are told that his *Chronological History of New-England in the Form of Annals* began a new epoch in American biography and historiography; and that it was a beginning long overdue. Undoubtedly there is some merit in this view. By all accounts, the *Magnalia* was an anachronism on the day of its publication. Foxe's *Book of Martyrs* achieved instant success. It helped unify the country, it became by royal decree a companion volume to the Bible in every parish church, and it remained the national epic for half a century, serving Englishmen as the *Aeneid* served the Romans, to recall their heroic origins and summon them to a great destiny. The *Magnalia*'s summons fell on deaf ears; it scarcely aroused the antagonism its author anticipated. When in 1820 the Reverend Thomas Robbins, librarian of the Connecticut Historical Society, persuaded a publisher of antiquarian curiosities to venture the first American edition, he expected a small sale at best. By that time, the name of Cotton Mather had become a catchall for puritan hypocrisy and repression. As for the *Magnalia* itself, "a small part of the community," Robbins sighed, "even knew of [its] existence." To his surprise, the edition sold steadily though slowly, and a second was called for in 1853. Robbins speculated, accurately, that the interest centered not so much in the church history as in the general fascination with the growth of America. The Puritans, he noted, quoting Virgil, had dedicated themselves to a holy labor—"And now we may say, by the favour of HEAVEN, THE WORK IS DONE. The world looks with amazement on a great Countrey, . . . more extensive than Rome," inhabited by an equally "great population . . . all looking for Salvation in the name of the DIVINE NAZARENE." [22]

Robbins's speculation expresses an enormous irony. Like Virgil's epic, Foxe's timely, often reprinted, and broadly quoted *Book of Martyrs* is relevant only to a brief period of national history. Mather's outdated *Magnalia* embodies a vision that remains one of the most powerful unifying elements of the culture. I refer of course to the persistence of the redemptive meaning of America. The generation that bought up Robbins's 1820 edition discovered in Mather a prophet of their own ideals. Harriet Beecher Stowe speaks for a goodly number of her contemporaries when she records the "happy hour" in which her father

> set up in his bookcase Cotton Mather's *Magnalia*, in a new edition of two volumes. What wonderful stories those! Stories, too, about my own country. Stories that made me feel the very ground I trod on to be consecrated by some special dealing of God's providence. . . . The heroic element was strong in me, having come down by ordinary generation from a long line of Puritan ancestry.

Much later, she commemorated that sense of special heroism in such novels as *Oldtown Folks* and *Poganuc People*. "God's mercies to New England," she wrote, foreshadowed the glorious future of the United States of America . . . commissioned to bear the light of liberty and religion through all the earth and to bring in the great millennial day, when wars should cease and the whole world, released from the thralldom of evil, should rejoice in the light of the Lord. The millennium was ever the star of hope in the eyes of the New England clergy; their faces were set eastward, towards the dawn of that day, and the cheerfulness of those anticipations illuminated the hard tenets of their theology with a rosy glow. They were the children of the morning.[23]

Whether or not they heard of the *Magnalia*, Americans through the eighteenth and nineteenth centuries shared Stowe's view of history. Not even the enlightened Thomas Prince really escapes the influence. He, too, was a descendent of the Puritan children of the morning. His *Chronological Annals* opens with an outline of mankind's seven-stage ascent towards the New World, and his famous discourse on *The People of New England* celebrates the centennial of Winthrop's arrival with all the figural optimism of the first settlers. The rhetoric (characteristically balancing regional filiopietism with futuristic Americanism, as in Mather's *Magnalia*) continues una- bated into and beyond the Revolution. Every crisis called forth a reassertion of the design. Whatever their political differences, rebels and loyalists, federalists and republicans urged their audiences to remember the Puritan "fathers": "What has been done . . . we may safely conclude will terminate in something great and glorious"; "We have seen in what order the type has been fulfilled; what doubt then can remain of the completion of the antitype in the same order?" John Adams was voicing the most potent platitude of the era when he announced—as the country's self- styled Moses-Lycurgus-Nehemiah—that the *Arbella* fleet had inau- gurated the "grand scene and Design in Providence, for the Illumination of . . . Mankind over the Earth."[24]

I will discuss the implications of this persistence in language and outlook in the next chapters. Here I wish only to suggest that the entire tradition points back to the crucial difference between Mather and his English counterparts, from Bale to Clarke. The unique quality of Mather's rhetoric, the distinctive strategy in his Life of Winthrop, lies in his use of the term "American." By a nice coincidence of philology and literary history, the term in its modern meaning appears initially in the *Magnalia*. Mather was the first major writer to infuse it with the imaginative power it has carried ever since, something both more comprehensive and more privileged than what Foxe meant by national election. "Englishman" was a metaphor for the temporary conjunction of sainthood and nationality. "Americanus" was, and has remained, a symbol of their fusion: a federal identity not merely *associated with* the work of redemption, but *intrinsic to* the unfolding pattern of types and antitypes, itself a prophecy to be fulfilled.

The credit does not belong to Mather alone, of course. Insofar as the *Magnalia* may be said to have anticipated the outlook of Stowe's generation, it was foreshadowed by the writing of the first emigrants. They had grown up in Foxe's England, they professed allegiance to the English Reformation, they felt they had inherited the mantle of national election, and they fled England as from a second Babylon. All these elements enter into the label of "non-separating congregationalists" by which we have come to identify them. In its original European context—as William Ames conceived of "non-separation" in Holland and John Cotton first coined "congregationalism" —the label was largely defensive, apologetic. In the opinion of adversary sects, it was an oxymoron covering a series of glaring paradoxes: a remnant representing the Reformation at large, congregationalists on a temporal mission, pilgrims in a national convenant, *de facto* separatists retaining their ties to the Church of England, an exclusive band of saints decrying the otherworldliness of separatism. These charges might be amply documented. And yet, as the emigrants adapted it to their peculiar New World situation, the label is a fitting one. Like the concept "Nehemias Americanus," "non-separating congregationalism" calls our attention to a paradox in order to assert a synthesis. Like Mather's title, it is an epitome of the prophetic fusion of *allegoria* and *historia* to which the colonists aspired.

Simply stated, the synthesis rests on a reordering of rhetorical forms. Non-separation affirms a historical movement in providential time; congregationalism, the timeless journey of the soul. The two terms therefore stand at opposite extremes. The ideological genius of the emigrants lay in their perception that the definitions were malleable. By reformulating the equations, they could make them interchangeable—transform them into mutually sustaining arguments for their vision of themselves, and of the New World wilderness before them, as *miracula apocalypsis*. Because they were congregationalists, they explained, visible members of the true church, their social enterprise was aligned with the work of redemption. And because they were so aligned, the spiritual progress of each saint among them was manifest in the progress of their venture. Thus congregation and society merged in a church-state designed by its very nature to resolve the contradictions inherent in Reformed activism. As the emigrant leaders elaborated their rationale, they gradually recast the negative connotations of non-separating congregationalism—exile, powerlessness, intrasectarian acrimony—into a comprehensive program for theocracy. While the English Puritans in Holland moved restlessly, often despondently, from one occupation to another, one congregation to the next, while they wavered between their conflicting commitments to purity and militancy, church and nation, the American settlers consolidated the New England Way. To be a "true New-England man," they declared, meant more than being a pilgrim and more than being a successful colonist. Their expedition superseded the opposites from which it sprung in the process of resolving them. They had come to America not to break with either the world or the kingdom, but to fulfill both.

To this end, between 1630 and 1660, the emigrants laid the foundations of the *Novanglorum moenia*, the walls of New England's Jerusalem. Having united the visible and the spiritual, they were free to actualize the metaphors of visible sainthood (for the individual) and national election (for the community). They proceeded, accordingly, to invoke the covenant of grace in defining the bonds of civic harmony and the covenant of works in standardizing the saint's preparation for heaven. Some of their most impassioned political appeals may be found in their sermons of redemption; their political sermons constantly urge self-scrutiny and conversion. What in England, Holland, Germany, and Geneva was an *a priori* antithesis became in America the twin pillars of a unique federal eschatology. Foxe's perishable ship of England has as its counterpart in Puritan New England writing the world-redeeming ark of Christ. The world's tempests might buffet this ship, and the helmsmen felt it their duty to threaten disaster if the crew flagged or veered off course. But, unlike Foxe, they understood those warnings teleologically, as the temporal means towards an absolute goal that precluded shipwreck. Christ was simply "not willing that our Nation should perish." The whirlwinds around them were intended to guide them faster to port. In the event of negligence, they could "Request for, and Rely on, the Aids of Grace"; in the face of adversity, or in danger of attack, they could trust in the protection of the Everlasting Covenant. Since they had "the Name of God written on their foreheads," they could assume that though "the storm may be sharp, all that are embarked shall be saved." They needed only to "be patient for a while, for a very little while, for it [would] not be long afore the storm be over, and then [they would] have glorious daies" and "*Ierusalem* . . . come down from heaven." [25]

The emigrants of 1630 had not quite charted their voyage to the end of time. As Mather shows in the Life of Winthrop, they filled in the outlines gradually, in debate with Puritans abroad and dissenters at home, and in adapting to the unexpected difficulties of the wilderness. Nonetheless, the great sermon Winthrop preached before they arrived in the New World, *A Model of Christian Charity*, shows that they carried their vision with them on the *Arbella*. The *model*, in accordance with exegetical tradition, is at once social, christic, and figural. *Charity* betokens simultaneously the effects of grace and the good works that knit together the civic order. The city on a hill indicates a true church and a covenanted society, *ecclesia* and commonwealth entwined in God's promises to His latter-day plantation. Throughout, the rhetoric aims at a middle way, a "socialized Eucharist," [26] which is neither compromise nor metaphor but a unity of extremes. Within the first decade the rhetoric became an institutional reality. From the start, the colonial leaders surpassed the federal covenanters in their demands for outward conformity, as befit visible saints. Their legal code astonished English jurists for its "judaical" severity. From the start they surpassed the separatists in their standards for church membership, as befit a community charged with a historical mission. Their spiritual qualification tests went far beyond those of Plymouth, both in rigor and in presumption of certainty. As their magistrates (according to the *Magnalia*) strove to a saintliness beyond that of European divines, so their ministers exceeded European magistrates in their social concern.

Their duties followed from their special prerogatives. In New England, they explained, interdependence of church and state meant mutuality, not interference. How could they *not* combine their sacred and secular interests? "Considering what means of grace and glory are here plentifully afforded . . . we may now be . . . blessed in Christ Jesus, both in this and in another world. And indeed we cannot but stand amazed at the free grace of God," seeing that He "hath so linked together the blessing of the Covenant (which is his to give) with the duty and way of it, (which is ours to walk in) that . . . the one . . . will work in us a carefull endeavour of the other." Here, in short, where Christ brought the promise of heaven in one hand and prosperity in the other, piety and moralism were inextricable. Thus the ministers could teach social reform by preaching the ways of salvation: *"You do commit the safety of this cause to the Lord himself, in the same way that you do commit unto him the Salvation of your own soules."* Thus also, the magistrates encouraged the spirit by enforcing proper behavior: the fact that this "Land is IMMAN-UEL's, *speaks forth* [the magistrates'] *priviledge and duty: Their obligation to walk with God and their salvation in so walking."* Here, Christ performed "his *invisible work* . . . [in] a *Visible Sion."* Here only, "When God moves the *Wheels of Providence* . . . He is wont at [the same] . . . time to move the *Wheels of Grace."* [27] In sum, these non-separating congregationalists, *as New Englanders,* laid claim for themselves to the identity of the figural Israel, where to be a believer was *ipso facto* to be a "true Israelite," and where, conversely, to be a member in good standing of the society was *ipso facto* to show oneself a saint.

Lord Saye and Sele, an early patron of the colony, simply could not believe that the emigrants were serious about all this. Surely, he wrote Winthrop in 1640, your venture is basically no different from others: "it is as likely that you have in providence been cast upon that place, to remove from thence upon due occasion, as to stay there, and much more likely, when in some other [enterprise] you . . . receive a more . . . comfortable subsistence." Anne Hutchinson objected from the opposite point of view. The colonists, she charged, had substituted righteousness for redemption, social for christic conformity. She, too, was a watcher for the Second Coming; along with most Antinomians of the period, she had heard the voice of John the Baptist predicting the fall of Antichrist. But as a saint she knew that she must attend *now* to the Baptist *within*. Avoiding the delusions of the self, she would "see nothing, . . . have nothing, doe nothing, onely . . . stand still and waite" for the Holy Spirit to bring her, of its own accord and in its own time, the millennium of the soul. That secured, she proceeded to instruct others:

> Here is a great stirre about graces and looking to hearts [i.e., preparation], but give mee Christ, I seek not for [outward] graces but for Christ, I seeke not for [federal] promises, but for Christ, I seek not for sanctification, but for Christ, tell not mee of . . . duties, but tell mee of Christ.

These doctrines may not have flouted reason and scripture, as Winthrop claimed they did,[28] but they obviously countermanded the New England Way.

Perhaps the clearest refutation of Anne Hutchinson appears in the work of her teacher, John Cotton. His sympathy with her position at several key points is well known, as is the general mystical strain of his thought. His christology diverged from Hooker's and Shepard's in its emphasis on transformation, not preparation. His soteriology was based on "resurrection" rather than on reformation, in opposition to Winthrop and Richard Mather. Yet for all this he epitomizes the theocracy's harmony of extremes. Following Anne Hutchinson's banishment, he became one of the colony's foremost legislators, more than any other theocrat responsible for limiting toleration and setting the directions of due process and civil rights. His treatise on *Christ the Fountain of Life*, which exalts the Holy Spirit above scripture, details the duties of "worldly business"; his *Covenant of Grace* stresses the importance of the Law; his *Churches Resurrection, or the Opening . . . of the Revelation* links personal and corporate piety in the context of the future reign of the saints. Nothing more clearly attests to the coherence of the New England Way than the changes it wrought upon Cotton's thought. And nothing more clearly than his susceptibility to those changes—as he demonstrates this in his sermons to Boston congregation, in his official apologias to Puritans abroad, and in his replies to his patron Lord Saye and Sele and his disciple Anne Hutchinson—vindicates the exemplary status which his contemporaries and successors accorded him. Soon after he arrived in 1633, he wrote to his close friend John Davenport that "the Order of the Churches and of the Commonwealth was so settled, by common Consent, that it brought to his mind, the New Heaven and New Earth." [29] He expounded this hope with growing conviction until his death almost thirty years later.

Cotton adjusted his outlook to that of his colleagues without ever abandoning his mystical tendencies. It is a tribute to the strength of the New England Way that, far from being divisive, such discrepancies in emphasis flowed into a common vision. Whether the clergy accented the Spirit (with John Davenport) or the Law (with Peter Bulkeley), they shared the same federal eschatology. Within that framework, they offered their solutions to the controversies that continued to plague them throughout the century, and, after 1660, explained away the untoward course of history. Their halfway covenant, for example, which scholars have established as the *locus classicus* of the theocracy's decline, marks a high-point in the formulation of American identity. The problem is familiar to every student of the period: too many of the founders' children did not have the "saving experience" which would qualify them for church membership. The clergy found the answer in the "first principles of New England." In *their* case, they decided, the churches could grant provisional membership by *inference* of conversion. The spiritual legacy *had to* continue from one generation to the next, until this second flight from Babylon would issue in the Second Coming. In spite of themselves, as it were, the still-unregenerate children were the heirs of salvation. As scions of the American Israel, they had received grace "through the loyns of godly Parents." [30] By virtue of their baptism they *already* bore the name of God upon them, through His pledge to the enterprise as a whole.

For those who remained troubled nonetheless, there were ready answers:

[To parents:] I will show you the *Hand-writing of God*, which you shall carry & argue before Him: There it is; Isa. 44. 3. *I WILL POUR MY SPIRIT UPON THY SEED, AND MY BLESSING UPON THY OFFSPRING*. . . . [Here,] *Children*

Confederate in their Parents . . . [to] *inherit* the *Glory* of their *Ancestors.* . . . You may be assured, that the vertue, the blessing, the efficacy of the Covenant shall never be disanuled; he will be a God, not to you onely, but your seed also; this your Covenant shall draw in your children to partake of grace with you, never to be broken off. The oyle that is powred upon the head will run down to the rest of the members.

[To children:] Strongley, Vastly, Ungainsayably Engaged are those persons, to say of the Great GOD, *He is my God,* who can say, *He is my Fathers God.* . . . To comply with the Demands of Heaven, the *Children* are Called! Oh! Admire *Sovereign Grace* in such a Dispensation. . . . The Lord will not only be as Ready to Do for *Us,* as He did for our *Fathers,* but will do more for us. The *Covenant-Mercy* of God, unto the Children of Godly Ancestors, oftentimes the *further* it Rolls, the *bigger* it grows.[31]

This genetics of salvation, which interprets succession as progression, is a striking instance of sheer ideological persistence. Equally striking is the imagery that carries the argument. The mercy that grows in time applies to each American saint; the oil of grace that covers the community as one man in Christ flows from generation to generation. We can hardly miss the continuity between these phrases and Mather's visionary leap, in "Nehemias Americanus," from Winthrop's deathbed consolations to the New World promise.

The same phrases, expressing the same vision, return towards the end of the century in the Mathers' attack upon Solomon Stoddard. The Connecticut minister, following Calvinist doctrine, had distinguished the federal convenant from the promise of grace, and defined church sacraments as a means of salvation, which ought to be open to all, rather than as an occasion for a gathering of the remnant. To Increase Mather, this amounted to nothing less than a call to God's people to return to Babylon. He recognized, of course, that Stoddard's ideas applied well enough "to the Imperfect Reformation in other Lands." There, precisely, lay the apostasy. Stoddard, he cried, would "deprive us of our Glory for ever"—he would equate other lands with this "Type and emblem of new-Jerusalem." When Stoddard objected that even in America, after all, the saints comprised only a fraction of the people, Increase retorted angrily that in America that fraction sufficed. As the incarnation of the New England Way, it "could stand for the entire land" and "redeem the whole." To see the Bay theocracy in any lesser light was to set oneself against the work of redemption. It was to try to "rob New England"—the sacred "New England of the type," *"Beautiful as* Tirzah, *Comely as* Jerusalem, *Terrible as an Army with Banners"*—"on which hangs all the glory of the house of Israel"— whose *"divine Originall* and *Native beautie* . . . [might] dazzle the eyes of Angels, daunt the hearts of devils, ravish and chain fast the Affections of all the Saints"—to rob *that* "New England of its glory at the end of history." [32]

Historians have described the Stoddard-Mather debate as symptomatic of the shift from Puritan to Yankee culture. For the Mathers, however, and the latter-day orthodoxy, it was an apodictic recapitulation of the colonial cause. From that special vantage point they continued to defend their Way against all the tendencies of the new age—pleading with their still-unconverted children or siblings to repent (so as to participate in the "great *ACCOMPLISH-MENTS* approaching"); denouncing laggards and mockers (their *"Everlasting Recompenses* will be very much adjusted by the Regards which [they] had for the Flocks of Jesus here"!); consoling the afflicted and the despondent (the world would soon "look with quite another Face than it does at present"). For all social ills they proffered a single American cure-all: "May we, as far as we can, Anticipate the Dayes of the *New Jerusalem*"; may we *"Labour to be found in such Frames, and in such* Wayes, *as the* State of PEACE *now advancing upon the world, would oblige us unto."* Every Christian should live in that anticipation, of course, but we especially. " 'Tis the prerogative of New-England above all the Countries of the world," because "such *Principles* as we have at last produced in the *American* Desarts" ensure "a *great* REVOLUTION . . . e're long." [33] We strive not only in the shadow but *as* the shadow of that event.

The continuity in approach over three generations expresses an extraordinary social achievement. As Cotton, Winthrop, and their colleagues transferred vision to reality, they welded together the traditional Protestant dualities as did no other community before or after them. On the one hand, they blended Lutheran piety and Calvinist institutionalism; on the other hand, they combined

Luther's prophetic eschatology, directed toward the apocalyptic Son of Man, and Calvin's "realized eschatology," centered upon the crucified Jesus. So conceived, the New England Way marks the high-point of the evolution of the theory of national election. Luther had spoken of a fleeting opportunity, one which would pass quickly to other countries if the Germans did not seize it at once and hold fast. "Gather in," he pleaded, "while it still shines." The Marian exiles had supplemented the appeal by their more fully articulated nationalism and by their Calvinistic stress upon discipline. The New World orthodoxy changed the perspective from antiquarian to prophetic history, enlarged the belief in godly rule to mean the reign of the saints, and redefined the sense of opportunity —"New-England's design in this vast undertaking"—as God's long-promised summons to His people, as irreversible as it was irresistible, to erect New Jerusalem in America.[34]

Social historians have documented the immediate, practical results of their effort. Family and tribe, piety and politics, worldly hierarchy and spiritual democracy, all the cultural norms of the community were fused, for over half a century, with extraordinary success. Plymouth fell victim to social mobility; the early history of Virginia and Maryland is marked by violence and drastic fluctuations in government, trade, and population. As Timothy Breen and Stephen Foster have shown, "Political chaos seems the rule in the seventeenth century until one comes to the Puritan colonies, especially to Massachusetts Bay under the old charter." [35] Indeed, much of recent historical research indicates the need for a positive restatement of the generational crisis of seventeenth-century New England. We have come to understand that the gradual collapse of the church-state was not directly due to the weakening of orthodoxy. Edmund Morgan, David Levin, Robert Pope, David Hall, Emory Elliott, and others have argued that the second and third generations sustained the piety of the first. Decline in church-membership after the mid-1650s followed at least partly from the *seriousness* with which the children responded to the demands of the fathers. Their sense of inadequacy, their hesitations about professing sainthood, suggest intensity of belief, not indifference. The members of the old guard themselves confirm this, and most vigorously of all, perhaps, Cotton Mather, who had most cause for complaint.[36]

In view of this remarkable hegemony, the recurrent vexations recorded in the Life of Winthrop, as well as those which Mather omits or glosses over, attest to the sustained imaginative vitality of the New England Way. Somehow, through all the difficulties of the young plantation, the orthodoxy upheld, and was upheld by, their vision of the American Jerusalem. They moved from one crisis to the next—physical, institutional, ideological, generational—with their eyes fixed on that prospect. If their numbers diminished on the way, their energy and conviction continued unabated, and there is every reason to suppose that they exerted a considerable influence upon the populace at large. "GOD intended to write upon these Churches the Name of *New Jerusalem*": with that assurance, no one—not Antinomians, nor recalcitrant children, nor Stoddard, nor history itself—could rob them of their glory. Rhetorically, they remained secure in their identity, "the New England, of the type," possessed of "the Priviledges of the Kingdom," and, indeed, "already Initiating our selves at the works of that *Kingdom*"; "God's Name," they explained, "hath been written upon us in Capital Letters from the beginning" of time.[37]

AMERICA MICROCHRISTA

The New England Way, as the term itself indicates, drew sustenance from two sources. One of these was ideological, the way of federal eschatology. The other was geographical, including not only Massachusetts Bay but the continent at large, which gave the newness of New England its eschatological import. Together, they rendered the colony an instrument whereby, according to a recurrent pulpit invocation, "Christ may bestow upon America . . . that salutation, 'O my dove!' " Traditionally, the dove signifies Christ's beloved (Cant. 2 : 14), the Holy Spirit, God's covenant with Noah, and the saints' deliverance after the final "fiery flood." The colonial clergy applied the image, punning on Columbus/*columbina* (Latin for "dove"), specifically, "peculiarly," to their redemptive journey toward a new heaven and a new earth—the new Age of the Holy Spirit in the New World. Mather frequently draws out this application: in his biography of Francis Higginson, for example, the "American Noah," and, at the start of the *Magnalia*, in his description of the transatlantic crossing as the voyage of a second, greater "family of Noah," which changed geography into *"Christiano-graphy."* "The *Old World,*" he explains, referring to Noah's time as a type of Israel's degeneracy,

> was destroy'd, because the grand Prophecy of our SAVIOUR was forgotten in it, and a *New World* brought on for the Revival of that Prophecy. . . . [Now,] a *Noah* is the Reviver of the *New World.* And in His very *Name,* as well as in many other Typical Circumstances, what have we but the Prophecy of our SAVIOUR [i.e., Jesus as prefiguration of the Son of Man] again given unto us? And such a prophecy as we [in America] are invited this Day to take a very particular Notice of.[38]

Mather's christianography rests upon a far-reaching tenet of colonial rhetoric. For the New England clergy, the meaning of the continent was an exegetical, not a historical, question, or more accurately, an issue of prophetic (as opposed to secular) history. "America's Name," they declared, and its destiny, "is to be seen fairly Recorded in the Scriptures," embossed in the prophecies of Isaiah, Zechariah, and Daniel, and, of course, "particularly in the Book of . . . *Revelations.*" For example, since in Nehemiah's time "Jerusalem was to the westward of Babylon, so New Jerusalem must be to the westward of Rome"—and what could "westward" mean at this stage of redemptive history, but America? Or again, when the Psalmist spoke of a new nation to be placed at the head of all others (Psalm 18), surely he was offering above all "Hopes for *Americans.*" Surely, too, Americans might find hope in John's promise that the earth's fourth corner would sound the final, millennial trumpet. The crucifixion itself suggested as much:

> The mystery of our Lord's garments, made four parts, by the soldiers that cast *lots* for them, is to be accomplished in the good sense put upon it by Austin, who, if he had known America, could not have given a better: *Quadripartita vestis Domini Jesu, quadripartitam figuravit e jus Ecclesiam, toto scilicet, qui quatuor partibus constat, terrarum orbe diffusam* [The parting of the garment of our Lord Jesus Christ into four pieces was a type of a like division of His Church which is distributed through the four corners of the globe].

So understood, the entire story of the New World, from beginning to end, was the story of Christ's *magnalia*. When Christianity had spread through Asia, Africa, and Europe, "the *Devil* got a forlorn Crue over hither into *America*, in hopes that the Gospel never would come at them here." [39] Now that time was drawing to its close, Christ was undertaking His final conflict with Satan (antitype of His conflict in the wilderness), by summoning His remnant across the Atlantic ocean.

   This use of figuralism had momentous implications for hermeneutics in general, as we shall see. In immediate geographical terms, it meant that America was consecrated from eternity for the New England Way. The Puritans' argument was not fortuitous. Without it, their case for "New England" was a weak one at best. Even granted the premises of their theocracy, they had no right to acclaim the *country* as the new promised land. To all appearances, what they called America was just another plot of ground in a fallen world. The essence of colonial Puritan historiography lay in the conviction that it was not. Other countries, the argument went, had a double affiliation. In a primal, absolutist sense they belonged to God, but insofar as they were "dead in sin"—that is, temporally, legally, and providentially—they belonged to separate federal constituencies. The New World, like Canaan of old, belonged wholly to God. The remnant that fled Babylon in 1630 set sail for the new promised land, especially reserved by God for them. Why else did He so long conceal it, but to make its discovery the *finale* to His work of redemption? Did mere chance explain the fact that its discovery coincided with the two greatest human achievements since Christ, the Reformation and the development of the printing press, which gave the world access to the Bible? Was it by accident that heaven inspired Columbus to call the New World "St. *SAVIOUR*"? [40] Did not even some European divines (the best of them) "talke of *New-England* with delight," perceiving as they did in its "*national*—as well as *congregational*—pattern of virtue . . . a true type of heaven itself"?[41] Was it not by design that the Book of Revelation found its greatest interpreters just before the voyage of the *Arbella*? Was not God's will manifest in the pestilence that cleared the land of Indians just before the fleet landed?

   In the face of these events, surely no one could believe that the American past, like that of Britain and Germany, lay in the realm

55401

of providential history, to be investigated by impartial antiquarians. Luther and Foxe had each hoped to confirm his country's election by setting straight its chronicles. Tudor and Stuart patriots undertook to display "the glory of the British original" by providing a historical background as ancient as Rome. They traced post-apostolic Christianity from the Lollards to Elizabeth, and resurrected the medieval chroniclers—Bede, Gildas, Geoffrey of Monmouth— in order to prove that British heroism began with Trojan Brut. John Leland defended the historicity of King Arthur in the hope that England's splendor would revive when another native king regained the throne; later, the author of *Eikonoklastes* planned to rouse his noble and puissant nation with an epic of Arthur's mighty deeds. But could a true believer derive America's meaning (any more than he could Canaan's) from heathen chronicles? Could he find in Indian legends the story of America's saving remnant, for whom God was showing "more Love and Zeal . . . then for any other people in the World"? [42]

Unmistakably, the New World was part of the history of salvation. As for the Indians, the settlers wavered in their opinion: they might be the ten lost tribes of Israel or Satan's misled crew. The debate centered on the prophecies about the Conversion of the Jews vis-à-vis God's promise that His remnant would conquer the ends of the earth. In either case, the significance of America remained firmly rooted in eschatology. One way or another, that is, country, saint, and church reflected one another, in the definition of the colony. Each of the three identities was fundamental to the whole, but what most clearly radiated the special nature of the undertaking, its *somma luce*, was its christianographical locale. Sainthood and church-membership implied one another, and both implied the New England Way; the idea of America implied all three in the proper apocalyptic context, justified the non-separating congregational theocracy, expressed the relationship of England to New England, and assured the settlers of success. Christic selfhood was a tremendous barrier against the terrors of self-discovery, but, as the English saints were to discover, it left the individual prey to the mutability of providence. The American Puritan self was a garden enclosed from the threat even of secular failure.

In part, it was precisely the enormity of the threat that prompted the emigrants' extraordinary definition of themselves. The English Protestant may have trembled at the uncertainty of his sainthood, but he knew, proudly, that he was an Englishman. So did the emigrant, but not proudly; he fled England as Bunyan's Pilgrim fled the City of Destruction. It seemed to him "literally *Babel, and so consequently Ægypt* and *Sodome*"—a country grown "fat for the slaughter," imminently to be "abased and brought down to hell." According to Nathaniel Ward, John Rogers, John Wilson, Charles Chauncy, Anne Bradstreet, and Thomas Hooker, "God [was] packing up his gospel," His angels were crying destruction upon England, His Son was shaking the heavens above that wicked and presumptuous land, turning the Sun to darkness and the moon to blood—"So *farewell* England *old*" and "*welcome . . . to New.*" "All the other Churches of Europe are brought to desolation," wrote Winthrop before his departure, "and it cannot be but a like judgment is coming upon us":

> the Lord hath admonished, threatened, corrected, and astonished us, yet we grow worse and worse, so as . . . he must needs give way to his fury at last: he hath smitten all the other Churches before our eyes. . . ; we saw this, . . . but have provoked him more than all the other nations round about us: therefore he is turning the cup towards us also. . . . I am verily persuaded, God will bring some heavy Affliction upon this land and that speedily.

America, he concluded, was to be a refuge for those whom God *"means to save out of this generall callamitie,"* as the ark had saved Noah from the flood, and as New Jerusalem would harbor the elect plucked out of the final conflagration.[43]

The New Englander, then, had the failure of European Protestantism behind him, and before him, as his refuge, what he called "wilderness" and "desert." The terms speak for themselves of his fear; the adjectives with which he formulaicly surrounded them are more explicit still: *howling, hideous, boundless, unknown, Satanic, wild, forlorn.* Cut off from family and friends by "soe vast an Ocean," "thousands of leagues . . . both turbulent and dangerous," spiritually divorced from the Church of England and physically separated from England's comforts and culture, working a "remote,

rocky, bushy, barren, wild-woody" soil [44] which he had by precarious patent from a hostile English king—who was he? Granted that
his true home was heaven, he still needed a *federal* identity.
Commonsensical Puritans like Lord Saye and Sele never questioned
their nationality. Purists, enthusiasts like Anne Hutchinson felt
more or less indifferent about it. But the non-separating emigrant
considered his social commitment crucial to his selfhood as
Christian: that commitment made visible his sainthood, his allegiance to the Reformation, and his historic destiny. Under these
circumstances, he could hardly see himself merely as a pilgrim
seeking salvation, or as an exile awaiting return, like the Marian
expatriates. He had to justify himself by justifying America.

His solution, which combined and transcended the meanings of
pilgrim and exile, was as sweeping as it was simple. He had
discovered his personal identity as Puritan by recourse to christology; now he overcame the problem of his American identity by
recourse to soteriology: by imposing upon the communal effort the
prophetic type (at once fulfillment and *figura*) of the Messiah's
advancing millennial army. The relationship between psychic
uncertainty and rhetorical self-assertion is transparent in the tone of
crisis that characterizes much of the literature. With every setback,
the assertion of American selfhood rose to a higher pitch. It is no
accident that the myth of the fathers developed with the failure of
the Protectorate, or that apocalypticism reached its height first with
King Philip's war and then with the Andros regime. The underlying insecurity is most pronounced in the most impassioned self-
affirmations. I quote from two defenses of the errand: one written
during the widespread defections back to England following the
triumph of Cromwell; the other written four decades later, soon
after the loss of the original colonial charter and the rise of
Stoddardism. The first is from Johnson's *Wonder-Working Providence:*

> as Israel met with many difficulties after their returne from
> Captivity, in building the Temple and City, so [did] these
> N. E. people. In a desolate and barren Wildernesse, exceed-
> ingly weakned with continued labour, watching and hard diet,
> [they suffered] such distresses, as to appearance of man seemed
> to be both hopelesse, and helplesse. Their griefe was further
> increased by the sore sicknesse which befell among them, so

that almost in every Family Lamentation, Mourning, and woe
was heard. It would assuredly have moved the most lockt up
affections to Teares, had they past from one Hut to another,
and beheld the piteous case these people were in.

But Christ was resolved to fight for them; wherefore with
bold resolvedness these Soldiers of Christ set forth, elevated by
him many Millions above that brave Warrier Ulysses. The
immovable Resolutions continued in these men, to re-build the
most glorious Edifice of Mount Sion in a Wildernesse, know-
[ing] this is the place where the Lord will create a new Heaven,
and a new Earth, in new Churches and a new Common-wealth.

The noble Acts Jehova wrought, his Israel to redeem,
    Surely this second work of his shall far more glorious seem.

The second is from Joshua Scottow's *Narrative of Massachusetts Colony:*

That this Design was Super-humane, will be evidenced by
the *Primum Mobile*, or grand Wheel thereof. The Setting up of
Christ's Kingdom was the main spring of motion, and that
which gave the Name to *New-England*, and at such a time,
when as Divine *Herbert* in his Temple Prophetically sang

Religion Stands on Tiptoe in our Land,
Ready to pass to the **AMERICAN** *Strand.*

The agency of the great God appeared, who raised up such
as were fit to lead this People in this wilderness; we had our
Mose's, and *Aaron's,* our *Zorobabels,* and *Joshua's,* our *Ezrah's,* and
Nehemiah's. Men of narrow spirits, of mean capacities and
fortunes, had not been capable to officiate in so great a worke.
That such, and so many Gentlemen of Ancient and Worshipful
Families should Combine in so desperate and dangerous a
Design, attended with such insuperable Difficulties, in the
plucking up of their Stakes, leaving so pleasant and profitable
a place as their Native Soil, parting with their Patrimonies,
Inheritances, plentiful Estates, to come into this Desert, &
unknown Land, and smoaky Cottages, to the Society of wild
Indians; what less then a Divine Ardour could inflame a
People thus circumstanced to a work so contrary to Flesh and
Blood.

Infinite Wisdom directed this, Divine Courage and Resolu-

tion managed it, Super-humane Sedulity attended it, and
Angelical Swiftness finished it, according to predeterminate
Design.[45]

Johnson refers to Ulysses in order to evoke a standard figural
interpretation of the *Odyssey*: the flight from heathen allurements to
one's true home and faithful Penelope. Scottow recasts the lines
from Herbert to say just the opposite from what Herbert intended.
The rhetoric of Scottow's entire passage is a defense against the
poem's prediction that the settlement at Massachusetts Bay will be
no more than another imperfect human undertaking:

> Yet as the Church shall thither westward flie,
> So Sinne shall trace and dog her instantly:
> They have their period also and set times
> Both for their vertuous actions and their crimes.
> . . . .
>
> Thus also Sinne and Darknesse follow still
> The Church and Sunne with all their power and skill.[46]

More formidably than Johnson's Mount Sion, Scottow's **"AMERI-
CAN"** stands as a barrier against poetic irony, a barrier raised by
the myth-making imagination upon self-doubt. In both cases, the
anxiety about "Sinne and Darknesse," and about "a work so
contrary to Flesh and Blood," is brought under control by the
assertion of a "predeterminate design." Paradoxically, that is, the
image of America provides the ultimate guarantee that things are
not *really* what they are in fact.[47] Like Johnson, though with greater
dependence upon prophecy itself, Scottow solves the problem of
federal identity by raising the locale *in toto*—past, present, and
future—into the realm of redemptive history.

The American Puritan elaborated his rationale from one generation to the next with all the energy of one who must defend his
selfhood not only in face of a harsh environment but against the
opinion of the world. Was he an exile? America became for him the
Land of Vision, like the Isle of Patmos. Did Satan rule the country
and its "savage" inhabitants? The Puritan errand was an emblem
of Christ's hastening deliverance of mankind. Were the colonists
cultivating a rocky soil in the world's remote corners? Scripture
foretold that a chosen remnant would make the desert blossom like

the rose, and gather the harvest from the ends of the earth. Were they separated from their brethren, often scorned by them for their flight into "the outer darkness"? It was ever God's way to bring light out of darkness; He had selected the new continent for just that purpose, to radiate back across the Atlantic a model of universal christendom. Did they find themselves besieged by Indians, plagued by schism and natural disaster? God was especially severe with His servants; He showed His love by scourging them with His corrective providential lash.

Their consolation sounds loud throughout the seventeenth century; and always, with a rising fervor (and desperation), it affirms the daring personal-national meaning which the orthodoxy imposed upon the New World. Their use of Job in this respect marks a dominant theme in the literature after midcentury. It was reinforced by many similar *figurae:* Joseph, Samson, Jacob, David, Nehemiah, and above all the afflicted Jesus, type of the Messiah of the Second Coming. In its every aspect their strategy pointed toward the same astounding purpose—no less astounding for the fact that it followed from the logic of their rhetoric. Having raised the country into the realm of sacred history, they proceeded one step further and imposed upon it the norms of spiritual biography. As the saint represented the entire church of the elect, so conversely America was seen to reflect the calling and temptations of each of its elect settlers. It was itself the exile redeemed from captivity, itself the saint sloughing off the influence of the Old Adam, exhibiting the good works which signaled its glorification, awakening after a long slothful sleep into the light of grace, assuming at last its true identity, and therefore engaged in a "fatal enterprize against all the devils and damned"—since "when the Devil sees that we shall shortly be where the wicked cease from troubling, [then] that wicked one will trouble us more than ever before." As the prophet of Patmos had written (Rev. 12 : 12), the tempter's wrath would grow "great as the time to exert it grew short."

Mather, we remember, applies this prophecy of Armageddon to Winthrop's final conflict of soul directly before he received "the great consolations of God." Such internalization of apocalyptic imagery is consistent with Reformed practice. What is remarkable —and distinctive in Mather's biographical technique—is that he means us to apply the prophecy also to America's soul (or

character, or destiny). This assumption underlies the figural
connective between Winthrop's glorification and Winthrop-Ne-
hemiah's quintessential achievement, his role in the construction of
the *Novanglorum moenia*. This vision of America explains Mather's
application of the same text (Rev. 12 : 12) to the Salem trials,
which he recounts toward the end of the *Magnalia*, as though the
witchcraft episode were part of the New World's climactic temptation. His friend Samuel Sewall, noting how "wonderfully suited"
was "the going of Christ into *America*" in these latter days, speaks of
New Jerusalem as "the Heart of America," and of "*America's* plea"
for the Second Coming as "the strongest" now being raised to God.
Before the migration, the continent was like Rachel, "desolate and
unmarried"; now "she may receive Jesus Christ as Her Husband
. . . and her Children [like Rachel's] shall be more and mightier
than her Sisters":

> 'Tis certain, CHRIST will speedily fetch home his beautiful,
> and belov'd, and long'd for Rachel. . . .
>   Come! our HIMMANUEL, constantly to keep House at
> *Boston* in *New England*.[48]

Cotton Mather was no less certain. America, he declares over
and again, stands at last revealed as the first among Christ's
beloved, "*pulcherrima inter mulieres*," the most beautiful of His brides.
Considering the glorious nuptials shortly to begin, he foresees "the
Holy City, in AMERICA"—*as* "America"—"a *City* the Street
whereof will be *Pure Gold*." This prospect, he continues, is neither
wishful thinking nor mere similitude. It is based on a long study of
scriptural texts pertinent to both the covenant of grace and the
work of redemption, all of them leading to the same inescapable
significance: "AMERICA is Legible in these Promises." To celebrate his discovery, Mather turns, as did his grandfather John
Cotton in 1640, to the Song of Songs, Solomon's enraptured
prothalamium for the marriage of heaven and earth: "*Awake,
Awake, put on thy strength, O* New-English *Zion, and put on thy Beautiful
Garments, O* American *Jerusalem*," "*Put on thy beautiful Garments, O*
America, *the holy City!*" And to America-Rachel-Penelope's chil-
dren, the "*New-English* Israel," in whom reside the "Pray'rs and
Hopes, for America," he brings the glad tidings that

> The Devil was never more let *Loose* than in our Days; and it
> proves the *Thousand Years* is not very *Far off*. SHORTLY didst

thou say, Dearest Lord! O Gladsome word! . . . [Considering our tribulations,] I may Sigh over *this* Wilderness as Moses did over *his, We are consumed by thine Anger.* . . . [Yet] if God have a Purpose to make here a Seat for any of *Those Glorious Things, which are spoken of Thee, O Thou City of God;* then even thou, *O New-England* art within a very little while of Better Dayes then have ever yet Dawn'd upon thee. Our *Lord Jesus Christ shall have the uttermost parts of the Earth for his Possession,* the *last* [shall] be the *first,* and the *Sun of Righteousness* come to shine *Brightest,* in Climates which it rose *Latest* upon![49]

In this vision of the Theopolis Americana the idea of national election takes on a literalness undreamed of by Luther or Foxe. It is the kind of literalness, in fact, assumed by the colonists about themselves. Luther believed that the Germans might help create the first truly Christian kingdom; Foxe and Milton hoped that England would lead the world in the destruction of Antichrist. The New England Puritans gave America the status of visible sainthood. The subsequent impact of their concept cannot be overestimated. Whatever the extent of its influence, it contributes significantly to the link between the New England and the American Way, to the usurpation of American identity by the United States, and to the anthropomorphic nationalism that characterizes our literature—not the secular anthropomorphism of parenthood (British homeland, German fatherland), but the eschatological anthropomorphism of spiritual biography: American dream, manifest destiny, redeemer nation, and, fundamentally, the American self as representative of universal rebirth.

4

From Hermeneutics to Symbolism

The Puritans' image of America marks the highpoint of their effort to find a rhetoric adequate to their sense of mission. Their claim to visible sainthood led them to stress the importance of christology; their rejection of mere separatism required them to define their venture soteriologically; and they combined both modes of identity, personal and historical, through their concept of national election. Having Americanized their rhetoric, they found in America the assurance of their destiny. Hence Mather's peculiar use of the adjective in "Nehemias Americanus"—not to modify the *exemplum* (as would be the case in European ecclesiastical biography) but to make the *exemplum* indicate the spiritual uniqueness of the locale. What might seem to be a play on words is in fact a wholesale inversion of traditional hermeneutics. To understand Winthrop, we must see him simultaneously as a saint, as a latter-day Nehemiah, and as the representative of a new chosen people; and Mather's rationale for blending the three perspectives—christology, soteriology, and national election—lies in his vision of the New World. Turning exegesis inside out, he transfers the source of meaning from scripture to secular history. Both he and his forebears, needless to say, would have denied the inference. They staked the outcome of their errand upon the *figural* import of "Americanus," and having thus anchored their meaning in prophecy, they felt secure that the future would vindicate them. Amazingly, the future proved them right. Amazingly, too, they succeeded in large measure because they so thoroughly committed themselves to the radically unorthodox implications of their rhetoric.

AMERICANA

The most searching critique of colonial rhetoric came from Roger Williams. He began by denouncing the practical effects of federal eschatology: the settlers' habit of mingling church and state, separatism and non-separation, the prerogatives of saint and citizen. All this was merely symptomatic, of course, and eventually Williams developed his arguments into a full-scale attack on the theocracy's claim to the title of New Israel. The emigrants, he pointed out, had based their claim on a federal covenant. They had a right to it, certainly, and by that right they might expect God to reward their obedience with large harvests. But they spoke of spiritual blessings as well, of a figural Israel in a new promised land. Quoting countless authorities from the Church Fathers to Calvin, Williams outlined the crucial distinction. Spiritually understood, Israel was "A *Non-such* and an *unparalel'd Figure* of the *Spirituall State*," whereas, he stressed, "*America* (as *Europe* and all nations) lyes dead in sin." The saints in New England, like all saints, belonged to the figural Israel. But *as New Englanders* they could no more arrogate that identity to themselves than could their neighbors, the Indians (Williams called *them* Americans), or the inhabitants of the Old World they had abandoned. "Nature knows no difference between [men] . . . in blood, birth, bodies," geography, or political arrangements. Any state, in any land, was "a ship at sea with many hundred souls"—"papists and protestants, Jews and Turks" and Indians—"whose weal and woe is common." What, then, was all this talk of a "new found land of Canaan," divinely granted to a New Israel for their "everlasting possession"? To declare that prophecies were unfolding through the agency of "a *people*, naturally considered"—that a ship of state represented the millennial ark of Christ—"if this be not to pull *God* and *Christ* and *Spirit* out of Heaven, and subject them unto *naturall*, sinful, inconstant men, . . . let Heaven and Earth judge." [1]

Williams debated with the baffled outrage of a man who just could not fathom his opponents' obstinacy. To some degree, we sense the same tone in the arguments of many others at home and abroad, from Thomas Morton's satirical *New English Canaan*[2] to the stern denunciations of English Presbyterian and Independent dignitaries. We can understand both their bafflement and their outrage by recalling the tensions in Reformed christology. The doctrines of *sola scriptura* and *sola fides* threatened to liberate the self in the most fundamental way, by encouraging a willful, arbitrary mode of exegesis. To counter the threat, the leading clerics imposed an absolute control over hermeneutics. What the Catholics, they charged, termed multileveled interpretation was nothing more than a license for subjectivity—for "empty dreams," "monkey-games," "wild adventures," "fantastical conceits." *They* intended to restore hermeneutics to its proper function, as an "anchor that never faileth" in the believer's stormy voyage from self to Christ. Accordingly, they instituted a single regimented "full sense" of scripture, a sort of catchall *littera-allegoria*—"*unum, simplicem, germanum et certum*"—by which the exegete could "never err or go out of the way." To ensure its application, they issued two sweeping strictures. The first defined the proper exegete as a believer. "The word is nothing without the Spirit," warned Richard Sibbes. Unregenerate readers kill the letter, reduce significance to dead fact. Hermeneutics presupposes a reader transformed in the image of the spirit he sets out to discover. The second stricture defined the process of discovery. Since the significance was put there by God, exegesis meant not invention or ingenuity, but orthodoxy. "When we proceed from the thing to the thing signified," wrote William Whitaker, in a famous treatise on hermeneutics, "we bring no new sense, but only bring to light what was before concealed in the sign." [3] In other words, literalism precludes personal interpretation. It serves as a wall of flame to secure the pristine Word against any snare of the intellect, all flights of the imagination.

This double identification of perceiver and fact would seem to leave no room for self-assertion. As though they intuited the chaos inherent in modern symbolism—fragmentation, self-contradicting multiplicity, eccentric cosmosophies—the Reformers rejected the secular and the subjective *a priori*. Only biblical facts yielded figural meaning, and only the believer who had interpreted himself figurally, as part of sacred history, could discern the meaning of biblical facts. From our modern perspective, however, having witnessed the growth of symbolism since the Reformation, we can hardly avoid detecting a fundamental ambiguity in their position. "When we proceed from the thing to the thing signified, we bring no new sense, but only bring to light what was before concealed in the sign." The very coherence of Whitaker's statement indicates the subjectivism inherent in Protestant thought. For finally, the connective between the thing and the thing signified is not the sign, but the regenerate figuralist in whom the concealed full sense is already manifested. Whitaker gears his formulation towards the passive voice of discovery ("what was before concealed"); his impersonal *we* reminds us that the self, like the word, is nothing without the spirit. And yet he makes it plain that the exegete is central: it is he who proceeds from sign to signification, he who brings the spirit to the fact and carries the light of meaning in himself.

This balance of extremes is precarious enough to suggest a resolution opposite but equal to that which the Reformers proposed. What if, for example, the saintly and duly reverent reader, bent on discovery, not invention, *did* find some "new sense" as he proceeded from the thing to the thing signified? Moreover, what if that new sense enabled him to discern signs hitherto concealed, and hermeneutically applicable to his present, secular situation? He would then have the whole system of exegesis at his disposal; he could restructure all of sacred history to bear out *his* signification; he could marshal all the literal-spiritual texts of the Bible to sustain his private vision. Neither Sibbes nor Whitaker considered that eventuality, but they should have. About seventy years before Whitaker's treatise, Luther had changed ecclesiastical history by discovering a new sense of the apocalypse in the concealed meanings of Daniel and Revelation. The New England Puritans went still further, at least with regard to language. By the time Sibbes wrote, they had discovered America in scripture; and had proceeded from the thing to the things signified—from Noah to Abraham to Moses to Nehemiah to "Americanus." Along the way, they changed the focus of traditional hermeneutics, from biblical to secular history.

The change in focus followed from the prerogatives they assumed as *American* exegetes. Luther announced his discovery in an act of rebellion, but his method and conclusions conformed to standard practice. The Reformation, as he conceived it, pertained exclusively to the universal church. He used "Romish Babylon" in the way the English Puritans were to use "British Israel," as a metaphor denoting the temporary conjunction of *Historie* and *Heilsgeschichte*. Basically, he knew, Roman (like German) history was not the history of the church. The Puritan colonists loudly proclaimed their orthodoxy, but when they announced that "America" was a figural sign, *historia* and *allegoria* entwined, they broke free of the restrictions of exegesis. Instead of subsuming themselves in the *sensus spiritualis*, they enlisted hermeneutics in support of what amounted to a private typology of current affairs. They were not only spiritual Israelites, with Luther, Foxe, and all Christians. They were also, uniquely, American Israelites, the sole reliable exegetes of a new, last book of scripture. Since they had migrated to another "holy land," as Thomas Tillam hymned upon his first sight of Massachusetts—"the *Antitype* of what the Lords people had of old"—they conferred upon the continent they left and the ocean they crossed the literal-spiritual contours of Egypt and Babylon. Since they were a "second, far more glorious Israel," their enemies at home and abroad became more sinister Pharaohs and Sanballats. Since they inhabited the earth's millennial fourth corner, "to which that blessed promise truly's given," and of "which the Old and New Testaments do ring," they regarded all other locales—Asia, Africa, Europe, places and peoples still unknown—as backward spiritual dependencies, awaiting the fulfillment of their venture.[4] In short, beginning with America, they recast the whole dead secular world in their own image.

The image required confirmation through what we would now call symbolic interpretation. The New England colonist not only had a private vision to convey, he had to convey it in metaphors that overturned the conventions from which those metaphors arose. He had to prove the Old World a *second* Babylon; otherwise, his readers might consider it (along with America) to be part of the universal spiritual Babylon. He had to *convince* them of the supernatural quality of the Atlantic. How else could they surmise the baptismal efficacy of the ocean-crossing? Most important, he had to demonstrate the eschatological import of the New World, to create his distinctive desert-garden *allegoria* from the details of his landscape. And the demonstration could only persuade symbolically—not through the shared atemporal significances of allegory (as in Bunyan's *Pilgrim's Progress*, or Nathaniel Holmes's popular *New World of the Church*), but through a highly personal inference drawn from secular experience. He responded accordingly. "Our eyes have *seen* our Sion," he declared to a deaf or incredulous Europe.

> Look upon [our] townes & fields, look upon [our] habitations & shops and ships, and behold [our] numerous posterity, and great encrease in the blessings of the Land & Sea. . . . Yea,

there is not only a *spiritual glory,* visible only to a spiritual eye, but also an *externall, and visible glory.* . . . And indeed, if we cast up the account, and lay all things together, God hath been doing the same thing here that is prophesied of Jacobs remnant. . . . He that hath said, *I will make the Wilderness a Pool of water, and* [in] *the dry lands I will plant a Cedar,* hath fulfilled that word before our eyes. And we may conclude that he intended some great thing when he planted these Heavens, and laid the foundations of this Earth. And what should that be, if not a *Scripture-Pattern* that shall in due time be accomplished the whole world throughout. [5]

In retrospect, it seems safe to say that such descriptions represent the process of the creation of the symbol of America. But the theocracy's entire rationale hinged on their being read hermeneutically, as a record of figural facts rather than as mere spiritualizations or hyperboles. Early New England rhetoric is a titanic effort to secularize traditional images without abandoning the claims of exegesis. The clergy compensated for their extreme subjectivism in substance by an extreme orthodoxy in approach. The perceiver, they insisted, had to identify with the divine meaning of the New World if he was to understand his environment correctly. He had to "cast his account" as an American, and his "conclusion" had to balance private and corporate redemption in the context of American destiny.

To that end, the orthodoxy instituted what might be called, for want of a better term, a rhetoric of inversion. Figuralism affirms the oneness of *allegoria* and *littera-historia,* as well as the interchangeability of private, corporate, historical, and prophetic meaning (e.g., "Israel" as the believer, the entire community of the elect, the latter-day church, and the saints in New Jerusalem). The Puritans used this approach consistently, comprehensively, as a means of transforming secular into sacred identity. Thus they personified the New World as America microchrista. Thus also they combined the genres of political and spiritual exhortation, and equated public with personal welfare. In effect, they invented a colony in the image of a saint. Discarding the difference between plural and singular, moving freely between historiography and spiritual biography, they inverted the notion of *exemplum fidei,* who stands for the elect

community, into the notion of a church-state that is an elect
Christian, *in imitatio Americae*—a newborn believer, who, by virtue of
his being American, represents the community of latter-day saints.
Elsewhere, for example, the jeremiad was a dirge over the
irrepressible agencies of common providence. Here it was a
celebration of God's promises, with New England a composite *figura*
embracing private, public, and prophetic identity.[6] Similarly, the
colonial histories read like spiritual biographies of an elect land.
Edward Johnson's *Wonder-Working Providence* (1651) describes the
country's coasts, towns, rivers, churches as the arms, heart, veins,
and soul of a believer marching at the head of the army of Christ.
Joshua Scottow's *Narrative of the Planting of the Massachusetts Colony*
(1694) follows the colony's development from a divine "embrio" to
a Holy Babe that grows into "the Righteous man." [7] Joseph
Morgan's *History of the Kingdom of Basaruah* (1715) uses Bunyan's
framework, the allegory of the Calvinist Everyman, to set out the
chiliastic prospects of the New World.

In its narrative sections, the *Magnalia* marks the high point of this
unprecedented genre of federal hagiography. Mather portrays the
venture as a case of conversion, ascending through temptations and
rededications towards paradise regained. He speaks of the emigrants' flight from the Old World as an evangelical call, and of
their ocean-crossing as a spiritual rebirth. Their progress in the
New World he describes in terms of the *imitatio*. The settlers go "into
the wilderness to a sacrifice unto the Lord," and fall upon "the
thorns of worldly vanities and vexations." Their enemies—witches,
heretics, Indians—appear in the various guises of the devils and the
damned: "a serpent by the way, an adder in the path"; the
Philistines destroyed by Samson; Azazel assaulting Jesus in the
desert; the flying monsters that preyed upon God's exiles; red-
skinned Esau, who plotted against Jacob and whom the Lord so
hated that He laid waste his heritage; the dragons of the wilderness
trodden underfoot by the heirs of salvation; the unburied carcasses
strewn beneath the eagles of grace; the army of Lucifer that
challenged the heavenly throne; the Satanic legions gathered for
their last furious but futile assault upon the children of Light.
Throughout, the action interrelates christology and apocalypse.
The conflicts which lead the corporate believer to his salvation also
reverse Satan's victory over the world; the paradisaic images

through which Mather conveys the success of the venture pertain simultaneously to the redeemed soul and the Mount Zion of Revelation.[8]

As the jeremiads and histories recast colonial progress into the journey of the latter-day saint, so conversely the sermons and treatises on grace inverted the process of personal redemption into a mode of historical expression. Thomas Hooker, for example, was New England's leading physician of the soul, and his "Sermon of 1638" has been singled out as being characteristic of his work. Yet the sermon applies the doctrine of grace principally to the problems of the *communal* enterprise. The distinguishing mark of the saint, Hooker begins, is that he can "see God in all." Knowing that the Lord acts towards him in love, he comes to relish punishments no less than deliverances. All standard pulpit fare, until the preacher brings the thesis to bear upon domestic hardships: Indians, lack of provisions, the "sad and sharp winter." Do you not see, Hooker demands, that the Lord delivered us in every exigency, sent us "drinke out of the rocke and meat from ravens"? Therein lies our proof "that marcy indures forever," our assurance that we will prevail: "God will doe good unto us, notwithstanding all the develes." This is the language of grace, but its message is political and temporal. To see God in all is to have experienced and understood New England's part in the divine plan. It is a sight of grace which confirms the perceiver's sainthood, his membership in the church-state, and, comprehensively, his participation as an *American* Puritan in a venture whereby (in Hooker's words) the "Prophecies are to attain their performances." [9]

Hooker's spiritual perception test lent itself to many variations. John Norton employs it in *The Believers Consolation* and *The Evangelical Worshipper* to make preparation for salvation a gauge of the colony's "outward," "day to day" prosperity. Thomas Shepard and John Cotton use it on several occasions to equate the problems of the elect with God's quarrel with New England. In the most massive and brilliant treatise of the century on the covenant of grace, Peter Bulkeley demonstrates that, as a "people in Covenant, i.e., Grace with God," the colonists are destined to shine forth, *through* their "times of tryall," as a holy, wise, and blessed people above all others.[10] The practical applications of this formula appear everywhere in the personal literature. The captivity narratives, for instance, transform what elsewhere would be considered evidence of private regeneration into a testimonial for the colonial cause. Mary Rowlandson proves through her capture and long imprisonment that "New England's present troubles are both justified and temporary." She does so by recourse to familiar jeremiad texts; by assuming the role of prophetess, repeatedly reminding the theocracy of its covenantal obligations; by scriptural allusions that link the believer and community; and above all, by perceiving God's "wonderful Power in carrying us along, preserving us in this Wilderness." For her as for the theocracy, "the 'worst of evils' will work 'together for the best good'." She charges her readers to "lay by something from [her] experience" so that they may profit "by all this affliction." [11] Her rhetoric renders her at once a microcosm of colonial history and a guide to the American future.

Essentially the same pattern of inversion dominates the narratives of sea-crossing. The emigrants detail the wonders of the deep not primarily to show God's favor to the saint, and not to recount oceanic marvels (as in French, Spanish, and Southern narratives), but, combining the spiritual and naturalistic levels, to extol the enterprise in general. Their emphasis on the hazards of the Atlantic reflects their sense of destiny: God "let us see all his power"; with His "owne immediate good hand [He] . . . asswaged ye violence of ye sea. . . . It was an extraordinary and miraculous deliverance," beyond that of the Israelites in "the streights of the Red Sea." These phrases come from private manuscripts (letters and journals); strictly speaking their form is autobiographical; but the attitude is that of the election-day orator, and the authorial *persona* is clearly representative. As an exemplar of the American Israel, he relives scriptural history: God leads him "From *Egypt* land through Seas with watry Walls"; in "Thickest fogge and darkest night" he fears no evil, for Christ "sayes peace ye waves, and . . . for all their height they fall downe flat." Repeatedly, the "miraculous providences" that save him "magnifie the grace of Christ in this great Worke." "We that dwell in America," declared Thomas Shepard, having come safely through so many dangers at sea, "as upon Eagles wings," may rest secure in our salvation. "We have . . . been like a little vessel in a storm," Mather concluded, after having entered a number of such personal testimonies in the *Magnalia:*

> The swelling waves have dashed, and raged, and roared; the
> rude billows have been going over us, and we have been ready

to sink. But just *then* our compassionate Lord Jesus Christ hath *awaked* for our safety, and marvellously calmed our circumstances! O thou land, strangely saved by the Lord, say now, as in Psal. cxxxvi. 23, "O give thanks unto the Lord, . . . because his mercy endureth for ever!" [12]

Mather's use of personal experiences to impute grace to state and country alike mirrors the inverted figural pattern of the narratives upon which he draws.

AMERICANUS

The inversion seems most pronounced in the autobiographies, because of their obvious deviation from the norms of the conversion-story. The English Puritan autobiographies, we know, show everything "as happening before, during or after conversion"; "Conversion arrests the downward cycle of events and embarks man upon the . . . 'way' to paradise." For many of New England's founders, the embarkation was a literal one. Figurally and structurally, the migration to America displaces conversion as the crucial event. Shepard's diary, for example, pivots on his exodus from Europe. Having seen "the Lord departing from England," he reports, he decided to "come over, to live among God's people as one come out from the dead"; after his extraordinary adventures at sea, he feels certain that he has in fact undergone a "heavenly translation," and now stands a New World believer, "come and risen from the dead." Shepard's equation of new life with New World, and of baptism with the Atlantic as a greater Red Sea, became a staple of early colonial autobiography. It has its counterpart in the sermons on grace, with their recurrent application of nautical language to the process of conversion. To be sure, the application is traditional. Yet as several critics have observed, its frequency, specificity, and poignancy in colonial writing is extraordinary. "Time and again practically every minister resorts for his imagery to the sea and ships and sailors." Time and again the imagery echoes recorded experiences: shipwrecks on rocky shores, vessels foundering in mid-passage or forced by tempests into an unexpected route, mariners fighting the Atlantic gales or struggling to repair a sinking ship, and finally, of course, "Wonder of Wonders," the arrival "safe to shore," into the bosom of Christ's Holy Commonwealth. [13]

The purpose of these images, like those used by Shepard, Hooker, and Mather, is to unite *allegoria* and *historia* in the framework of the American venture. A good many of the emigrants adjusted their autobiographies to that framework. One of them, Roger Clap, rose by his wits from soldier to officer and legislator, and the *Memoirs* he left his children, like Franklin's *Autobiography*, are an encomium to the opportunities of the New World. Clap makes his life the occasion for displaying the works of Christ in America, correlating the signs of his redemption with "God's regular disposition" towards His new chosen people. His decision to ship for America, as he relates it, was part of a moment when Christ so plainly showed men the "absolute Necessity of the *New-Birth* . . . that our Hearts were taken off from *Old-England* and set upon Heaven." He speaks of his subsequent hardships in terms of "the then unsubdued Wilderness": his perseverance is an emblem of "the settlers' determination," his success a token of "*their* eventual triumph," and his spiritual experiences indistinguishable from God's blessings upon the community. In sum, Clap turns self-portrait into New England chronicle by presenting the pattern of colonial history as the justification for his life. His opening sentence describes his *Memoirs* as a tale of "GOD'S Remarkable Providences to me, in bringing me into this Land, and placing me here among his dear Servants." His intention is "to declare . . . the *wonderful Works of God* in . . . this Wilderness." Just how remarkable those providences were, and how wonderful those works, he indicates at the end of the autobiography. Urging his children "to build a millennial New England," he envisions a grateful posterity, "more heavenly than their Predecessors," that "will doubtless greatly Rejoice" in "the first Planters of *New England*" as "*the Generation whom the Lord hath Blessed.*" [14]

The diary of John Hull, another self-made man, tells much the same story. Like Clap and Shepard, Hull emphasizes the miraculous ocean-crossing rather than his conversion, and links his regeneration to his spectacular worldly ascent within a theocracy destined for "great prosperity . . . maugre all adversity." More successful than Clap, he is more willing to deal with misfortunes— or rather, to explain them in the context of the federal covenant. An "epidemical cold" means that God is chastening His people. Financial problems show how He has been "trying, nurturing, lopping, and pruning his poor children, by his own fatherly hand, for their good." At other points, Hull girds himself for affliction by comparing the colony with Job, who also suffered from "the power of Satan, by God's permission," and consoles himself for having decided "to foresake all" in Europe by recalling "the faith and courage of this people so lately come into this wilderness." His diary falls into two parts: "Passages of God's Providence About Myself" and "Passages of [His] Providence Toward the Country." In effect, however, Hull joins both kinds of providence, personal and public, eschatological and prophetic, in the comprehensive social myth which he several times recapitulates—how old England had seemed to him and the other emigrants "as Babylon to Israel," how they then undertook "this work the Lord had to perform," and how He was now directing them into New Jerusalem.[15]

The similarities between Hull's account and Clap's extend through most colonial diaries: among others, those of Major William Vaughan, the merchant Joshua Scottow, the magistrate Simon Bradstreet, Obadiah Russell, tutor at Harvard college, Captain Lawrence Hammond, John Eliot, the "apostle to the Indians," the poet Michael Wigglesworth, and reverends Josiah Flynt, Jonathan Pierpont, Joseph Green, and Peter Hobart.[16] These two examples will do, I hope, to convey the formula that links them all. Precisely to affirm their sainthood the authors identify with the enterprise at large. Their method complements Mather's in the Life of Winthrop: it invokes the national epic heuristically to complete the epic of the soul. For the laymen Hull and Clap, no less than for the theocratic elite, self-examination leads to the assertion of a *social*-divine selfhood which certifies their calling as introspection alone could never do. This is not to say that they considered the confirmation complete. Both the personal writings and what I termed the genre of federal hagiography remained vulnerable, finally, to the course of history. Since they could no more than assert the success of the errand, their form is closer to Bunyan's autobiographical *Grace Abounding* than it is to his self-contained narrative of *Pilgrim's Progress*. Theoretically, their rhetoric had eliminated the anxiety of process by elevating secular into sacred history. But theory alone—in history as in autobiography—could not altogether compensate for the palpable insecurities of day-by-day events: planting and reaping, suppressing schismatics, raising children, fighting Indians, maintaining order in an increasingly complex and heterogeneous society.

This limitation in time, with the ominous void it allowed between *figura* and fact, explains the prominence of the exemplary Life in colonial literature. To be an American is to assume a prophetic identity; to have been an American is to offer a completed action that makes destiny manifest. As *Pilgrim's Progress* proves what *Grace Abounding* can merely imply, so the Life of Winthrop provides the cornerstone, retrospectively, and the capstone, prospectively, of the New World Jerusalem. Thus the colonial elegy differs from its European antecedent, as Kenneth Silverman has noted, because it speaks of regional rather than of personal matters.[17] More than that, it uses the saint's glorification to project the country's coming glory. In accordance with the technique of inversion, the elegists translate private loss into an affirmation not (primarily) of immortality but of political continuity. They render the hero's death an occasion for reviewing the past and predicating the future. The American accomplishments which are now seen to have been the *visibilia* of his election become, by that token, a guarantee to the bereaved community of the common cause, a promise tendered to each one of his survivors that his/their mission will prevail.

This is most simply seen in the use of parallels. "John Winthrop," reads one elegy (anticipating Mather's Life), directed us "to the promised land . . . out of the Babylonian Captivity." Benjamin Tompson celebrates Governor John Leverett as the pilot of the colonial ark, and as the Joshua who cleared the heathen from "This Holy Land"; we lament his death, but his accomplishments remain our legacy:

> This will be omen of your future peace
> Heaven will Create or rayse up more of these.

So, too, Sewall commemorates Samuel Willard:

> As *Joseph* let his Brethren see
> *Simeon* both alive, and free:
> So *JESUS* brings forth *Samuel*;
> . . . .
> Distressing Fear caus'd us to Pray;
> God help'd us; He will help us aye.

Similarly, John Fiske pictures Nathaniel Rogers in the "heavenly Canaan," resting "by our Josua," in order to remind the settlers, in *their* temporal Canaan, serving *their* Joshuas, that God will bless

their venture, as He has Rogers's, "in the end." Fiske's elegy
to John Cotton is even more fortifying, since the loss is greater.
He compares him to "a knott / Of Hony sweete" in the American "honi-comb," a "plant of Gods own hand" flowering on
New England's "vine." The minister's death has left the country
(once in "Cotton clad") "Naked," but still a *typus Christi:* still Israel,
a vine, a honeycomb. When Fiske prays that we "may follow
afte[r him,]/surviving worlds ocean," he recalls the Atlantic passage
that brought Cotton to the New World; and though he fears
"pinching times t'ensue," ultimately, he assures the inhabitants of
New Israel, we "maust see" God's "waies of mercy." [18] "Let his
Mourning Flock be comforted," writes Benjamin Woodbridge in
another elegy "Upon the Tomb of . . . John Cotton":

> Though *Moses* be, yet *Joshua* is not dead:
> I mean Renowned NORTON; worthy hee
> Successor to our MOSES is to bee,
> O happy *Israel* in AMERICA,
> In such a MOSES such a JOSHUA.[19]

The communal emphasis of the early New England elegy
characterizes all forms of colonial verse. Its function as federal
hagiography stands most fully revealed in the development, soon
after mid-century, of the legend of the founding fathers. I have
explored this development elsewhere at some length; here I want
simply to mention in passing that it constitutes an imaginative
achievement of a very high order. Less than thirty years after the
Arbella landed, before all the leaders of the Great Migration had
died, there evolved the legend of a golden age, one that effectually
transported all the archetypes of biblical and classical antiquity to
the Massachusetts Bay shores. Its sustained intensity, its coherence,
and the rapidity with which it grew, amounts to an astonishing,
possibly unrivaled cultural maturation. In part, no doubt, we can
ascribe this to the emigrants' driving need to confirm their identity,
to convince the world that their hermeneutics was *not* some
blasphemous warping of dogma for quixotic sectarian ends. It is no
accident that the legend dates from 1660, with the failure of
Cromwell's Protectorate. What happened then in England to the
idea of the elect nation—the natural, almost felicitous demytholog-
izing process discussed in chapter 3—could simply not happen in

New England. The orthodoxy had invested too much of themselves
in their image of America: not only their hopes in founding a city
on a hill, but their "national" background, their communal future,
and their personal calling. Their recourse during this period of crisis
to the legend of the fathers marks a momentous victory for their
secular hermeneutics and, by implication, for the concept of
American identity.

We have a valuable gauge to the novelty of their approach in
Samuel Clarke's revision of the first two large-scale New England
biographies. During the Restoration, the English Dissenter tran-
scribed John Norton's Life of Cotton and Increase Mather's Life of
his father, Richard, for a collection of Lives of eminent divines. In
Clarke's version, both Lives tell the old tale of the pilgrim's progress
to heaven. Cotton was another Abel, *figura* of the persecuted
universal church; Richard was an *"Imitation in the Lord."* The
original Lives tell another story as well—about the "unparallell'd
undertaking" of an entire community, "the greatest undertaking"
of all time, "a History of such experiences, each one whereof is more
than a Wonder." Norton compares his hero with Jesus led into the
wilderness only to amplify the comparison into a historical configuration. The New World setting establishes the continuity from old
Israel to new, and Cotton himself stands revealed as the champion
of a "time now come wherein God purposed to [s]uperadd unto
what hath formerly been." Virtually every aspect of his life becomes
an occasion for paying homage to the mission. Norton links
Cotton's youthful promise to his stature as father of the theocracy;
he makes Cotton's conversion experience interchangeable with his
"tempestuous Flight" across the Atlantic; and he describes him, in
New England, as another Moses, directing "the removal of . . . a
Nation," and as a second John the Divine, predicting the defeat of
Antichrist "and the joys of the City of God." [20]

In short, what Clarke deleted turns out to be the purpose of
Norton's biography: the affirmation of the New England Way
through the pilgrimage of its representative saint. Significantly,
Clarke deletes the same kind of passages from the Life of Richard
Mather. In fact, he omits altogether the motives for and the
circumstances of migration—which is to say, he omits about
one-fourth of the biography, and its central *motif.* Passing briefly
over his father's new birth, Increase concentrates instead on the

summons to America, and on Richard's principal arguments for engaging with the other "First-fathers" in "so great and hazardous a Design." The arguments rise with dramatic intensity from the duty to flee persecution, through the world's present need for a purer model of church-state, to the divine call to leave England, before its desolation, for an appointed sanctuary. Richard's reasoning is verified by Jehovah in Person when "by a mighty hand and an outstretched Arm" He brings His "chosen vessels" (the pun is deliberate) to the New World. America itself Increase describes as "the desired Haven" to which the "Lord, after manifold Trials" of His saints, brings them "in safety . . . to special service for his Name." [21] The European Puritans usually reserved such phrases for descriptions of heaven. Here they denote the figural link between New England and New Jerusalem, with Richard Mather himself the exegetical text that verifies the *figura*.

The persistence of rhetorical technique from one generation to the next, from Hooker and Norton to Increase Mather, would seem to contradict the facts of social change. The contradiction sharpens when we consider that the concept of American selfhood presupposes a figural (rather than a platonic) alliance of the real and the ideal. The settlers expected *history* to verify their dream. Their obsessive compilings of wonder-working providences express their conviction that a more heavenly generation, as Roger Clap put it, would one day regard their errand as postdated prophecy. History betrayed them, we know. That they persisted nonetheless requires us, I believe, to redefine their achievement in a positive way. I said earlier that in part their imagery served a compensatory function, that the sweep and confidence of their language hinted at various internal problems and distressing shifts of attitude abroad. But surely this dialectic between rhetoric and fact is common to most cultures, and the Bay Puritans were not the only New World colonists to face a recalcitrant reality. In the broadest cultural perspective, colonial "reality" is a composite of social challenge and imaginative response. As both these factors are reflected in early New England literature, they reveal above all the undiminished commitment of the old guard, and the protean richness of their rhetoric.

For the fact is, that the orthodoxy found a ready answer to declension in the rhetoric itself. They could treat the entire issue as a problem in hermeneutics. The apparent discrepancy between promise and fulfillment, they explained, was an error in perception. Since appearances meant nothing without the spirit, and since the spirit yielded a significance that was transcendent and immutable, their task was not to invent new interpretations, but to devise strategies which would sustain the discovered meaning. Of course, they could not deny the untoward course of history, but then they did not need to. They could make their denunciations *support* their vision, their affirmations feed on decline. Historical extremity became their opportunity to display the creative potential of their imagination. Shifting their approach, accordingly, from social pragmatics to imaginative assertion, they salvaged their image of America by making the image itself the historical link between thing and thing signified. Hooker's "Sermon of 1638" arrives at a foregone conclusion, but it confronts actual problems. Even when he confronts his backsliding contemporaries, the theocrat of 1690 overleaps the present into the legendary past and the prophetic future. He offers a test not of perception but of symbiotic identification; and he succeeds not because the facts conform but because the rhetoric compels. What remains, finally, is the vision of the errand as it has been ingested, spiritualized, and made manifest in the mind and art of the regenerate "Americanus."

AMERICA

Let me illustrate the nature of this transformation by contrasting Mather's biographical method with Edward Johnson's. Written though they were some fifty years before the *Magnalia*, the brief biographical poems in *Wonder-Working Providence* clearly embody the same principles of inversion that inform Mather's Lives. All of Johnson's heroes are both saints and exemplary colonists, all are "shaddowes of good things now come," and in every case Johnson uses the American teleology to conflate the visible with the invisible church, social and christic identity. As the narrative progresses, the poems actually turn from personal into institutional biographies— about Harvard, or various congregations, or the New World at large—and the History closes with a prophetic forecast that is also a survey of the lives of America's exemplars:

because you shall be sure the day is come indeed, behold the Lord Christ marshalling of his invincible Army to the battell:

some suppose this onely to be mysticall, and not literall at all, but these N.E. people ingage[d] with the main battell of Antichrist [have already shown] what the issue will be. Babylon is fallen. And now you antient people of Israel, look out of your prison grates, let these Armies of Christ provoke you to acknowledge he is certainly come, that you may enjoy the glorious nuptials of the Lamb.[22]

Now, on the surface of it, all this might be transposed to the *Magnalia*. The critical difference between the two works that emerges upon closer inspection reflects the authors' relationship to their culture. Mather was writing during the collapse of the church-state, sustaining himself in his defense of "our invaded Churches" by his declared affinity with the great men of the past. No more than a handful of Johnson's heroes were dead when he eulogized them. Whereas Mather's biographies are retrospective, Johnson's sustain the forward sweep of the chronicle: for individual and community alike the consummation lies in prophecy. Whether the reward is heaven or the chiliad, the sanctifying tasks that precede the reward devolve upon the still unfulfilled American enterprise:

> They prosper shall that Sions building mind,
>   Then [John] Ward cease not with toyl her stones to lay,
> For great is he thee to this work assign'd,
>   Whose pleasure is, heavens Crown shall be thy pay.
> . . . .
> Christ call'd his people hither for these ends,
>   To tell the world that Babels fall is nigh;
> And that his Churches through the world shall spread,
>   Maugre the might of wicked men and devils,
> Then [George] Moxon thou need'st not at all to dread,
>   But be aveng'd on Satan for his evils,
> Thy Lord Christ will under thy feet him tread.[23]

As in the Life of Winthrop, the imagery is millennial. But for Mather the future follows directly from the achievement of the past; the walls of the Theopolis Americana have their "imperishable" foundation in the promise *fulfilled* in Winthrop's career. For Johnson they rest unavoidably upon the flux and struggle of the present. John Ward still has a lifetime of hardship to endure; earlier, the author feels it necessary to tell him that he is not "yet of hope bereft." So also the poem to George Moxon acknowledges many conflicts ahead; the rhyme-words "spread" and "tread" are linked by the actual, the temporal, and hence the "dread" *process* of fulfillment. Johnson tells us that what he has written (guided by "the very finger of God") will be "a great strengthening to the Faith of those who are appointed of the Lord." His intention is to offer "the People," through sketches of their leaders, "heavenly things your earthly toyle to cheere." [24] The sketches themselves make transparent the need for a vision that stands independent of experience. Even as they give cheer and strengthen faith, they highlight the dangerous open-endedness of prophetic identity, the distance between the appointed *telos* and the toil of becoming.

The difference in perspective, therefore, opens into antithetical images of the representative American. Mather's portrait of Winthrop offers a viable type, an acknowledged member of the City of God who, as exemplary New Englander, becomes a vehicle for investing providence with prophecy. The representative men of *Wonder-Working Providence* turn our attention from the absolute future to the conditional present. All too clearly they stand for the *effort* to fuse fact and promise, the secular and the hermeneutical, and Johnson himself makes it plain that the uncertainty of the fact compels the assertion of the promise. At the start of his narrative, he tells us that the emigrants planned their venture with undue optimism. The Lord, he explains, hid "from the Eyes of his people the difficulties they are to encounter withall in a New Plantation that they might not thereby be hindered from taking the worke in hand." Once they have undertaken the work, they obviously need men like Johnson to keep it in hand:

> With eyes full of anguish, they face to the right . . . so many dreadfull Engines set by Satan to intrap their poor soules; Then casting forth a left hand looke, the labour and wants accompaning a Desert, and terrible Wildernesse affright them. . . . When with thoughts of retreating, they turn their backs about, the experienced incumbrances and deep distresses of a dangerous Ocean hinders their thoughts of flight, besides the sterne looke of the Lordly Prelates, which would give them a welcome home in a famishing prison.

In such passages, and there are perforce a good many of them in *Wonder-Working Providence*, the very effectiveness of description obscures Johnson's purpose. *Because* Samuel Stone regrets having his "youth and learning's spent / In desart Land," the author reminds him of the glories that await him. "Stop not in discontent," he calls out to Richard Bellingham. Others he admonishes to "Wait patiently," to "Hold out till death," not to falter, nor allow old age and infirmity to discourage them.[25]

In short, Johnson's portrait of the American has two very different aspects. One is allegorical: the colony as saint, advancing by "Scripture light" to "lasting blisse." The other is historical: the saint as colonist, "poor, despised," burdened by anxiety, nostalgia, and doubt, occasionally luxuriating in "ease and sleep," often inclined to "trifle" time away, and always in need of rhetoric to goad him on. Johnson tries valiantly to harmonize the two aspects, only to make us more aware of the dichotomy between the *allegoria* and the *littera-historia*. The dazzling works of wonder in the foreground tend to sharpen our perception of the shadows of human weakness, of insecurity, failure, and desertion. Sir Henry Vane "in new world tri'd a while" but suffered "defeat." So also "Christ sent over the much honoured and upright hearted servant of his Richard Saltingstall" but he soon grew "weary" and left. Those who remain do not easily adjust. The poem to Ezekiel Rogers beseeches him not to mourn for England; the hesitant John Knowles must be inspired to continue with what Johnson reveals, despite himself, to be a precarious venture; the planting of Sudbury was attended by floods and crop losses, and Johnson finds he must rouse its aging minister, Edmond Brown, by signs of the approaching Conversion of the Jews. Not infrequently, his tone rises from reprimand to veiled threat. "Why do's thou stand and gaze about so long?," he demands of Nathaniel Ward. Do the "worrying wolves," the "daily" trials, deter you?

> Despayr not; Christs truth they shall not mar,
>   But with his help such drosse from Gold refine.
> What, Man, dost mean to lay thy Trumpet downe[?]
> . . . . / . . . .
> Hold out or sure lesse bright will be thy crowne;
>   Till death Christs servants labour is not done.[26]

Despair not, they shall not mar: but the mortal dross intimates that we are not witnessing the wonders of redemption, after all, but an experiment in providential history. Herbert's incipient "sin and darkness" lie just beneath the glitter of the metaphors. Indeed, we might fairly posit that Johnson's motive in prodding his compatriots is to cheer *himself* through similar crises. Whatever the case, his sense of urgency and immediacy contrasts vividly with Mather's assured retrospective tone; and the contrast provides an index to the cultural developments that separate the two men. The exemplary Lives of *Wonder-Working Providence* emphasize the enormous labor that still is *not* done—remind us how much the exegesis of America depends on "humane" events. The *Magnalia*'s exemplary Lives function to obviate that dependency. Of course, Mather cannot quite get around temporal limitations. No amount of embellishment can make it seem that Christ's battle for America, like Joshua's for Canaan or Aeneas's for Rome, is over and done with. What Mather does instead is almost as bold. Drawing upon the furthest reach of the mode of inversion, he makes his saints' Lives—considered not individually now, as I have been treating the Life of Winthrop, but in the conglomerate, as a *progression* of heroes—emblematic of the story of America.

To appreciate this effect in full, we must return to the biographical approach with which this study began: Winthrop as a member of an ongoing historic enterprise—in a favorite image of Mather's, one of many players on the stage of the New World theater.[27] So considered, the biography represents the smallest unit in a Chinese box of biographical forms. It is one of a series of portraits of New England magistrates, and the group of magistrates (book II) is in turn one of a series of group portraits, including also the leading colonial divines (book III) and the most notable Harvard graduates (book IV). And these groups of biographies, as we have seen, are enclosed within the gargantuan federal hagiography that shapes the narrative sections (books I, V, VI, VII). Mather's mode of integration is fairly simple in concept. The series of biographies, and biographical groupings, demarcate the successive acts in the drama of the corporate American pilgrim. Like Winthrop, every one of the "principal actors" stands for the venture at large; conversely the progress of the errand is embodied in a procession of representative American saints. The result is a twofold biographical scheme.

Mather's chronological ordering of his Lives (e.g., the Winthrop biography followed by the Lives of Winthrop's successors) heightens our sense of narrative development. At the same time, his biographical method constantly returns us to the pattern of the *imitatio*. As the two perspectives merge, they form what may best be understood as a futuristic *imitatio*—a completed and justified *christic* configuration whose import lies in its promise for the future.

In the broadest sense, Mather's organizing principle is generational.[28] His unifying metaphors derive from the process of preparation. The metaphor of exodus dominates his portraits of the first-generation heroes; he links his second-generation heroes through the metaphor of adoption, the filial bond. Succession, that is, means progression. The flight from depravity issues in the commitment to continuity and fulfillment. Mather enforces this motif in many ways throughout the biographies, most successfully by the imagery of implantation and fruition. The fathers, as he describes them, are both planters and seeds, the sons both harvesters and harvest. Sifted from Europe and engrafted on to the New World landscape, the emigrants flower like green olive trees, cedars of Lebanon, lilies of the valley. Their heirs, who "had their whole growth in the soyl of New England," bring the mythical-green glow to its full lustre. Each "more than ordinary man" among them points towards the "more than ordinary thing to be done . . . in an American wilderness"; each carries the promise that "the American hemisphere may anticipate the state of New Jerusalem"; and all of them are *de facto* saints. Mather's work, therefore, becomes in itself a guarantee of the success of the venture. The fame of the New World garden it celebrates *already* resounds "from one end of heaven unto another"; its representative men, founders and heirs, stand in relation to one another as thing to thing signified in the New World scripture. Together, they prove that "the further the grace of God is continued [among us] . . . the greater *effects* of that grace will be still appearing." As prophetic types, they bring assurance that *"now, within the last few sevens of years, things grow nearer to accom-*plishment." [29] What will be is present in what has been, in the acts and monuments of the *Magnalia*'s called, adopted, implanted, sanctified, and *now*-glorified exemplary Americans.

Mather's filiopietism, then, renders the present intermediate between fulfillment and greater fulfillment. As another Nehemiah,

Winthrop reminds us that the scriptural past is filiopietism antedated; as the father of the New World Israel, he assures us that the future is postdated filiopietism. "*Our Fathers, Where are They?* They are now in Heaven*," urging us to consummate "the great affairs . . . now come into [our] hands." John Eliot who "fought the devil in once his American territories," was always "sounding the silver trumpets of Heaven." Now Eliot himself is in heaven, with "tidings to the old founders of New-England, that . . . the number of our churches was continually increasing." John Eliot's celestial discourse engages many another trumpeter of the apocalypse, American Nehemiahs all: Henry Flint, for one, that "solid *stone* in the foundations of New-England [who] is gone to be a glorious one in the walls of the New-Jerusalem"; Urian Oakes for another, whose dedication to our "fam'd Utopia" assures us that "wide America" will hold the capital of the new age; and again, John Davenport, who rendered "the renowned church of New-Haven like the New Jerusalem"; and once more, Edward Hopkins, in whom "New-England saw little *dawnings,* of emblems, and earnests of the day, 'that the greatness of the kingdom under the whole heaven shall be given unto the people of the saints of the Most High'." [30]

Together, Mather's Lives constitute a corporate auto-machia— linking New England, *exemplum fidei,* and "the American hemi-sphere"—whose outcome is secure as spiritual biography. Like hermeneutics, his filiopietism helps us "see with open face God's secret for time past" and His "performances for [the] future, as if they were accomplishments at present," so that "two Eternities (as it were) meet together." Mather has no need, therefore, as did Johnson, to bait his wayward contemporaries with the prospect of the hastening millennium. His work speaks for itself. "With such a *glory,* with such a *defence,*" the *Magnalia* is its own vindication. It not only signifies but embodies and vouchsafes the national *telos.* Indeed, in the rare instances when Mather turns to the immediate present, he stresses that adversity has nourished his faith. Expecting "nothing but scourges" for his labor, he cheerfully foresees "a recompense that will swallow up all discouragements!" To all enemies of the cause, at home and abroad, their hearts "full of serpents and venom," he proudly and "freely confess[es], 'tis COTTON MATHER that has written all these things; *Me, me, adsum qui scripsi; in me convertite ferrum"*—"It was I, I myself who wrote this! Hurl your spears at *me!"* [31]

As Mather well understood, his recompense depended on an individual act of will and vision. He articulated the Puritan dream more forcefully than his predecessors because history forced him back upon his own resources. To be sure, he tried to augment his authority by using filiopietism to confirm his representative role. In one way or another, he implies, all his heroes attest to the public leadership which by heavenly and dynastic right he ought to have inherited. But his strength lay in his realization that the claim sufficed in itself; and accordingly he centered the image of America where it really always belonged, in the symbolic imagination. Johnson saw himself as a guardian of society, Scottow as a defender of the Good Old Way. Mather declared himself the keeper of the dream. His concept follows from the premises of secular hermeneutics, but he carries them to their final, logical inversion. He rescues the errand by appropriating it to himself. "The more stones they throw at this book," he writes, "will not only be the more proofs that it is a tree which hath good fruits growing upon it, but I will build myself a monument with them." *Book, tree,* and *monument:* figurally interpreted, they proclaim the walled garden of the representative American, flowering in the stony wilderness; the monument to the New World Jerusalem, validated by its imperviousness to the adversities of time. "Whether New-England may *live* any where else or no," Mather declares summarily, "it must *live* in our History!" [32]

Mather's assertion of representative identity marks the furthest, most audacious extension of colonial Puritan hermeneutics. His play on *live* affirms more than the exegetical dichotomy between the dead fact and the word revivified in the spirit. It asks us to consider American identity a rhetorical (rather than a historical) issue, to make Mather's proofs *our* monument, his vision our *history,* and to perceive *any where else* as a synonym for meaninglessness.[33] It is the most improbable request in his more than four hundred publications, and the only one to which his American audience has acquiesced. His History has indeed remained ours, as the supreme colonial expression of what we have come to term the myth of America. Mather set out, with the ambition of an epic bard, to leave posterity an outline of the country's divine origins, a pantheon of its first fathers, a variety of heroes embodying its cultural norms, and an action appropriate to the cosmic scope of the venture. He succeeded by submerging all of these epic conventions in a genuinely distinctive mythical mode. The golden ages of "primitive" myth—and of literary epic as well (Troy, Latium, Eden)—come to us from an irrevocable past. Insofar as they apply to the present, they reshape it into an *exemplum* of universal history, a recapitulation of some primal action. The meaning of the present (and the future) is accessible only through memory, since that action has already been fulfilled. Mather's myth comes to us from the inevitable future. It reshapes the past into a foreshadowing of greater things to come, a developing drama whose meaning is accessible only through anticipation. Interweaving autobiography and sacred history, it confirms Mather's role as prophet by asserting the communal purpose, and proves the continuity of purpose by the presence of his vision.

Mather compared himself in this respect with the Old Testament seers; but again, his concept of an *American* mission impelled him to a distinctive prophetic mode. Jeremiah derives his authority from popular tradition. The myth he represents is the commemorative expression of his race. His function as communal spokesman builds on the conflict between vision and fact; and accordingly his outlook is dialectical, insistent on the irreconcilable dualism of what his people is and what it ought to be. The very need for prophecy, that is, arises out of an engagement with history and community; the very concept of fulfillment centers on the *problem* of the present. Even as he outlines the paradise to come, Jeremiah invokes the myth in terms of contradiction. He appeals to the past in order to call attention to the hiatus between past and present. His representative stature, the authority both of his denunciations and of his predictions, is that of a tradition at odds with the course of history. Mather's entire rhetoric is geared toward obviating that discrepancy. He earns his authority as communal spokesman not by his relation to any existent community, but by personal assertion. His myth is essentially projective and elite, the invention of expatriate idealists who declared themselves the party of the future, and then proceeded, in an implicit denial of secular history, to impose prophecy upon experience. They themselves hesitated to make full use of their approach. They had devised their rhetoric, after all, as a means of social control; to some extent at least they felt obliged to confront the conflicts inherent in their venture. Mather's work shows no such tension. The problem he sets himself in the *Magnalia* is one of imaginative self-completion. Since he himself constitutes the link between promise and fulfillment, he can resolve the anxieties of the present simply by confirming his representative stature.

Mather's method issues in a peculiarly self-contained concept of heroism. Mythographers tell us that the heroic "superindividual" provides a model of tribal identity, and that mythic rituals, by reenacting the exploits of the patriarchs, transform biography (in Lévi-Strauss's phrase) into "a form of history of a higher power than itself." Some such motives inform Mather's biographies. Only *his* superindividual is America itself, microcosm of the worldwide work of redemption, and macrocosm of the redemptive work underway in each of its chosen people. Thus he obviates history by inverting it into a still higher form of personal narrative. Perhaps the best description of this form is auto-American-biography, where the central term, "American," referring as it does to a futuristic ideal, transforms the tribal ritual from a social mode of personal fulfillment into a personal mode of social fulfillment. In sum, it reconstitutes national prophecy and spiritual biography as prophetic autobiography. American Puritan hermeneutics begins by asserting the unique status of the community; it finds its amplest expression, at the end of the theocratic experiment, in the unique powers it confers upon the solitary "true perceiver."

In the *Magnalia*, those powers also extend, of course, to the epic heroes who convey Mather's vision. Traditionally, the epic hero culminates the myth-making process. As in the case of the christic antitype, he serves to remind his imitators of their *in*completeness; the transcendent model toward which they aspire accentuates their own limiting historical conditions. Mather's heroes, on the contrary, delineate the myth in process. Considered in context, they are successive harbingers of the Theopolis Americana at hand. Each of them, in his distinctive historical situation, emerges an emblem of destiny manifest. The retrospective *imitatio* therefore opens into a relativistic configuration; it justifies itself, as John Higginson noted, "in relation to future times"—by reference to a fuller and better reformation of the Church of God, than it hath yet appeared in the world . . . [when] the *sincere,* though *weak* endeavors of the servants of God, that went before them, will be also accepted of the saints in those times of greater light and holiness; and when the Lord shall make Jerusalem . . . the joy of many generations, then [our present methods] . . . will be owned and improved unto an higher degree of *practical godliness,* that shall continue for many generations succeeding one another.[34]

The hero's stature, so conceived, derives from the capacity to signify something *fuller, better, greater, higher.* Ultimately, the New World itself reveals the scope of his action. To identify with John Winthrop or with Cotton Mather is not merely to assume the characteristics of a life finished and glorified, a mode of imagining sufficient unto itself. It is this too, but more largely it is to become part of a teleology. For Mather, Winthrop is a prophetic exemplar, and he a greater Nehemiah who would define us, as Americans, in relation to the still unfolding New World *magnalia,* somewhere midway between the theocracy and paradise regained. And wherever the midway point falls along the inter-Sabbatical line, the concept of "Americanus" designates a comprehensive social-divine selfhood that surmounts the anxieties of secular time, since the very notion of "social" has been transformed (by association with the idea of the new continent) into the realm of rhetoric—of sacred past and sacred future unified in the self-celebrating imagination. In other words, to see Mather and Winthrop as Nehemiah is to identify with them as "the American." The two terms converge in that the regenerate American defines himself, figurally, through their mutuality. The magistrate is the Nehemiah of New England then, as Mather is the Nehemiah of New England now, as the New England Way is the Nehemiah of the Reformation, and as the Reformation is the Nehemiah of the universal church, preparing to greet the Son of Righteousness, antitype of all Nehemiahs, Who is to consecrate the apocalyptic marriage of the new heavens and new earth. Of all this both Winthrop and Mather are representative, because the substance of their heroism lies in the myth of America.

5

The Myth of America

In retrospect, it seems clear that the Puritan myth prepared for the re-vision of God's Country from the "New England of the type" into the United States of America. Founded as it was on prophecy, the colonists' view of the New World not only facilitated but dictated the emergence of different forms of expression. It depended for its verification upon more heavenly generations to follow, with ampler terms of exegesis, and a more illustrious American text to interpret. Mather's continual reference to himself as an American, like his concept of Winthrop as "Americanus," signifies not a secularization of "New Englander" but, on the contrary, an amplification of the figural import of the colony; just as the title of his New World epic, *Magnalia Christi Americana*, draws out the exegetical implications of the subtitle, *An Ecclesiastical History of New-England*. His method in this regard (as in others) is symptomatic of the movement from colonial to national identity. Early New England rhetoric provided a ready framework for inverting later secular values—human perfectibility, technological progress, democracy, Christian socialism, or simply (and comprehensively) the American Way—into the mold of sacred teleology. And the concept Mather advanced of the American who stands for the New World, in despite of, or beyond, the forces of secular time, justified the claims of a long procession of solitary keepers of the dream. The greatest of them are also the leading figures in our cultural tradition, from the Great Awakening through the American Renaissance, Edwards through Emerson. Each of them, in his own way, responded to the problems of his times by recourse to what I have described (with reference to the *Magnalia*) as the genre of auto-American-biography: the celebration of the representative self as America, and of the American self as the embodiment of a prophetic universal design.

UTOPIA/MILLENNIUM

Most dramatically, perhaps, the impact of the Puritans' rhetoric appears in the contrast between their vision of America and that of other New World colonists. All others conceived of their venture as Europeans, in the context of providential history. This is obviously true of the mercantile colonies, like New Sweden and New Amsterdam, whose "newness" meant dependency or at most imitation of the parent country.[1] It is equally true, in an even more revealing way, of the colonies to the South. Like the New Englanders, the Maryland and Virginia settlers regarded the continent with a wonder commensurate to the unique prospect before them. They personified the New World simultaneously as a nourishing mother and an undefiled virgin (a mixed metaphor that adds pungency to the later concept of the rape of the land)—providing material plenty, perennial good health, and moral purity against a backdrop of Edenic lushness. Richard Hakluyt's rhapsodies about the "sweet embracements" of "Virginia, that fairest of nymphs," echo through the travelogues of numerous lover-voyagers. "Neither higher nor lower inducement might be wanting": the fecund soil yielded harvest upon harvest; in Maryland (wrote George Alsop) the deer were tamer and more plentiful than prostitutes in London; the unexplored interior beckoned with promises of "an endless Succession of Natural Pleasures"; the territories already under cultivation spread before the "ravished" planter like so many "Beauties of naked Nature." [2]

Such phrases, all of them commonplaces of Elizabethan literature, are virtually unthinkable in colonial New England. The Puritans could be just as erotic in their imagery, but they conceived of the American paradise as the fulfillment of scripture prophecy. The Southern myth was essentially utopian. Like Bacon's *New Atlantis*—or its counterparts in the work of Burton, Andreae, Rabelais, and Campanella—it mingled the euphoria of Renaissance exploration with the secular aspirations of classical and medieval Europe. Like More's *Utopia*, it offered a probable basis for natural and rational progress, emphatically outside the realm of revelation. When, accordingly, the Southern writers invoked the image of Eden or Canaan, they used it in a way that Roger

Williams and all Protestants approved: *either* exegetically, as a figure of heaven, *or* metaphorically, to denote a haven from civilized corruption, *or* literalistically, to suggest topological (rather than typological) comparisons, as in Robert Beverley's description of Virginia:

> it is very near of the same Latitude with the Land of Promise. Besides, As *Judoea* was full of Rivers . . . So is *Virginia*. . . . Had that fertility of Soil? So has *Virginia*. . . .
>
> All the Countries in the World, seated in or near the Latitude of *Virginia*, are esteem'd [for their] . . . Clymates. As for Example, *Canaan, Syria, Persia,* great part of *Indies, China* and *Japan,* the *Morea, Spain, Portugal,* and the Coast of *Barbarry* . . . These are reckon'd the Gardens of the World.[3]

In sum, the Southern "paradise" meant a benevolent, unspoiled retreat, convenient for adventurers, entrepreneurs, farmers, and idealists in quest of the good society.

The questers varied widely, of course, in their concepts of the good society. Some hoped for an economic panacea; others planned to organize a model state (Anglican, humanist, or aristocratic). Still others chose a pastoral golden age, rooted in literary and philosophic tradition, and fringed by speculations about the Westward location of the garden in Genesis. But as utopians they all shared a single, decisive difference in outlook from the Bay millennialists. Basically, they were seeking to improve imperfect human institutions. Their social goals called "for present gains," their errand concerned the issues of providential history, and their exemplary ruler, under any circumstance, was no more than a Good Magistrate—an outstanding patriot-administrator, as Richard Lewis remembered the governor of Maryland, expert in "Social Virtues," well educated, a public benefactor, and "the best dancer in the province." Appropriately, when their expectations failed they recorded their disillusionment not in jeremiads but in dystopian satires, deriding the local Yahoos, mocking the vanity of human wishes and the pitfalls of Candide-like innocence, and in general warning prospective emigrants that America was not, after all, "such a Lubber-land as the Fiction of the Land of Ease, is reported to be, nor such a *Utopia* as *Sr. Thomas Moore* hath related to be found out."[4]

The southern dream of utopia survived these early disillusion-
ments, we know, and eventually fed into the legend of the Old
South. But it always retained its European cast. The cult of
romantic medievalism, the nostalgia for an "organic" agrarianism,
the rage for regal Old World genealogies, the model of the
gentleman planter, the reverence for Cavalier fashions—through all
its manifestations, the Southern myth stood fundamentally opposed
to the hermeneutics of Puritan American identity. Quite reasona-
bly, Southern apologists after the Civil War saw themselves as
regional Europeans without a country. Where they did not simply
recoil into fantasy or antiquarianism, they took their stand with
"cosmopolitan culture," poetry versus science (where *poetry* meant
the English literary tradition and *science* meant the American Way),
and a political conservatism that opposed the inner "timeless"
values to the futile cycles of human history. The South, said John
Crowe Ransom, is "the most substantial exhibit on this continent of
the European and historic order." Elsewhere, he amends this to the
"continent north of Mexico." His claim is far too sweeping, even as
amended, but it accurately expresses a feeling shared by many
other Southern intellectuals since 1865, of being gentiles in New
Israel, non-Americans somehow trapped by birth in what they were
told was God's Country.[5]

In this context, Ransom's allusion to Mexico is a significant clue
to his culture. Southern utopianism had a main source in the
Spanish views of the New World. Here, too, and on a far grander
scale, the Edenic motif was pervasive. Here, too, America promised
to be a Lubberland of Ease; and much more powerfully than the
Virginia and Maryland narratives, the Spanish tales of conquest,
glowing with the legends of classical antiquity and chivalric
romance, seem a concerted effort to prove that life imitates art. I am
speaking mainly of the lay orders, of course; the missionaries came
to save souls. Nonetheless, the religious venture and the secular
coincided in what was at bottom a common European enterprise.
Spain held the rights to the New World, according to official
doctrine, because the Pope had granted them to the Spanish
monarchy for the purpose of converting the heathen. But conversion meant civilization, and civilization required conquest. Thus
soldier, explorer, colonist, and missionary bound themselves jointly
in the service of the crown. Columbus felt it no contradiction to

connect his voyage to the Antilles simultaneously with prophecy, romance, and the market for slaves and spices. In the words of the conquistador-historian Bernal Díaz del Castillo, who followed Cortés through New Spain as a quizzical squire follows his wonder-working knight-errant, "We came here to serve God, and also to get rich." [6]

In this Spanish-Christian venture, the missionaries' role was a crucial one. Where they preceded the army, they pacified the population; where they followed the army, they consolidated the conquest. They were delivering the natives to Christ by delivering them to Christ's earthly viceroy, the Spanish king. The most idealistic of these clerical imperialists were the Franciscans, whose outlook resembles the Puritans' more closely than does that of any other emigrant group. Inspired by the end-time prophecies, the Franciscans came to create a "millennial kingdom," in the belief that they could redeem Europe (now declining under the influence of the Protestant Antichrist) by leading the Indians from their bondage to the Aztec pharaohs into the "blessed" service of Spain's "messiah-kings." The major expression of their view, Geronomo de Mendieta's *Historia Ecclesiastica Indiana*, bears strong formal similarities to Mather's *Magnalia Christi Americana*. Both men write as witnesses to the increasing disparity between prophecy and experience, both evoke an idealized colonial past and sustain their faith in spite of present corruptions. But the titles themselves attest to the substantive differences in approach. Mendieta locates his ideal in the reign of Charles V, who inaugurated the "Golden Age of the Indian Church"; accordingly, he begins not with a flight from Europe, but with the triumphant transplantation of European culture. Moreover, his redeeming agency is a coalition of historical forces rather than an army of Christ; unlike Mather, he never equates colonization with the progress of the saints. His very millennialism, therefore, compels him to shift his allegiance. Confronted with the consequences of colonial rule—*hispanitas* in flagrant opposition to *Christianitas*—he salvages his dream by abandoning the notion of Spain's "universal mission" and turning instead towards the desecrated Indian Church. In sum, Mendieta sees the drama of New Spain as the struggle between two peoples, neither of them "American" and both already old, a struggle motivated like any other by greed and passion and like any other without resolution short of the apocalypse.[7]

The Franciscan venture was short-lived. By far the most effective Spanish missionaries were the Dominicans, led by Bartolomé de las Casas, who protested the Europeans' barbarities from a pragmatic point of view. Historians have praised Las Casas's policies as enlightened and humane, and we cannot but agree when we consider the fate of the Massachusetts Bay Indians. But the contrast should not obscure the Dominican's purpose. The Puritans, despite their missionary pretenses, regarded the country as *theirs* and its natives as an obstacle to *their* destiny as Americans. They could remove that obstacle either by conversion (followed by "confinement"), or else by extermination; and since the former course proved insecure, they had recourse to the latter. The Spanish, for all their rhetoric of conquest, regarded the country as the Indians' and native recruitment as essential to their design of colonization. When at first their methods threatened to decimate the population, Las Casas offered a way of stabilizing the Spanish rule. Appealing to European legal codes, he argued that "from the moment of [the natives'] entering into Spanish obedience, [they deserve] all guarantees of liberty and justice." So protected, the New World inhabitants would be incorporated, the king's revenues increased, and New Spain would flourish as "the best and richest [country] in the world." [8]

By *best* Las Casas meant *most religious,* but in effect his proposals reached no further than the *parcere victis* principle of Virgil's Anchises: "spare the conquered and war down the proud." Earlier, Cortés had attempted by deceit and violence to secure the country as a feudal stronghold. After the Dominican complaints, the king ordered his soldiers to subdue the Indians without force (if possible), his administrators "to preserve and augment" their numbers, and his missionaries to instruct them, as "our vassals of the Crown of Castile," in the Spanish language and religion. These decrees were never fully implemented, of course; nonetheless, they suggest the strategy behind the success of New Spain. Whether they regarded the natives as noble or savage, as royal subjects or as a cheap labor supply, the colonists saw themselves as Spaniards in an inferior culture. By that prerogative, they converted, coerced, educated, enslaved, reorganized communities, and established an intricate caste system, bound by a distinctly Spanish mixture of feudal and Renaissance customs. The first Viceroy of New Spain, Antônio de Mendoza, set the pattern: a zealous Christian, he owed his title of *pater patriae* to his influence with the clerics at the Spanish court; an aristocrat and patriot, he considered the Church a "useful adjunct . . . in maintaining control"; an advocate for the New World, he undertook a full-scale "projection of institutions from [the] parent country" [9] by alternating threat and bribe in his subjection of the natives.

Like Winthrop, Mendoza exemplifies the values of the community he governed. The "protection" granted to the Indian "vassals" served to integrate them into a social structure so thoroughly colonialized that even after the decline of Spain it retained its viceregal character. Through the eighteenth century, its spiritual, intellectual, and artistic life remained indistinguishable from that of Spain. There are great Spanish poems about the Indians and great American-born writers of Spanish literature. Carlos de Sigüenza y Góngora and Pedro Peralta y Barnuevo equal or surpass Increase and Cotton Mather as scholar-intellectuals; Edward Taylor cannot claim the genius of Sor Juana Inés de la Cruz, nor Anne Bradstreet the skill of Antônio Vieria Juan del Valle y Caviedes and Bernardo de Valbuena. Yet unlike the Puritans, none of these creoles can be said to have begun an American literary tradition. With independence, their descendants, *Americanos* at last, faced a profound identity crisis. We were "not prepared to secede from the mother country," wrote Simón Bolívar in his famous Jamaica Letter of 1815:

> Emperor Charles V made a pact with the discoverers, conquerors, and settlers of [Latin] America, and this . . . is our social contract. . . .
>
> When the French invasion . . . routed the fragile governments of the Peninsula, we were left orphans. . . . Finally, uncertain of our destiny, and facing anarchy for want of a legitimate, just, and liberal government, we threw ourselves headlong into the chaos of revolution. . . . I look upon the present state of [Latin] America as similar to that of Rome after its fall. . . . But we scarcely retain a vestige of what once was; we are, moreover, neither Indian nor European, but an

intermediate species *[una especie media]* between the legitimate owners of this country and the Spanish usurpers.[10]

An intermediate species: by implication, Bolívar's definition points up the distinctiveness of the colonial New England legacy. The Civil War left the Southern apologist stranded in a historical no-man's-land, midway between a defeated dream and a dream he refused to accept. Independence from Spain left the Latin American similarly stranded in time, trapped between the loss of historical bearings and the need for historical renewal, at once a victim of and a rebel against the past. He had nothing because he had everything—culture from Spain, politics from France, religion from Rome, antiquities from missionary histories of the Aztecs. In this context, intermediacy involved a *historical* gesture at cultural *discontinuity:* a deliberately transitional form of nationalism, and a concept of the American as "the son of Nothingness" [11] which bespoke the still-potent image of Antônio de Mendoza, Spanish aristocratic father to a subject Indian people. In the postrevolutionary Northern United States the sense of intermediate identity was just as pervasive, but its meaning was reversed. Here it entailed a *mythical* mode of cultural *continuity:* Hawthorne's Endicott, the iron-breasted harbinger of the Revolution; the hero of Franklin's *Autobiography*, whose success story at once recapitulates the nation's past and predicates its future; Natty Bumppo on the prairie, transcending all contradictions of race and culture because, as *our* representative American, he synthesizes the values of nature and civilization.[12] These cases are very different from one another, but all three confirm American selfhood as an identity in progress, advancing from prophecies performed towards paradise to be regained. The Spanish called their transatlantic dependencies "the Indies," after the native inhabitants, and the historical consciousness this suggests tells us much about the plight of their creole heirs. Sir Walter Ralegh urged English settlement for gold, glory, and gain, and his hopes express the motives behind the Europeanization of the South. The myth of America is the creation of the New England Way.

Scholars have long debated the differences between Puritan and later forms of eschatology: Revivalist postmillennialism, Revolutionary "civil millennialism," Romantic naturalist millennialism, and so on. But the debates themselves *support* the sense of cultural continuity; in the process of making distinctions they call attention to the extraordinary facts that create the need to argue over what ought to be obvious, that Puritanism did not survive intact into the nineteenth century. No one should be startled to learn that Sylvester Judd's best seller of 1843 is anti-Calvinist. What is startling is that the Theopolis Americana he foresees looks so much like Mather's—that despite the predictable differences between them, both men employ the same mode of hermeneutics, and both affirm the same federal eschatology. "We have now seen the *Sun Rising in the West*": the phrase is Mather's, but it appears also in Judd's *Margaret*, with the same exegetical pun on the sun/Son, and the same figural inversion that raises America into sacred history. Before Judd, the phrase had appeared, *mutatis mutandis*, in Johnson's premillennial *Wonder-Working Providence*, in Edwards's postmillennial *Thoughts on the Revival*, and in Jacob Duché's civil-millennial *Observations* on the coming Revolution. It was to recur throughout the second half of the nineteenth century, in numerous paeans to "The Great Nation of Futurity" and predictions about "the American way spreading over the face of the earth." [13]

Any profitable study of cultural diversity, I would suggest, must begin in a recognition of this common pattern: not only the persistent influence of millennialism, but the overall consistency of rhetoric and approach. Samuel Sherwood was a man of his time: he believed in religious liberty, laissez faire economics, and democratic government. Yet he called his countrymen to arms in 1776 in the conviction that America's victory would initiate the chiliad. Thomas Bray differed politically, temperamentally, and theologically from Sherwood, and both of them from Timothy Dwight; their exegeses of the Revolutionary wars are virtually interchangeable:

> Let your faith be strong in the divine promises. Although the daughter of Zion may be in a wilderness state, yet the Lord himself is her *Light*. The time is coming when Jehovah will dry up the rivers of her persecuting enemies, and the *Ransomed* of the *Lord* shall *Come With Singing unto Zion, and Everlasting Joy*.

> God Almighty, with all the powers of heaven, are on our side,
> to encounter the dragon. God brought his church into this
> wilderness as an eagle's wings, and He has tenderly nourished
> and cherished her from the cruel hand of oppression, by
> executing his judgments in a most terrible manner on [her]
> enemies, and leading [her] to Canaan, for an everlasting
> inheritance.

> How shall these evils be averted? Think of the manner in
> which GOD *bare* your fathers to this land *on eagles wings*. Recal
> their numerous deliverances. A work thus begun, and thus
> carried on, is its own proof that this great continent is soon to
> be filled with the praise of the Millennium.

Through the nineteenth century the proof seemed increasingly
self-evident. The hermeneutical method that underlies Samuel
Baldwin's *Armageddon: Or, The Existence of the United States Foretold in
the Bible, Its . . . Expansion into the Millennial Republic, and Its Dominion
Over the Whole World* (1854) shapes the distinctive American
approach to virtually every major area of concern. The "self-made
man" of business, for example, was not simply a secular version of
the visible saint. He was a sort of mercantile *imitatio Americae*,
representing a union of personal and historical ideals, both of these
grounded in the belief that America "was ready for the ultimate
confrontation with God." So also Brook Farm was far more than an
experiment in Romantic socialism. In Hawthorne's words, that
"little army of saints," having taken up the Puritans' "high
enterprise," intended to carry it "onward and aloft" to its consummation. The "beacon fire" lit a century before was at last to
illuminate the entire earth.[14]

By that light, too, historians and poets recast the concept of
translatio studii, the classical theory that civilization moves in a
westward course, from Greece to Rome to Western Europe—and
thence, according to certain seventeenth- and eighteenth-century
European thinkers, to the New World. Traditionally, in both its
pagan and its Christian contexts, the *translatio studii* stems from the
cyclical-providential view of history; it offers an explanation for
mankind's "sad Vicissitude," the "fatal Circle" that circumscribes
the course of empire. Religion stands ready to pass to the American

strand, wrote George Herbert, but there, too, sin and darkness will dog her progress. From the Revolutionary period onwards, Americans responded to that threat precisely as Scottow, we have seen, did in 1694. Substituting redemptive for providential history, exegesis for analysis, they declared that America was the last act in the drama of salvation. The course of empire became for them the millennial schedule. Most of the prophecies, they pointed out, had already been "literally fulfilled": the discovery of America, the New England migration, the flowering of the desert into "IMMANUEL's *land*." Now, "THE MILLENNIUM IS AT HAND, SAY WE, TO MAKE OUR POSTERITY HAPPY, . . . [in] A GLORIOUS CONTINUANCE OF OUR OWN DISPENSATION." Elsewhere, industry had led to luxury, and luxury to decay; here "Flux and sad Decay / Can never come."

> This is a land where the more noble light
> Of holy revelation beams, the star
> Which rose from Judah lights our skies . . .
> . . . .
> They [the prophecies of Isaiah, Amos, Jeremiah, and
>   Revelation] sing the final destiny of things,
> The great result of all our labors here,
> The last day's glory, and the world renew'd.
> . . . .
> . . . A *Canaan* here,
> Another *Canann* shall excel the old,
> And from a fairer Pisgah's top be seen.[15]

These lines come from Freneau and Brackenridge's "Poem, On the Rising Glory of America" (1771), which has justly been acclaimed a representative document of the Revolutionary period. The outlook they express distinguishes the utopian literature that swept the country a century later. Although it adopts many forms of the European genre, the American version differs in three fundamental respects: the location is not anywhere (or nowhere) but *America;* the society fulfills the movement of history, rather than some philosophical scheme; and beneath the technological jargon, the rhetoric is predominantly biblical. Summarizing the scientific *miracula* he has witnessed, the American hero of Bellamy's *Looking Backward* exclaims: "this is indeed the 'new heavens and the new

earth wherein dwell righteousness,' which the prophet foretold."
The author himself tells us in his "Postscript" that he intends his
book "in all seriousness, as a forecast . . . of the next stage in the
. . . development of . . . this country; . . . the dawn of the new
era is already near at hand, and the full day will swiftly follow."
The basis for Bellamy's forecast, and for the "New Nation" fervor it
inspired, lies in the conviction that the very concept of utopia,
properly understood, expresses an unfolding redemptive design.
Cotton Mather argued this at large in the *Magnalia* and in *The
Wonders of the Invisible World*; so did Thoreau, and Emerson, and J.
Sullivan Cox, a leading advocate of manifest destiny: "the Utopian
dreams which visionaries have pursued and sages exploded, will
find their beautiful theories rivalled & outdone by the reality,
which it has pleased God to bestow upon the United America. . . .
Here glory finds his final home"; "the scriptural prophecies are
confirmations of the hopes obscurely represented by secular utopias
throughout the centuries; these latter are, as it were, intuitions of
the divine plan." [16] For Bellamy, as for his predecessors, the
proof-text of the plan was the promise of America.

Considered in its immediate context, *Looking Backward* reflects
late nineteenth-century economic theory; in the long view, it is a
variation on a pervasive cultural theme. In accordance with that
theme Bellamy's supporters and critics debated his proposals:
Roberts and Michaelis claimed that his socialist principles betrayed
the dream, Satterlee argued that they were inadequate for America,
Geissler and Schindler insisted that they flowed from the ideals of
the Puritan fathers. Other enthusiasts before and after Bellamy
make the connection between utopia and "United America" still
clearer. Moore's *Age of Progress* (1856), for example, dedicated to
"AMERICAN PATRIOTS" on behalf of "Universal HUMANITY," moves
from the discovery of the New World (following the failure of the
Old) through the final conflicts with Satan to the redemptive
triumphs of "the Great American Republic . . . as the great chosen
instrument of the Eternal." The issues that Moore covers bespeak
his time: slavery, the Mexican War, the uses of steam and
electricity. His rhetoric and historiography reveal his heritage.
They continue through a host of comparable visions of the future:
the "Grand American Commonwealth," the "Cooperative Association of America," the "Ideal American Democracy," the "Ameri-

can New Era Union," the "Ideal Nation of America." From a
hundred different perspectives—shareholding, education, agrarianism, state or corporation control, free enterprise, various brands of
religion—these writers see themselves as latter-day Nehemiahs,
summoning the nation towards its Jerusalem. For all of them, to be
utopian is to define oneself, in the words of Arthur Bird's *Looking
Forward* (1899), as an exemplar of

> the United States of America,—bounded on the north by the
> North Pole; on the South by the Antarctic Region; on the east
> by the first chapter of the Book of Genesis and on the west by
> the Day of Judgment. . . .
>
> The Supreme Ruler of the Universe . . . has marked out the
> line this nation must follow and our duty must be done.
>
> America is destined to become the Light of the world.[17]

SOLA NATURA

Most directly, the Puritan view of intermediate American
identity shapes the tradition of national biography. Daniel Boorstin (echoing the Reformation polemics) condemns American biography as a cross between medieval Saints' Lives and the Greek
legends of the gods. George Bancroft conveys its purpose more
precisely when he speaks of Washington's trials as "the dark,
solemn ground on which the beautiful work of his country's
salvation was embroidered." From the Revolutionary period onwards, the Lives of public leaders constitute a progressing spiritual
biography of America. The biographers' concern with moral
character or chronicle history is virtually subordinated to "the ideal
American," "the embodiment of the true spirit of the nation," the
"epitome of American history," the "incarnation of the People"
who "acted in the name of the People while they acted through
him." This outlook applies to all levels of biography, from the sagas
of folk heroes, like Daniel Boone, the Moses of westward migration,
to campaign biographies, which throughout the nineteenth century
set out self-consciously to create "an enduring symbol of the ideals
and aspirations of the Republic," a "cultural apotheosis in which
the nation can see an image of its best aims." The major Romantic
historians shared the same principles. As David Levin has shown,

they render the hero an "idealization of American motives," emblem of "all that is most noble in the American character." [18]

No doubt this concept of heroism draws upon various Romantic themes, including those of nineteenth-century European national-ism, just as the earlier American biographers drew upon the main currents of *their* time—or as Mather's Lives reflect the heroic models of late seventeenth-century England. But again, the concept of "Americanus" provides a distinctive pattern. Characteristically, the American hero fuses the "universal" virtues with the qualities of national leadership, and together they define him as a prophetic exemplar of the country. The English hero may (in some cases) represent both the spirit and his nation, but he does so in different ways, and in separate spheres of life. I noted earlier that this distinction between secular and sacred identity received special emphasis after the failure of the Protectorate, and all evidence suggests that the emphasis continued through the Enlightened concept of "divided mind" and the Victorian concept of the "divided self." [19] It may be illustrated by the twofold approach of Romantic biography, "essential" and "social." Essential biography sets out to show, in the words of Keats and Carlyle, that "A Man's life of any worth is a continual allegory . . . a life like the scriptures figurative," "a whole epitome of the Infinite." Social biography displays the hero as "a microcosm of the great events" in history, and studies lesser men as specimens of broad anthropological categories. In 1813 James Stanfield advocated a systematic correla-tion of such studies, in an effort to enlist biography in some comprehensive "humanistic science" of the secular self.[20]

Seven years after Stanfield's influential essay, the Reverend Thomas Robbins reissued the *Magnalia* to an audience for whom, as for Mather, the events of national history seemed indistinguishable from the spiritual patterns of scripture. In 1834, another Connecti-cut minister, Jared Sparks, a leading historian of the Revolution and New England's literary arbiter, undertook to compile a *Library of American Biography*. The Lives of our "great Americans," he announced, from Winthrop through Washington, would "embrace a perfect history of the country," embody the highest Christian virtues, and so provide a blueprint for mankind's future. Sparks's formulation may be said to represent the American version of Romantic biography. It follows directly upon the long procession of eulogies which formally endorsed George Washington as "the type of man the new nation could produce." When Horatio Nelson died a national British hero in 1805, his biographers honored him either as a model patriot *or* as a martyred servant of the Lord.[21] The biographies of Washington are portraits of the saint as the *figura* of a communal errand.

Their strategy may be illustrated by the parallel they most often employ, that between Moses and Washington. The Israelite, went the refrain, was the precursor of the *greater* "hero of AMERICA," heaven-sent to deliver his people, "the posterity of Jacob," from the "*worse* than Egyptian bondage of Great Britain." With surprising exegetical precision, most panegyrics draw out every possible aspect of the type. (The details correspond even in the number of people who crossed to freedom through a "sea of blood.") And in accordance with hermeneutical practice the *littera-historia* serve above all to illuminate the "thing signified": not only has Washington "done more" than Moses, but his achievements assure the still greater deeds of Washingtons-to-come. Given this assurance, there was no difficulty in shifting the controlling parallel to other heroes of scripture and classical antiquity—Joseph the provider, Joshua the conqueror, Plutarch's great men—since (as in Mather's Life of Winthrop) all of them could in some way add lustre to the national mission. To demonstrate "what it meant to be an American," was to announce "how America ranks among the nations of the world." By the same logic, the parallels could be shifted at will, as in a figural kaleidoscope, to bring other national representatives into focus (Adams, Jefferson, Patrick Henry, Jackson, Monroe, Fisher Ames). Not even the retrospective image of the crucifixion, especially prominent in the Lives of Brown and Lincoln, detracts from this theme. Nature threw aside her "Old-World molds" when she formed Lincoln, wrote James Russell Lowell in his popular *Ode* to "our Martyr-Chief,"

> And, choosing sweet clay from the breast
> Of the unexhausted West,
> With stuff untainted shaped a hero new,
> . . . .
> New birth of a new soil, the first American.[22]

Lowell meant by *first* American neither *earliest* nor *greatest* nor *most Christ-like*, but *most like America*. With other eulogists, he saw Lincoln as embodying "this supreme climax in the history of civilization." The newness he boasted of ("Nothing of Europe here") was figural: the martyr-chief was the New World counterpart of "the Hebrew seers, . . . heralding the close of a dispensation . . . from which is emerging the mystical dawn of a new day." Lincoln's emergent quality, that is, "new birth of a new soil," links him with a long line of representative Americans, leading back through Washington to the leaders of the Great Migration. Of course, his contemporaries did not regard Lincoln as a Puritan. Teleology demanded a lesser dispensation upon which the present could improve, as well as a seminal "ancient ground" from which the country blossomed. Cotton Mather served as a scapegoat for national evils overcome, the heroes of the *Magnalia* as harbingers of the republic. "Let us thank God," wrote Hawthorne, "for having given us such ancestors; and let each successive generation thank Him, not less fervently, for being one step further from them in the march of ages." For Parson Weems's generation, Thomas Hooker was a John the Baptist to Jefferson, while Winthrop and Washington were shadow and substance of the founding father. For Lowell's generation, Lincoln stood as antitype to all of those *patri patriae*, and therefore first of Americans to come.[23]

Above all, Lincoln's qualities as first American seemed to his contemporaries to derive from the New World that molded him. He "exerts the enormous power of this continent in . . . every act," wrote Emerson; Whitman saw "foreshadowings [in him] of the future races that shall fill these prairies." With Lowell, they believed that Lincoln represented God's people because nature had shaped him in the image of the country. "New birth of a new soil," he was regenerate *in imitatio Americae*. Nowhere is the Puritan vision more clearly in evidence than in the hermeneutics of the American landscape, and nowhere else is the Puritan concept of intermediate identity more strongly affirmed—where intermediacy, we recall, indicates not a historical limitation but a comprehensive prophetic selfhood. Europeans of Lowell's day believed that the divinity in nature was in the spiritual eye of the beholder. The American made his sainthood visible by identifying the literal-spiritual contours of the land. For the European, nature might evoke the spiritual qualities in the viewer's mind, enlarge *his* soul, fill *him* with ideas commensurate with *his* deepest feelings. But in its historical reality, as the English or German landscape, nature remained part of his specific, concrete, and therefore limiting (if cherished) personal or national past and present. The American scene by definition transcended past and present. "Marked by God" for man's "most magnificent dwelling place," the New World provided the "conclusive proof" of the "perpetuity and destiny of our sacred Union," and so enabled the viewer to "see far into futurity." Its natural wonders, truly perceived, were oracles of the "new order . . . to be." The Old World was distinguished for its hoary ruins, fittingly enough. Here, as in a new, last Book of Revelation, "the Angel of the Future spreads his white wings, whilst all things intimate that nature awaits a coming history." [24]

Perry Miller has argued that our Romantics saw nature as "the American TEMPLE." [25] It would be more accurate to say that they saw AMERICA as the temple of nature, and then, not a temple in the tropological sense, as a general moral guide, but in the exegetical "full sense," as christology and sacred history combined. All Romantics regarded nature as the temple of God. All of them, that is, were the heirs of natural theology—the traditional Christian view, shared by Catholics and Protestants alike, that creation is God's "other book," a Holy Writ of living hieroglyphs. The tradition leads forward to Romantic naturalism through a process of redefinition which, for our present purpose, may be simply stated. As the Bible gradually lost its authority after the Renaissance, *sola scriptura* became *sola natura*. The Reformers used the Bible to validate the conclusions of natural theology. The Deists claimed that Newton's universe *was* the mind of God. The Romantics confirmed (or denied) the lessons of scripture by appeal to the imagination in harmony with nature. New England has a distinguished place in this tradition. Cotton Mather's *Christian Philosopher* is something of a summa of Ptolemaic natural theology; Jonathan Edwards's *Images or Shadows of Divine Things* attempts a major synthesis of theology and the New Science; Emerson's *Nature* is an important adaptation of natural theology to post-Kantian Romantic thought.

But the line from Mather to Edwards to Emerson more largely

demonstrates the sustained influence of Puritan secular hermeneutics. Mather's naturalism expresses what he called the "true
American *Pietism*," the eschatology of the Bay planters as this
adumbrated the "Principles and Practices of the Immanuelan
People." He organized his work, accordingly, in a threefold pattern,
integrating the processes of personal salvation, scientific understanding, and sacred history; and he centered the configuration
upon the regenerate American perceiver. In other words, the
context of *The Christian Philosopher* lies in Mather's conception of
himself and of the colonial errand. In his *Diaries*, he portrays himself
as the beleaguered, Christ-like harbinger of the New World
Jerusalem; his "Biblia Americana" delineates the work of redemption through twelve exegetical discourses. The sixth and central
discourse, as Mather conceived the work, would correlate the recent
discoveries in science with scripture prophecy. It was to be preceded
by a history of Jerusalem through Nehemiah's time, and followed
by a discussion of the major end-time events, all of which, he
declared, "have had their most punctual *accomplishment*," except for
the chiliad. Between these celebrations of old and new Israel, he
placed the natural observations that have demonstrated, he declared summarily, "the blessing of CHRIST on the Labors of an
American." [26]

The relationship this implies between natural theology and
federal teleology follows logically from the Puritan concept of
errand. Right perception is a measure of personal regeneration, and
personal regeneration a measure of one's commitment to the
establishment of the New World kingdom. Edwards makes essentially the same assumption in *Images or Shadows of Divine Things*. Like
Mather, he believed that he alone, of all his contemporaries, truly
understood the course of New World history; and like Mather, he
arrogated the venture to the labors of the blessed self-reliant
American observer. Edwards's interpretation of the scriptural
phrase "new heavens and new earth" is characteristic of his
method. Exegetically, as it appears in the Book of Revelation, the
phrase applies both to conversion and to the apocalypse. Thomas
Browne and other European exponents of natural theology (from
the seventeenth through the nineteenth century) render the phrase
a touchstone to the understanding of the temple of creation, an
emblem of the process by which the religious scientist, or the

naturalist poet, comes to see the earth as an image of heaven. Edwards incorporates all these meanings in his interpretation. "This new world," he writes, "is probably now discovered that the new and most glorious state of God's church on earth might commence there," for "When God is about to turn the earth into a Paradise he does not begin his work where there is some good growth already, but in a wilderness." The image refers us, first, to Edwards's postmillennial soteriology, and then to his christology, his notion that the spirit begins its work "at the lower end" of personality, in the "utmost, meanest, youngest and weakest part." The two concepts combine in the analogy (one of his favorites) between the growth of the mind, the soul, and the church; and all three modes point towards the vision of a renovated nature.[27] And in doing so, they reinforce the primary meaning of Edwards's interpretation of the "new heavens and new earth," that the wilderness-to-become-paradise is America.

Edwards's convictions in this respect are well known. Alan Heimert has shown that Edwards differed from contemporary English revivalists by his focus on *corporate* mission, and that he turned personal experience, accordingly—in diary, autobiography, spiritual biography, case-histories of conversion—into a vehicle of prophetic fulfillment. As one common-sensical witness to the Revival remarked, with a baffled outrage reminiscent of Roger Williams, Edwards expected that "the *millennium* State . . . is NOW going to be introduced; yea, and [that] . . . AMERICA is that Part of the World which is pointed out in the *Revelation* of GOD for . . . this glorious Scene." I rehearse these facts because they bear directly upon Edwards's natural theology. He regarded his "new sense" of nature as a product of the unfolding age of the spirit. Among the chief gifts of the expanding millennial light was a keener insight into the two books of God. It was no mere tautology that the fulfillment of prophecy should bring with it a deeper understanding of the mysteries of scripture. Nor was it by accident that Newton devoted himself to the study both of gravity and of the apocalyptic timetable. Hence Mather's use of Genesis 1 as the structural model for *The Christian Philosopher*: during the Great Sabbatism, he reminds us, the climactic seventh age of redemptive history, Christ will "*feast* His *Chosen People* . . . with Exhibitions of all these *Creatures*" in the full spiritual significance of "their various

Natures." Hence, too, Edwards's emphasis on the first week as *figura:* the creation then of order out of chaos foreshadowed the emergence now, after "great confusion," of the end-time kingdom; and by its "clear and irresistible light" we have already begun to perceive nature in its *antitypal* beauty. "Things even before the fall, were types of . . . redemption. The old creation . . . was a type of the new." [28]

Now, the concept of the creation as *figura* is a Christian commonplace. What distinguishes both Mather and Edwards is that they invoke the *figura* with a specific federal eschatology in mind. The confusion Edwards speaks of is that of mid-eighteenth-century New England, languishing through a winter of acrimony and deadness of soul—"But we know the spring is coming." The evangelical "crowing of the cock to wake [us] out of sleep" betokens "the morning of the glorious times," when "God shall say, Behold, I make all things new, and there shall be a new heaven and a new earth"; when His angels shall shout for joy, more gloriously than at creation; and when His Son, "the Sun of Righteousness, the sun of the new heavens and new earth, . . . shall rise in the west, contrary to the course of . . . things in the old heavens and earth, . . . until it shines through the world," revealing "America a brighter type of heaven." [29]

Edwards, unlike Mather, was influenced by Locke; Mather, unlike (say) William Hubbard or Samuel Sewall, was influenced by the New Science. But all of them geared their natural theology to the same vision. Not Newton but America demanded their muse. In his brilliant election-day oration of 1676, *The Happiness of a People*, Hubbard declared that to be a New England Puritan was to pierce beyond nature's images or shadows to the "flourishing beauty" that would once again, with an even more "verdant lustre" than before, turn "the rough and barren wilderness . . . into a . . . fragrant Sharon." Twenty years later, Samuel Sewall, hailing the glories in store for America, remembered Plum Island, where his parents had landed in 1634, and he broke into a rhapsody that remains one of the finest tributes on record to the literal-spiritual beauties of the New England landscape. In 1721, Sewall's mentor in the interpretation of apocalyptic phenomena, Cotton Mather, wrote the first major work in the genre of the American natural theology. Jonathan Edwards, no less than his forebears convinced of New England's role in the drama of salvation, adopted and enlarged their underlying premise, that the "supernatural understanding" of nature constitutes an epistemology of Christ's *magnalia Americana*. "When God redeemed his people from their Babylonian captivity," he informed the audiences of the Great Awakening, "and they rebuilt Jerusalem, it was . . . a remarkable type of the spiritual redemption that is to . . . take its rise from this new world," and in time "wonderfully [to] alter . . . the course of nature." Therefore, whereas the Old World heaven and earth provide emblems of eternity, the New World yields "not merely emblems but prophetic tokens"—secular *images* that open into divine *shadows* of things to come.[30]

They were shadows for Americans first, but not, Edwards hastened to add, for Americans alone. Though we are to gather "the first fruits of that glorious day," he explained, "the progress and issue of it shall renew the world." Christ's weakest, utmost, youngest, and best-beloved bride will disclose to all nations "the new heaven as it makes [itself known] to those who stand upon the new earth." Echoing Sewall and Mather, Edwards contrasts Europe and America through the prophetic types of Leah and Rachel—the homely "elder sister [who] brought forth Judah," and the lovely "younger sister [who] . . . brought forth Joseph and Benjamin, the beloved children. Joseph, that had the most glorious apparel . . . and was . . . to push the peoples together, to the ends of the earth; i.e., conquer the world. . . . And Benjamin whose mess was five times as great as any of his brethren." With the authority of a spokesman for Rachel-America's beloved children, Edwards enumerates the material as well as spiritual advantages of the millennium: "inventions to facilitate . . . secular business," "more time for more noble exercise," "better contrivances" to "expedite . . . communication between distant regions." And as the representative exegete of a nature illuminated by the Sun risen in the West, he announces what may be taken as a central tenet of his personal narrative and his *Thoughts on the Revival*, as well as *Images or Shadows of Divine Things*: "The changing of the course of trade, and the supplying of the world with its treasures from America is a type and forerunner of what is approaching in spiritual things, when the world shall be supplied with spiritual treasures from America." [31]

Edwards's use of American commerce as a prophetic type is a striking instance of colonial hermeneutics. Equally striking is the implication this carries for the concept of American identity. We have been taught to contrast Edwards's Calvinist sense of depravity with Emerson's cosmic optimism. Yet this image of sacred treasures in the bosom of a beneficent nature suggests something distinctly Emersonian: a new man in a paradisaical New World. He is a fallen creature, to be sure, but comparable nonetheless, as a latter-day American saint, to (say) Emerson's Young American, aspiring in troublous times towards a lost organic wholeness which he only darkly understands and of which he remains still largely undeserving. The connection I speak of is not simply that between the Reformed and the Romantic concept of the self in process. Colonial hermeneutics bridges the considerable gap between christic auto-machia and Promethean self-creation in several important ways. It secularizes the scope and direction of the auto-machia; it recasts self-creation in terms of exegesis; and it obviates the traditional dialectic between secular and sacred selfhood by fusing both in the framework of auto-American-biography. For both Edwards and Emerson, the image of the New World invests the regenerate perceiver with an aura of ascendant millennial splendor; and for both of them, the perceiver must prove his regeneration by transforming himself in the image of the New World.

"The land," writes Emerson, "is the appointed remedy for whatever is false and fantastic in our culture. . . . The land with its . . . sanative influences is to repair the errors of a scholastic and traditional education." This might be Luther announcing the doctrine of *sola scriptura,* except that the source of divinity here is nature. Or it might be Wordsworth speaking of Grasmere, except that he would have applied the "sanative influences" to the kingdom within, as nourishment for the egotistical sublime. Emerson's land was uniquely sanative in itself, its influences counteracted (even as they completed) the traditions of the Old World, and it guaranteed regeneration for a people still to be formed. If nothing else, he declares, "One thing is plain for all men of common sense and common conscience, that here, here in America, is the home of man," here the "new love, new faith, new sight [that] shall restore [creation] to more than its first splendor." What makes this plain is not the men *in* America, but man *as* America, and America not as state of mind but, actually and unequivocally, as "the land," the Bible's *littera-historia* become American *natura-allegoria:*

> The continent we inhabit is to be physic and food for our mind as well as our body . . . ; the native but hidden graces of the landscape [are] . . . intruding a new and continental element into the national mind. Without looking then to those extraordinary social influences which are now acting in precisely this direction, but only at what is inevitably doing around us, I think we must regard the *land* as a commanding and increasing power on the citizen, the sanative influence, which promises to disclose new virtues for ages to come. . . . The Genius or Destiny of America is . . . a man incessantly advancing, as the shadow on the dial's face, or the heavenly body by whose light it is marked. . . . Let us realize that this country, the last found, is the great charity of God to the human race.[32]

This argument is "plain" in the manner of the Puritan plain style: the heavenly continental dial is itself our guide; God's altar needs not our polishings.

Bronson Alcott noted that these "first fruits of a new literature" joined nature and the soul through American images—he might better have said, through the Puritan image of America. Indeed, he may well have meant to. With other Transcendentalists, he believed that "God in his providence has given the American people . . . to prove what man may be"; they had only, for their part, to "be true to that cause which landed our fathers on Plymouth Rock." In any case, it was in the Puritan image that Emerson conceived the mission of the race. In that image, too, he cast his great essay on *Nature* (1836)—though not explicitly, of course. As with Mather's *Christian Philosopher* and Edwards's *Images or Shadows*, we must largely infer its American context; and as in the earlier works, we have ample warrant for the inference. We know that Emerson's hopes for the nation were never higher than during the 1830s and 1840s, that he rooted those hopes in the "living, prospective, titanic American nature"—the grand "feeling, which the geography of America inevitably inspires"—and that phrases and concepts from *Nature* echo through other of his writings which expressly contrast an outworn Old World with "America's ineffable power." [33] Granted these parallels, I would like to single out the central section on language, as a key to Emerson's contribution to the hermeneutics of landscape and selfhood that distinguish American natural theology.

"Words are signs of natural facts," Emerson begins; as *littera-natura* they signify higher spiritual facts, and together they comprise "the symbol of the spirit." Symbol it is, Charles Feidelson has shown, in all the formal Romantic ramifications of the term; but Emerson builds his method upon the demand for a single, certain, and comprehensive "full sense," diametrically opposed to invention. The perceiver discovers meaning by overcoming subjectivity. Nature must be the vehicle of his thought; the natural fact must verify the "issue of spirit"; and conformity to nature aligns him "with Truth and God." In short, he responds to nature insofar as he embodies its spirit in himself, and he symbolizes well insofar as he conforms to nature. Language, Emerson insists, is an exercise not in the powers of the individual imagination but in the philology of nature. To speak truly is to use nature's language in its pristine form. When we "make it plain," we convert the "outward phenomenon into a type," utter "perpetual allegories," and, since the "axioms of physics translate the law of ethics," convert ourselves into paragons of virtue. Thus the Me and the Not-Me mirror one another in the Oversoul, as the exegete and the biblical Hebrews reflect one another *in imitatio Christi.* The supreme benefit of a "life in harmony with nature," Emerson concludes, is that the spirit may "purge the eyes to understand the text"; the "fundamental law of criticism" is that "every Scripture is to be interpreted by the same spirit which gave it forth." [34]

These strictures are remarkable for the model of selfhood they imply, and for their deliberate evocation of the principles of exegesis. But their real force lies in their relation to the discourse as a whole—which is to say, in Emerson's teleology of nature. His exegetical approach is above all prophetic, his Romantic apocalypse of the mind a guide to vaster prospects ahead, because *his* scripture is the New World. Man "was prophesied in Nature," he writes elsewhere, "a thousand years before he appeared"; subsequently, humanity spiralled upwards from the worm by slow degrees: the Greeks deified nature, Christians craved a heaven out of it, and modern man would "marry mind to Nature." Yet even modern man remains incomplete, "applies to nature but half his force." Emerson assigns his countrymen the task of completing the journey—or as he might put it, American nature assigns the task through the vehicle of Emerson's thought. Like some election-day orator of early Massachusetts, he reminds Americans that they still have "a moral wilderness" to traverse "in preparation for . . . building a New Jerusalem." Then, combining the terms of Puritan and Romantic salvation, he rejects the disparity between fact and vision—dismisses all anxiety about process or incompletion—by announcing that the thousand year reign of "the truly Human hovers, now seen, now unseen, before us." The millennium, he would have us believe, *now* "exists for us, shines in on us at unawares." It requires no more than the American's

> obedience . . . to the guiding of . . . [his] great rivers and prairies. . . . Never country had such a fortune, as men call fortune, as this, in its geography. . . . Resources of America! why, . . . "The Golden Age is not behind, but before you." Here is . . . the Genesis and the Exodus. . . . America should speak for the human race. It is the country of the Future. . . . [The] sublime and friendly Destiny by which the human race is guided . . . has infused itself into [our] nature. . . . Remark the unceasing effort throughout nature at somewhat better than the actual. . . . Nature works in immense time . . . to prepare new individuals and new races. . . . The population of the world is a conditional population; . . . there shall yet be a better, please God. . . . Which [state] should lead that movement, if not New England? Who should lead the leaders but the Young American? [35]

Emerson's equation of landscape and redemptive history recalls the opening of the *Magnalia*, where Mather, we have seen, pictures the Ark of Christ en route to New England, changing geography into christianography. More directly, perhaps, it recalls Edwards's image of the redemptive natural-spiritual resources of the New World. In either case, Emerson's vision serves to reaffirm that of the Puritans. He tells us in *Nature* that the principles by which man fulfills himself "have always been in the world"; they "reappear to every bard" but to *him* as "gleams of a better light," as a mighty "influx of the spirit" that heralds a "Revolution in all things." If this seems a Romantic truism, we must remember that Emerson invokes it to support a federal eschatology. It is crucial to his message that "Prospects," the final section of *Nature,* speaks directly to "the American, . . . in his own country," and that it presents its Orphic "prophecy" through the voice of a New England bard. The European symbolist interpreted nature through the medium of the self; he understood creation as part of his own *Bildungsbiographie,* since he himself was the "Messias of Nature." [36] Emerson interpreted the self through the medium of American nature; his model of spiritual growth reflected a teleology that eliminated the tension between process and fulfillment. It gathered meaning by its proleptic identification with the destiny of the New World, of which American nature was the symbol.

By extension, this outlook also became the basis for a distinctive symbolic mode. What makes the type "completely different" from the symbol, Erich Auerbach has observed, "is that figural prophecy relates to an interpretation of history . . . while the symbol is a direct interpretation of life." The symbolist, that is, finds significance through the interaction of experience and imagination, the figuralist through a sacred design that is prior to, and independent of, the self. The American *resistance* to that dichotomy explains the persistent tendency toward what Ursula Brumm has termed typological symbolism, as well as toward that "peculiar self-consciousness," as John Lynen describes it, "which makes the symbolic process itself the center of attention." [37] In both cases, the tendency reflects Emerson's method of American nature, where the fact mediates prophetically between redemptive history and the self, and so requires the perceiver to create himself in the spirit of the New World scripture, even as he interprets the American experience as a metaphor for the journey of the soul. "The roots of letters are things," puns Thoreau. "Natural objects . . . are the original symbols or types which express our thoughts." By this standard he condemns as heretics the "American scholars [who] . . . confine themselves to the imported symbols"; they neglect a situation more favorable "on the whole" than that of paradise, a landscape "grander" and "more spiritual" than the European, a new earth whose creative "possibility far exceeds the accomplishments of the past," because it alone offers that "prospect of the future" which can fully awaken the "transcendental senses." Thoreau himself, of course, bypassed the natural supernaturalism of his European contemporaries for that of his Puritan New England predecessors (including Cotton Mather). His most comprehensive "symbol or type," Walden Pond, serves both as a shadow of the baptismal fount and as an image of the "Lethean" Atlantic, "over which we have had an opportunity to forget the Old World." [38]

I need scarcely argue Whitman's adherence to this outlook; he does so himself with unmatched eloquence in his prefaces. He considered *Leaves of Grass* a "language experiment" in the sense that it offered the "new words, new potentialities of speech," that would provide "an *American* . . . range of expression." He felt certain that the New World sublime, where he discovered "the law of [his] own poems," would make "Americans . . . the most perfect users of words." Upon this premise he vaunted his self-conscious symbolizing as a model of national self-fulfillment. The poetic results of his effort, together with *Walden* and *Moby-Dick*, constitute the major examples of American symbolism in the mid-nineteenth century. But I might note also that the critique par excellence of self-conscious symbolizing is Melville's *Pierre*, which leads through a maze of stone images or shadows to an epiphany of the New World landscape as the apocalypse. And perhaps the single most striking typological symbol in the literature is the "A" that illuminates the midnight landscape in the central scene of Hawthorne's *Scarlet Letter*. However tentatively or ironically, it prefigures both personal and historical redemption, lending "another moral interpretation to the things of this world than they had ever borne before, . . . as if it were the light that is to reveal all secrets, and the daybreak that shall unite all who belong to one another." [39]

Critics have always noted, rightly, that Hawthorne, Melville, and Thoreau differed widely from one another, and each of them, in his distinctive way, from Emerson. To posit a common design is not to simplify the differences—nor to imply that they are less important than the similarities—but, on the contrary, to provide a context for meaningful discrimination. What is remarkable, from this perspective, is that all of these very different writers learned from Emerson to make Romantic natural theology an expression of the national dream. The Europeans humanized the work of redemption, rendering unto nature what once had belonged to the church. Emerson expanded the principles of colonial hermeneutics by recasting them as the principles of modern symbolism. When his Puritan forebears gave the kingdom a local habitation and a name, they upturned traditional exegesis. Yet as C. S. Lewis has observed, new literary forms often burgeon out of cultures which seem most strictly aligned to the past, and in the Puritans' case the allegiance was not pretense but the foundation upon which the new forms developed. Their legacy was secularism and orthodoxy entwined. Edwards reinforced the secular aspect of their rhetoric by defining colonial progress in the framework of postmillennialism. Emerson sustained their hermeneutics through the quintessential Romantic doctrine of *sola natura*. With the full power of a tradition vindicated, *Nature*'s concluding Nehemiah-like summons, "Build therefore your own world," returns us to the christianographical opening of the discourse—"new lands, new men, new thoughts," [40] a naturalist teleology of the New World, by the exemplary American exegete, for New England and Young America first, and then the world.

FIGURA MEDIETATIS

Emerson's fusion of Romantic naturalism and Puritan hermeneutics is significant in the broadest terms. He is the most influential thinker of the period and the crucial figure in the continuity of the culture. Through him the distinctively American modes of expression matured; his achievement lay in his compelling synthesis of abiding national themes. The most important aspect of his synthesis, I have said, pertains to the idea of the American self. Let me illustrate this through a provocative contrast in Harold Bloom's *Anxiety of Influence*. Bloom describes Romantic British and American poets as the common heirs to "a severely displaced Protestantism"; but "British poets swerve from their precursors," he observes, "while American poets labor to 'complete' their fathers." Emerson is the direct inspiration here—and the long foreground to Emerson is the Puritan concept of intermediate identity. Theological displacement is defined by Augustine, in a famous passage, as the *"experimentum medietatis,"* a "trial of the center" in which the ego overcomes the soul. The Puritans applied this concept to the unsuccessful auto-machia, the false pilgrim's regress from Christ to the self; following Augustine, they found their main examples in Lucifer and Prometheus. The Romantics, we might say, redefined the *experimentum medietatis* as a victory of the soul. Having claimed the self as its own absolute—in Coleridge's words, a "manifestation of the Eternal and Universal One" [41]—they outlined a Promethean auto-machia which ascended *through* the Center of Indifference to an affirmation of the self as divinity incarnate.

As Professor Bloom indicates, the Romantic view has its roots in the Reformation. The displacement begins in England as early as the seventeenth century, with the Puritan "vulgar prophets" who claimed the prerogatives of Christ, with the Quaker doctrine of the inner light, with the Diggers who used (or discarded) scripture insofar as it provided a viable metaphor for the soul, with John Milton's *De Doctrina Christiana* which announced that all believers are no less than Jesus sons of God. We can trace the line forward to the Romantics of our own time—to Carl Jung, for example, who warns us not to imitate Christ since, properly seen, the self is God; or earlier, to Nietzsche, who advised man simply to forget God, love himself through self-generated grace, and thereby enact in himself the entire work of redemption. So considered, the link between Puritan and Romantic is obvious enough. We have seen that the Reformers, having unleashed the individual, doctrinally, through the principle of *sola fides*, found their defense against subjectivism in the concept of *exemplum fidei*. They restricted the spiritual meaning of all facts, especially the fact of the self, to the external model of Christ's life and the figural patterns of scripture. Fundamentally, Romantic symbolism differs from Puritan exegesis not because it substitutes nature for the Bible, and not because it treats of secular events. For the Reformer, too, after all, nature was the book of God, and figuralism extended to the full range of human experience. The basic difference in the Romantic outlook is that it reverses the Reformed equation for personal identity. The Romantics subsumed the concept of *exemplum fidei* in the doctrine of *sola fides*. Their model of selfhood was the inspired perceiver. In effect, they freed the individual to choose (or invent) his identity, and then to impose his own patterns upon experience, including his experience of history, nature, the Bible, Christ Himself.

In this context, it seems all but inevitable that the Romantic poet should be overwhelmed by the anxiety of influence. The imitation of Christ became for him the process of duplicating himself, fashioning examples of faith in his own image—a deific creation *ex imaginatione* in which *caritas* depended upon autonomy, and plenitude was narcissism extended to infinity. Accordingly, the precursor poet assumed the role of the tenacious Puritan self, replete with "the appalling energy of . . . the Wholly Other [that was] yet also a possessing force." [42] The Puritan's dilemma was that the way from the self necessarily led through the self; occasionally, the struggle became so severe that he could resolve it only by abandoning all hope, or else (like the proto-Romantics just mentioned) by leaping, self and all, directly to Christ. For the Romantic, the way to the self led through the precursor poet. Only the strongest did not abandon either poetry or the self. No Romantic voiced the need to persist more eloquently than Emerson did; and yet in public at least he subsumed anxiety in prophecy. The influence he felt came, buoyantly, from national prospects. Intermediary between the Puritan and God was the created Word of scripture. Intermediary between the Romantic and God was the creating imagination. Intermediary between the Transcendentalist and the Oversoul was the text of America, simultaneously an external model of perfection and a product of the symbolic imagination, and in either aspect a guarantee that intermediary *American* identity bypassed the contradictions inherent in the effort at self-completion.

All this does not deny the Romantic tenets of Emerson's thought. What I would suggest is that he adjusts these to the tenets of early New England rhetoric. Characteristically, the self he sought was not only his but America's, or rather his *as* America's, and therefore America's as his. He undertook a figural trial of the center that led ineluctably toward a social *telos*, since what he meant by "social" (as America) was defined by the *figura*, in contradistinction to historical fact, and the nature of figural completion was for Emerson a matter of prophetic self-expression. "I must Create a System," cries Blake's archetypal artist, Los, "or be enslav'd by another Man's"; Schelling claimed that "each truly creative individual must create his mythology for himself." Emerson expressed himself by expressing the myth of America. Insofar as he echoed the European Romantics, he may be said to have posited a double standard of personal identity, American and un-American. The latter he analyzed in static terms, either as indices to the "genius of humanity"—pure intellects like Plato, who transcended time and place—or else as the agents of human history, public leaders like Napoleon, who embodied middle class greed. From this perspective, Emerson had no use for temporal distinctions. "History is a vanishing allegory, and repeats itself to tediousness, a thousand and a million times." With Thomas Fuller, he felt that "to look long on these turning wheels" was to "grow giddy," "lost in the hopeless confusion . . . of War, Faction, Misery." Only when he turned to America did history become meaningful, as an ascending spiral within which even the universal minds assumed a temporal, relativistic significance. Emerson's historical correlative for the soteriology of nature—man's progress from the worm to the "truly Human"—is the evolution of New England into the United States. Those who "complain of the flatness of American life," he wrote, "have no perception of its destiny. They are not Americans." As a true American, he never wearied of repeating the familiar story—how the continent was "kept in reserve from the intellectual races until they should grow to it," how Boston in particular, Winthrop's city on a hill, was "appointed in the destiny of nations to lead . . . civilization," and how the present generation was "continuing [the] holy errand into the wilderness." [43]

Emerson's sources for this *emergent* allegory of history were the writings of his colonial forebears. He acknowledged them proudly, as a spiritual tribute. Constituting as they did "a bridge to us between the . . . Hebrew epoch, & our own," the Puritans assured him of "the greatness of the New World." Their enterprise, "as great a gain to mankind as the opening of this continent," proved that "the Supreme Being exalts the history of this people." His son tells us that he "often spoke of a wish to write the story of Calvinism in New England," in order to commemorate the climactic "triumphs of humanity." Emerson's project is outlined in his essays and journals from the 1830s through the Civil War. The "two great epochs of public principle" were for him "the Planting, and the Revolution of the colony." "The new is only the seed of the old," he wrote in 1841. "What is this abolition and non-resistance . . . but a continuation of Puritanism . . . ?" In 1863, after non-resistance had given way to armed conflict, he declared the country to be "in the midst of a great Revolution, still enacting the sentiment of the Puritans, and the dreams of young people thirty years ago." The sacred light that "brought our fathers hither" was guiding "the visible church of the existing generation" towards an unprecedented harvest of the spirit. It would be irrelevant, in this context, to point out that the visible American church of 1863 was *not* a fulfillment of the New England Way. Emerson was obviously speaking of fathers and Puritans not in any historical sense, but as aspects of the American idea as this made itself manifest in his thought. Like Mather's, his filiopietism is a self-celebratory summons to the future. "GOD WITH THE FATHERS, SO WITH US," he writes in his eulogy to Boston, and then adds: "Let us shame the fathers by superior virtue in the sons."[44] As *figurae medietatis*, the sons labor to complete the fathers in a process of exodus, an organic unfolding of personal and national divinity, whose substance *is* the Emersonian-American self.

Emerson found the model of exodus in the Great Migration. His teleology requires, first, a clear sense of the past *as* the Old World. "Let the passion for America cast out the passion for Europe"— "extract this tape-worm of Europe from the brain of our countrymen"—and with it the stifling veneration of Europe's great men. Universal though they are in one sense, finally they must be understood in their prophetic sense, as *our* precursors. "To us has been committed by Providence the higher and holier work of forming *men*, true and entire men." All others, however high and holy, are adumbrations of the representative American who is "to prove what the human race can be"—the "exalted manhood" that has been decreed "The Fortune of the Republic." In 1833, after visiting Coleridge, Carlyle, and Wordsworth, Emerson recorded his sense of superiority to all of them and thanked God for bringing him to "the ship that steers westward." Milton may have been an obstacle to Coleridge's self-realization. Emerson considered Milton —along with Homer, Luther, Bacon, Swedenborg, Goethe—as part of an outmoded "feudal school." "Not Shakespeare, not Plato . . . would do." They "call to us affectionately"—"But now all these, and all things else hear the trumpet, and must rush to judgement"; now, "America is a poem in our eyes."[45]

The trumpet that Emerson heard required him—as the second major step in his teleology—to don the robes of a latter-day John the Baptist. Over and again in his essays, letters, and notebooks, he heralds the New World messiah who will adequately mirror "our

incomparable materials." America's "urgent claims on her children
. . . yet are all unanswered." "Where are the American writers"
who are to solve "the great questions affecting our spiritual
nature"? When would the country's divines "realize the spiritual
religion of the future"? When would its poets find a meter-making
argument adequate to its "ample geography"? When would its
philosophers and politicians reflect this "country of beginnings, of
projects, of vast designs and expectations"? Emerson posed these
challenges in his early and middle career. In 1868, at the age of
sixty-five, after Whitman and Thoreau had in some measure at
least answered his call—after Lincoln had shown himself "the true
representative of this continent," and Daniel Webster a "fit figure
in the landscape" (radiating, until 1850, "the American . . .
Adamitic capacity"), and John Brown a fusion of Revolutionary
ardor with the "perfect Puritan faith" (and so a "true history of the
American people")—even at sixty-five, Emerson was still seeking a
spokesman for the "new era," and still assuring his audiences that
"he shall be found." Since "America is essentially great and *must*
produce great men," he explained, "we shall yet have an American
genius." [46]

He expressed his faith most fully in "The American Scholar." In
Nature, he described the process by which the natural philosopher
"postpones the apparent order and relation of things to the empire
of thought." Here, in what he calls "one more chapter" in a
continuing "biography"—in effect, a prophetic biography of the
American self as scholar—Emerson envisions the advent of the
thinker through whom "this continent will . . . fill the postponed
expectation of the world." Accordingly, he begins the essay, as
Mather did the Life of Winthrop, with a sweeping review of the
past, from the ancient Greeks to the medieval troubadours to "our
contemporaries in the British and European capitals." Then,
following the westward course of history—and transmuting as he
does so the concept of the *translatio studii* into that of redemptive
history—he sets out what Oliver Wendell Holmes called "Our
intellectual Declaration of Independence":

> [America's] long apprenticeship . . . draws to a close. The
> millions that around us are rushing into life, cannot always be
> fed on the sere remains of foreign harvests. Events, actions,

arise, that must be sung, that will sing themselves. Who can doubt that poetry will revive and lead in a new age, as the star in the constellation Harp, which now flames in our zenith . . . shall one day be the pole-star for a thousand years?

In this hope I accept the topic . . . [of] the AMERICAN SCHOLAR.[47]

The distance between Emerson and Mather shows itself in certain revolutionary and Romantic phrases: "apprenticeship" as preparation for salvation, poetry in place of theology, "rushing into life" as a quasi-naturalistic conversion experience, the star in Harp rather than the millennial Sun of Righteousness. But these are new terms in an old context. The rhetorical strategy is the same, as is the underlying assumption, that the American enterprise, unlike all others, interweaves personal and corporate self-fulfillment. As the scholar's goal comprehends the particular natures of all men, so the delegated national function transcends secular nationhood by realizing the world's postponed expectation.

Those who heard the "grand Oration" testified to its overwhelming effect. "The Puritan revolt had made us ecclesiastically, and the Revolution politically independent," wrote Lowell, "but we were still socially and intellectually moored to English thought, till Emerson cut the cable." According to Dr. Holmes, "the young men went out from [the oration] as if a prophet had been proclaiming to them 'Thus saith the Lord.'" *Prophet* was the right term, if we construe it in Mather's special ahistorical sense. Emerson's essay is above all a testament to his overriding identification with the *idea* of America. His every appeal to self-perfection stems from and leads into his vision of the New World future. He equates the present time with all times in order to stress "the auspicious signs of the coming days" which "glimmer already through poetry and art, . . . through church and state." So, too, he calls the roll of genius, from Thomas à Kempis to Wordsworth, as preface to his plea for a greater New World literature: "We have listened too long to the courtly muses of Europe." If he castigates his countrymen for their base "materialities," he does so in order to sever the apparent from the ideal, to eulogize the country's natural treasures as images of a renovated earth. And when he declares that "the world is nothing, the man is all," it is only to reaffirm that "the unsearched might of man belongs, by all motives, by all prophecy, by all preparation, to the American Scholar." Rising from "hope" to "confidence," he declares, summarily, that a "nation of men will for the first time exist," in America.[48]

I need hardly say that Emerson's confidence is finally an act of faith in himself. Various critics have noted how closely he identified with the ideal he sets forth, how much he infused into it his own hopes and sense of vocation. Indeed, it has been argued that his Scholar is the protagonist of an unwritten *Prelude*, Emerson's version of the European Romantic autobiographical hero—"the Werthers and the Childe Harolds and the Teufelsdröckhs of the period." If so, the essay provides a sweeping contrast between American and European Romanticism. Wordsworth tells us that "The mind is to herself / Witness and judge"; but since the mind he speaks of is his own, he must come to terms with the specifics of his private and historical condition. Emerson can omit such considerations because he bears witness to the rising glory of America. By projecting himself in his hero, he recasts Romantic autobiography into auto-American-biography, creates himself as symbol of a corporate teleology. The myth of the primal One Man with which he begins is a Romantic commonplace. Emerson absorbs the One Man, as the "exponent of a vaster mind and will," into the Sun of Righteousness advancing towards the *nation* that *will* exist. Like Whitman, he vindicates himself by expecting "the main things" from future Americans; like Thoreau, he confirms his rebirth by considering it to be only a morning-star, herald of the ascendant western sun that "all the nations follow." For the European Romantic, the Sun of Righteousness is his own conquering imagination; *Urzeit* and *Endzeit* embrace in self-discovery. The cyclical form of Wordsworth's *Prelude* suggests how the poet in himself reconstitutes all that had been divided. The apocalypse that concludes Blake's *Jerusalem* equates the fourfold unity of the One Man with each man's recovery of creative vision:

> . . . we behold as one,
> As One Man all the Universal Family; and that One Man
> We call Jesus the Christ.[49]

Blake's concept of Jesus is an important clue to the distinction I would make. It goes without saying that not all European Romantics asserted a comprehensive selfhood. Many believed that they could achieve that "only in infinite approximation"; others were content to await some poet-messiah, a "liberated, reintegrated, and perfected man" who would express "in spirit what was, what is, what will be." But in virtually every instance, their ideal centered upon the self-determining, all-embracing *individual*. In these terms also, as Meyer Abrams has shown, the Romantics conceived of historical progression. Humanity was advancing in "a great circle from the One back to the One"; it developed in a process of "self-education" that applied equally to mankind and to each "reflective" person. In either case, the goal was autonomous self-realization, an internal-universal "Resurrection to Unity." And from either perspective, the goal reflected the design of Reformed spiritual biography, with its pervasive correlation, through Christ, between the journey of the believer and of the church, and, again through Christ, its constant interweaving of the imagery of personal salvation and the thousand year reign of the saints:

> All that which you call history . . . is all to be seen and felt within you. . . . Jesus Christ at a distance from thee, will never save thee; but a Christ within is thy Saviour. . . . Now the second *Adam* Christ, hath taken the Kingdom my body, and rules in it: *He makes it a new heaven, and a new earth, wherein dwells Righteousness.*[50]

These lines come from Gerrard Winstanley's *New Law* (1648); Professor Abrams traces them forward to the English and German Romantics, for all of whom, from Wordsworth through Carlyle, the new heaven and new earth signify, *as the millennium*, the regenerate state of soul. The comparable seventeenth-century source for Emerson is (say) Sewall's *Description of the New Heaven as It Makes to Those Who Stand upon the New Earth*, where history is prophecy in process, where the Redeemer is the antitype of Jesus, and where the New World is an actual locale awaiting its glorification. The European Romantic, despite his abiding faith in the future of mankind, was compelled by his commitment to the organic self to identify with the resurrected Jesus of the gospels, the model of the completed life. In spite of his commitment to the God within, Emerson's faith in American destiny compelled him to find his model of organic selfhood in the coming Son of Man. The Unitarians, he charges in his "Divinity School Address," would have us "subordinate [our] nature to Christ's nature." His "remedy" is to reverse the equation. He seeks not to become Jesus the Christ but to fulfill Him. The Nazarene is one among a host of precursors who have prepared the way for the "newborn bard of the Holy Ghost." Thus, as "noble provocations," He "serves us, and thus only." For the rest, we must call on "resources in *us*": first, the "certain truths" of the Puritan fathers; then, the historical dynamic whereby "Calvinism rushes to be Unitarianism, as Unitarianism rushes to be pure Theism," in a redemptive spiral which confirms that "America shall introduce a pure religion." Most amply, of course, our resources lie in the spirit which the New World itself "inevitably inspires." "What hinders that now," Emerson demands, addressing himself to the Young Americans in his audience, "now, everywhere, . . . you speak . . . with new hope and new revelation? . . . The Hebrew and Greek Scriptures, contain immortal sentences. . . . But they have no epical integrity; are fragmentary; are not shown in their order to the intellect. I look for the new Teacher." [51]

The patriotic European Romantic looked in a different direction. The Germans based their mystique of the *Volksgeist* on popular epic and legend; their sense of destiny led them back to the origins of the race, to cultural antiquities. Emerson, like Mather, interpreted the national past through the double focus of prophecies accomplished and prophecies unfolding. In this respect he was perhaps closer to the English Romantics, who resurrected the dream of national election (though they were far enough removed from its source to center their hopes on the French Revolution). But like Milton they distinguished, ultimately, between personal and federal identity, and accordingly they reenacted the drama of political commitment, disillusionment, and retreat to the kingdom within. By 1837, when Emerson wrote "The American Scholar," their high argument was a revolution of consciousness that eventuated "within the self and beyond nature." Blake's reintegrated Albion symbolizes spiritual wholeness. The "Characters of the great Apocalypse," writes Wordsworth, are "types and symbols of Eternity." When Shelley has Young Atlantis speak the final chorus of *Hellas*—"The world's great age begins anew"—he is saying not that the United States will fulfill history, but that "Freedom belongs to Thought." [52] As a visionary company, these poets had no country. As English nature poets, their allegiance was to the countryside, the details of rural life and landscape. As citizens, their country, as Milton said after the Restoration, was wherever it is well with one.

Emerson sustained his faith not because the American Revolution was more successful than the French, but because his vision annihilated division. The rhetoric he inherited enabled him to dissolve all differences between history and the self—as well as all differences within the self (civic, natural, prophetic)—and so to overcome political disenchantment by revealing himself as the representative American. Significantly, he conceived his essays on nature, the scholar, and the new religious teacher at the height of what he considered the barbaric corruption of the Jacksonian era. The 1828 election of Andrew Jackson was hailed as a spectacular triumph of the new democracy. His re-election in 1832 seemed to Emerson to undermine the very purpose of the Revolution; and the crash of 1837 convinced him that society had "played out its last stake." But with the latter-day theocrats he found that his rhetoric blossomed in adversity. In the face of "emphatic and universal calamity" he reread the "whole past . . . in its infinite scope," and declared: "Let me begin anew"! His method of self-renewal, like Mather's, consisted in arrogating the meaning of America to himself. God's angel is named freedom, he tells us in a review of the national history. He proclaims his discoveries in thought in the same prophetic tone with which he has God say: "Lo! I uncover the land / Which I hid of old time in the West." To the Romantic notion that "there is no history, only biography," Emerson added two crucial, and crucially related, stipulations: first, that "all biography is autobiography," and second, that "the American idea" concerns neither "caucuses nor congress, neither . . . presidents nor cabinet-ministers, nor . . . such as would make of America another Europe"; it belongs to "the purest minds" only, "and yet it is the only true" idea.[53]

Emerson's conflation of the private with the national dream characterizes the writing of most of the American Romantics, including the most belligerently antinationalistic among them. It is clear, for example, that Thoreau regarded America as the golden West of the imagination. It is no less clear that, even at times of active disobedience, he identified "the prevailing tendency of [his] countrymen" with the redemptive story of mankind, the ordained "journey" from the Fall to "Christ to—America." And it is central to his message that we *not* choose between these disparate personal and historical paths to salvation. Dante's *vita nuova* leads him out of the world's dark forest; Teufelsdröckh's leads him back to the City of Man, but as an alien and a wanderer, circumambulating "the terraqueous Globe," indifferent to time and place. *Sartor Resartus* insists that we distinguish the clothes from the soul, history from the kingdom, modern life from the Everlasting Yea. Thoreau insists upon the spiritual significance of his clothes, his locale, his way of life. They stand for the wilderness-condition that prepares for the American paradise. He does not walk anywhere, but *westward*, for "Westward is heaven, or rather heavenward is the west." His "new country" mode is distinctly national: migrant, free-enterprising, evoking the frontier dream even as it mocks Franklin's Way to Wealth. Mather's Winthrop is an American who has made himself a cornerstone of the New World Jerusalem, and therefore part of the author's exemplary autobiography. *Walden* is the archetypal Romantic autobiography of the self as "the only true America." [54] The bridge between these works is Emerson's Scholar-Teacher-Natural Philosopher, who compensates for political failure by collapsing nature and society, history, biography, and autobiography, into the eschatological Now which is Emerson as the representative American.

AMERICA NEHEMIANA

One major result of this mode of compensation appears in the contrast between the European and the American cult of genius. Perhaps the most misleading commonplace of recent criticism is that our major literature through Emerson is Antinomian. The Puritans banished Anne Hutchinson, we recall, because she set her private revelation above the public errand. The controversy foreshadows the fundamentally opposed concepts of greatness in Emerson and Carlyle. Emerson's hero, like Mather's Winthrop, derives his greatness from the enterprise he represents. Despite his distaste for, and fear of, the mass of actual Americans, he did not need to dissociate himself from America because he had already dissociated the mass from the American idea. Carlyle's hero gathers strength precisely in proportion to his alienation. He stands sufficient in himself, a titan born to master the multitude. As the Frankenstein's monster of left-wing Protestantism, he finds his place in a latter-day Antinomian brotherhood that includes Shaw's Superman and Ibsen's Master Builder; Nietzsche's Zarathustra, that "terrible teacher of the great contempt"; Byron's banished saint, whose immortal mind "makes itself / Requital for its good or evil thoughts." [55]

In contrast to all of these, Emerson posed the severely ethical code of the true American. European geniuses like Goethe and Carlyle, he complained, "have an undisguised dislike or contempt for common virtue standing on common principles." Accordingly, he reminded himself in his journals to "beware of Antinomianism," and declared in public that his rejection of popular standards was a battle *against* "mere antinomianism," in the interests of turning society towards the higher laws of chastity, simplicity, spiritual and intellectual awareness. "There was never a country in the world which could so easily exhibit this heroism as ours." Of course, Emerson never denounced Antinomianism with the vehemence of Winthrop, Mather, and Edwards. Once or twice he spoke of it with a condescending admiration, as a "vein of folly" that helps the enthusiast reach "the people," and often enough we feel a powerful Antinomian impulse in the absolutism of his claims. Nonetheless, his concept of representative heroism denies the tenets of Antinomianism, in any meaningful sense of the term. More accurately, his teleology redefines his Antinomian impulse, somewhat in the manner of Edwards (who was similarly accused of Antinomianism), as the revelation of the New World spirit. If Emerson differs from the chauvinist by his Romantic self-reliance, he differs equally from the Romantic Antinomian by his reliance on a national mission. The natural habitat of the *Übermensch* is the sublime, anywhere; Emerson's is America. "Greatness appeals to future," he explains in "Self-Reliance" (1839), and other essays.

> It is [therefore] for want of self-culture that the superstition of Travelling, whose idols are Italy, England, Egypt, retains its

fascination for all educated Americans. . . . The force of character is cumulative. All the foregone days of virtue work their health into this. What makes the majesty of the heroes of the senate and the field, which so fills the imagination? The consciousness of a train of great days and victories behind. They shed a united light on the advancing actor. . . . That is it which throws thunder into Chatham's voice, and dignity into Washington's port, and America into Adam's eye. . . . Accept the place the divine providence has found for you, the society of your contemporaries, the connection of events, . . . transcendent destiny; and . . . [become] guides, redeemers, and benefactors, obeying the Almighty effort.[56]

Emerson's exhortation to greatness speaks directly to the paradox of a literature devoted at once to the exaltation of the individual and the search for a perfect community. Self-reliance builds upon both these extremes. It is the consummate expression of a culture which places an immense premium on independence while denouncing all forms of eccentricity and elitism. The denunciation, as Emerson indicates, is less a demand for conformity than a gesture against Antinomianism. Anne Hutchinson's self-reliance, like Wordsworth's, Byron's, Carlyle's, and Nietzsche's, may hold out grand prospects for mankind, but it locates the divine center in the individual. The self-reliant American may declare his whim superior to the entire legal code, but he remains by definition the hero as guide and national benefactor.

Or heroine: as Michael Bell has shown, a commonplace of the American historical romance is the representative American woman—Judd's Margaret, for example, and Hope Leslie, the spirit incarnate of democracy, liberty, progress, and the divine " 'principle' behind the events of seventeenth-century New England." The supreme instance, of course, is Hester Prynne, Hawthorne's "living sermon" against the "haughty" and "carnal" Mrs. Hutchinson, who "could find no peace in this chosen land." To some extent, his argument builds upon the tradition of the biblical Esther—homiletic *exemplum* of sorrow, duty, and love, and *figura* of the Virgin Mary: "Hester meke / Who did the serpents hede of[f] streke"; "Hester la tres amé / Ke sauve la genz jugé." [57] But primarily Hawthorne's "sermon" traces the education of an *American* Esther.

As her name implies, she is "the hidden one" who emerges as the "star" of the new age. Christologically, the "A" she wears expands from "Adulteress" to "Angelic." Historically, as "the 'A' for America," it leads forward from the Puritan "Utopia" to that "brighter period" when the country will fulfill its "high and glorious destiny." More than any other aspect of the novel, this fusion of personal and federal eschatology makes *The Scarlet Letter* an American romance. Like Hester, Anna Karenina is a moral *exemplum* ("Vengeance is mine; I will repay, saith the Lord") as well as the victim of particular social and psychological forces. But for all of Tolstoy's didacticism the two levels of meaning conflict, and for all his nationalism he never asks us to think of Anna, or even Levin, as an emblem of Russia. Despite Hawthorne's celebrated irony, and despite his unresolved ambivalence toward the Puritan past and the democratic present, his novel yields an emphatically national design. His heroine is an intermediary prophetess, neither merely a doomed Romantic Dark Lady at her worst nor wholly a world-redeeming Romantic savior at her best, but a *figura mediatatis*, like the Grey Champion "the pledge that New England's sons [and daughters] will vindicate their ancestry." [58]

The representative quality of American Romantic heroism expresses the furthest reach of Mather's daring auto-American-biographical strategy in the *Magnalia*. By comparison, the European great man, for all his superiority to the mass, is sadly restricted. His very self-reliance implies an adversary Other, not only the great precursor poet but everyone to whom he is superior, everything from which he is alienated—history, the common laws, the representative men and women that constitute social normality. American intermediate selfhood has no such limits. Indeed, the very concept of "Americanus," from Mather through Emerson, advances a mode of personal identity designed as a compensatory *replacement* for (rather than an alternative to) the ugly course of actual events. By definition the flight of the "true American" to the imagination embraces individual and society alike, without allowing either for Romantic hero-worship or for the claims of social pluralism. Hester herself is an inadequate example of this kind of heroism. Because she is part of a larger, complex design, the problems of history assume a weight equal to, if not greater than, the prophetic solace she offers; it may be that an imperfect society actually usurps her representative stature. This, at any rate, is the implicit view of those who admire her as an Antinomian, and insofar as Hawthorne shared their admiration (in spite of his repeated, severe strictures to the contrary), he upheld the immemorial Old World convention, through *Antigone* to *Anna Karenina*, that the great soul reveals itself by confronting social realities and recognizing its limitations.

Undoubtedly, *The Scarlet Letter* owes much of its force to the tension between this tragic recognition and the optimism of its New World vision. My point is not to explore the tension, but to note the antithesis. Hester's Emersonian role as prophetess, if I may call it so, militates against the prospect of tragedy because it defeats contradiction. According to F. O. Matthiessen, the earliest example of Emersonian compensation is the *dictum* that "God is promoted by the worst. Don't despise even the . . . Andrew Jacksons." We can hardly avoid seeing in this formula the strategy by which Emerson, in his seminal essays of the 1830s—after having witnessed the Jacksonian "depravities," and now sensing his solitude amidst a "wide and wild madness"—proclaimed himself the keeper of the dream. Not by accident his phrases echo those in the *Magnalia*'s General Introduction, where Mather announces that "whether New-England may *live* any where else or no, it must *live* in our History!" Emerson's essays set forth a doctrine of self-reliance, at a crucial post-Revolutionary moment, that lend a new symbolic scope to the Puritan concept of American selfhood. Geoffrey Hartman has argued that the Romantic assertion of selfhood took the triadic form of nature, self-consciousness, and imagination. Its issue was not only the triumphant assertion of the imagination but, alternately, the "visionary despair" [59] of the "sole self," the recognition that, for all the power of negative capability, despite the heady reaches of the egotistical sublime, the world is always with us. The Emersonian triad is American nature, the American self, and American destiny, a triple tautology designed to obviate the anxieties both of self-consciousness and of the recalcitrant world.

I am speaking here of the mythic self, of course. All evidence indicates that an enormous private anxiety underlies the affirmation of national identity. The Emersonian night of the soul rarely occurs in the open, and never involves the struggle with an external foe. Publicly, the morning star is forever heralding an ascendant western sun, the protagonist is always young and always "here" (even when he shakes his white locks at the runaway sun) and the only engagement is with the future, which is already prophetically secured. The struggle takes place in private, in journals, sometimes in letters and marginalia. "If . . . the world is not a dualism," Emerson confided, "is not a bipolar Unity, but is *two,* is Me and It, then is there the Alien, the Unknown, and all we have believed & chanted out of our deep instinctive hope is a pretty dream." Stephen Whicher has recorded Emerson's long effort to retain his belief, at the expense of shutting out the tragic vision, which is to say at the expense of self-acceptance. Against the felt dichotomy between Me and It, "the yawning gulf between the ambition of man and his power of performance," between the promise and "the shabby experience," the *figura* and the secular fact, against the "double consciousness . . . of the Understanding & of the Soul" which he termed "the worst feature of our biography," Emerson chanted the representative self—a "dualism" that excludes the alien or unknown—personal and national identity twined in the bipolar unity of auto-American-biography.[60]

Privately, throughout the 1840s and 1850s Emerson recorded his "frequent humiliation" and feared he would have to "write *dupe* [about himself] a long time to come"—"the dupe of hope," "the dupe of brilliant promises." "If I should write an honest diary," he confessed, "what should I say? Alas that life has halfness, shallowness." In public, he explained why life "cannot be divided nor doubled," how "a certain compensation balances every gift and every defect," why the soul "always affirms an Optimism, never a Pessimism"—and, on that premise, announced that America was "yet only at the cock-crowing and the morning star." "This ineffable life which is at my heart," he wrote privately in 1842, "will not . . . enter into the details of my biography, and say to me . . . why my son dies in his sixth year of joy." In "Experience" he placed Waldo's death in the context of "the mighty Ideal before us." His "heart beating with the love of the new beauty," he proclaimed himself "ready to be born again into this new yet unapproachable America [he had] found in the West"—unapproachable today, but tomorrow (Nature had whispered to him) the city of "the lords of life." Over and again, during this period, his journals note that "we blame the past[;] we magnify & gild the future and are not wiser for the multitude of days." Over and again, his lectures ask us to "draw new hope from the atmosphere we breathe to-day," to "read the promises of better times and of greater men," and above all to "believe what the years and centuries say, against the hours. . . . Things seem to say one thing, and say the reverse. . . . Things seem to tend downward, to justify despondency"—but the "whole value of history, of biography, is to increase my self-trust. . . ." Again, we catch echoes from the *Magnalia*; and here as before Emerson amplifies their meaning through the more comprehensive, more reassuring concepts of Romantic symbolism:

> . . . to increase my self-trust, by demonstrating what man can be and do . . . Still more do we owe to biography the fortification of our hope . . . ; consider the task offered to the intellect of this country. . . . We do not seem to have imagined its riches. We have not heeded the invitation it holds out.[61]

My self-trust: the precarious leap from the first term to the last, from subjective to universal, begins a journey outward that precludes a return to the "sole self." The national treasures vindicate the individual dream; the autobiographical *exemplum* serves as national prophecy; and what fortifies the hope in both cases is the spiritual biography of America. Granted this configuration, it is not difficult to understand Emerson's suppression of the dichotomy between self-consciousness and imagination. The private state, no less than the public, is destiny manifest. "My estimate of America," he once confessed, like my "estimate of my mental means and resources, is all or nothing." To despair in oneself is a symbolic gesture of equal magnitude to the affirmation of the national dream. It is to declare oneself a *figura medietatis* of what we might call the negative apocalypse. The great example here is Melville's Pierre, whose discovery of personal ambiguity reverses the national myth embodied in his colonial and Revolutionary sires. "Out of some past Egypt," the narrator begins, "we have come to this new Canaan, and from this new Canaan, we press on to some [ultimate] Circassia." Much later he acknowledges that the Circassia his hero represents is the New World inferno. Vivia, the protagonist of Pierre's auto-American-biography—and epitome of

Pierre's titanic effort to cap the "fame-column" of his forebears—
emerges as the "American Enceladus," the "foreboding and
prophetic" symbol of the void.[62]

One of Pierre-Vivia's precursors is Vivenza, the American utopia
described in *Mardi* as "a young Messiah," "promising as the
morning." Another is the "Master Genius" Melville hailed in his
essay on Hawthorne: the "literary Shiloh of America" who would
demonstrate "the supremacy among the nations, which prophetically
awaits us." "We want no American Miltons," Melville declares
here, directly after praising Hawthorne for his Calvinism; indeed,
the very comparison insults any "true American author. . . . Call
him an American, and have done; for you cannot say a nobler
thing of him." Melville's career is a rapid growth towards this
vision, and then a long falling away. *Typee* and *Omoo* see the New
World through the eyes of Spanish voyagers;[63] *Redburn* and
White-Jacket transform the journey of the soul into a voyage of the
redeemer nation, "homeward-bound" for the millennium; their
language is unmistakably Emersonian.[64] The disillusionment that
begins in *Mardi* reaches its nadir in *Pierre*, with its savage critique of
Transcendentalism and its self-lacerating despair over what for any
European Romantic would be a triumphant Antinomian epiphany
—the realization that "all the world does never gregariously
advance to Truth, but only here and there some of its individuals
do; and by advancing, leave the rest behind." Thereafter, Melville's
tone varies from Swiftian irony to the grotesque, but the original
dynamic is transparent throughout, even in the mock-heroic voice
of Israel Potter ("prophetically styled Israel by the good Puritans,
his parents") who plays a diminished Revolutionary Ishmael to a
series of parodic "true Americans"; even in the comic apocalypse of
The Confidence Man—whose antihero, in one of his guises, is Emerson
himself—or in the bitter detachment of *Clarel*: "To Terminus build
Fanes! / Columbus ended earth's romance: / No New World to
mankind remains." [65]

Emerson, too, had those intimations of mortality—he also heard
the call of Terminus, "god of bounds," saying "No more! . . .
Fancy departs; no more invent"—as did Thoreau and Whitman. If
America is *not* "the Great Western Pioneer whom the nations
follow," Thoreau wrote near the end of his life, then "to what end
does the world go on . . . ?" It was a rhetorical question, of course;

and an emendation in an early draft of *Walden* suggests the basis for his persisting optimism. "I could tell a pitiful story respecting myself," he had written, "with a sufficient list of failures, and flow as humbly as the very gutters." His revision, a direct echo of Emerson, became the motto of the entire work: "I do not propose to write an ode to dejection, but to brag as lustily as chanticleer in the morning, standing on his roost, if only to wake my neighbours up." Whitman's mode of compensation is perhaps best seen in his technique of avoidance. No Romantic "archetypal autobiography," unless we classify "The American Scholar" in that genre, tells us so little about the author as does *Song of Myself*. "Apart from the pulling and hauling stands what I am," Whitman declares; but at the slightest danger of scrutiny he *flees, vanishes, slips away, eludes,* orders us (and presumably himself) to *stand back*. The self which Whitman does sing—which he anatomizes in epic catalogues—belongs to the "divine average," the christic-prophetic *I Am* as the New World: "America isolated yet embodying all, what is it finally, except myself?" [66]

When Whitman deleted "myself" from the equation, when he left America on its own, he found it difficult to sustain his optimism. "The people's crudeness, vice, caprices," he admitted, might prove the United States "the most tremendous failure of time," a country whose "destiny [was] . . . equivalent, in its real world, to that of the fabled damned." He found it just as difficult to sustain his faith in himself when he deleted "divine" from the average he claimed to express. "Considered merely as a poet," he feared, he might turn out to be "the most lamentable of failures . . . in the known history of literature." "All or nothing," Emerson had declared: Whitman, like his Master, found the all in the divine American selfhood he celebrated throughout his career: "a New Man, . . . typical of the future," "a gigantic embryo or skeleton of Personality,—fit for . . . native models," a "huge composite of all other nations, . . . Self-reliant, . . . assuming to himself all the attributes of his country," "the sole reliance of American democracy." As such, he could absorb the slayer and the slain with equanimity. He has heard the "cries of anguish," he tells us, suffered the "human aggregate of cankerous imperfection," beheld the cost—and, being "typical of it all," he has beheld also its last result. The good come out of evil, as he describes it, is "an aggregate of heroes" *now* "mounting the horizon like planets," "a cluster of mighty poets, artists, teachers, fit for us, national expressers." These, too, are part of his autobiography—a history of the sole self en masse, or *mutatis mutandis* a biography of the New World, in which

> . . . past and present have interchanged,
> I myself as connector, a chansonnier of a great future.[67]

Democratic Vistas is Whitman's largest statement of that vision. Written during an era more corrupt than even the Jacksonian, and more crassly materialistic than that of the early eighteenth century, it trumpets a Nehemiah-like summons equivalent in its way to that of Emerson's "American Scholar," [68] Edwards's Revival sermons, or Mather's jeremiads. "In this age of Seeming," Emerson admonished, "nothing can be more important than the opening & promulgation of the gospel of Compensations to save the land." Mather had compensated for *his* age of seeming by opening the prospects of the Theopolis Americana, Edwards by promulgating the eschatology of the new heavens and new earth. For Whitman, the gospel of compensation centered upon the "fervid and tremendous IDEA" of the New World. At the moment, he admits, it remains still partly veiled ("How long it takes to make this American world to see that it is, in itself, the final authority and reliance!"). But as *figura Americae,* "acme of things accomplish'd, and . . . encloser of things to be," Whitman brings in himself the fulfillment that *now* "resides, crude and latent . . . in the hearts of . . . the American-born people." Proclaiming his good news from atop the "towering selfhood" of "America Herself," he charts the vistas which from eternity "the Almighty had spread before this nation"—"imperial destinies dazzling as the sun," to which the present is a morning star. "You said in your soul," Whitman concludes, addressing at once himself and the New World at large,

> I will be empire of empires, overshadowing all else, past and present, putting the history of Old-World dynasties, conquests behind me, . . . I alone inaugurating largeness, culminating time. If these, O land of America, are indeed the prizes, the determinations of your soul, be it so. . . . We see our land, America, her literature, aesthetics, etc., as substantially, the getting a form, or effusement and statement, of deepest basic

elements and loftiest final meanings, of history and man . . . on which all the superstructures of the future are permanently to rest.[69]

The superstructures Whitman speaks of were secured by Emerson. Their foundation was laid in seventeenth-century Massachusetts. The American future which Mather proclaimed at the end of the *Magnalia* finds its fullest expression in the transcendental vistas, the democratic *magnalia Americana*, heralded in Emerson's essays of the 1830s. Undoubtedly, Mather would have scorned the theology of the young visionary who, a century after his death, took his post as minister of Boston's Second Church. But he might well have endorsed the strategy by which Emerson sought to redeem the nation, compensating for the betrayals of the post-Revolutionary generation much as he himself had sought to compensate for the collapse of the theocracy. For Puritan and Transcendentalist alike, autobiography and spiritual biography fused in the process of writing "our" New World history. And for both of them, auto-American-biography meant simultaneously a total assertion of the self, a jeremiad against the misdirected progress of the "dead" present, and an act of prophecy which guaranteed the future by celebrating the regenerate "Americanus." The closing scene of Mather's Life of Winthrop—where the venerated Davidic ruler addresses the tribes of the American Israel—is transparently a private wish-fulfillment. It is properly balanced by the biography's opening quotation: *"Quincunque venti erunt, ars nostra certe non aberit"*— "Whatever winds may blow, our art will surely never pass away."

For it is to art (in the broad mythico-cultural sense of the term) that Mather's achievement belongs.[70] The continuities I have been arguing do not spring from some amorphous American Spirit hovering ubiquitous in the New World air, like the white-hooded phantom of *Moby-Dick*. Let me repeat, to avoid being misunderstood, that "Nehemias Americanus" is not a type (either in the theological sense or in the poeticized, ahistorical versions of Jung, Lawrence, or Northrop Frye) of "The American Scholar." That there are major differences between Emerson and other writers of his time, let alone between him and Mather, goes without saying; and in America those differences were magnified by a particularly *dis*continuous culture. Indeed, it might well be argued that the

Puritan myth survived partly by accident. After the failure of the theocracy, a series of disparate developments fostered the need for the myth, in its many secular variations. I think here not only of the events that led up to the Revolution, but of the recurrent crises of corporate self-definition in the nineteenth century: the demand for a pantheon of founding fathers that would satisfy absolute moral standards without inhibiting democratic progressivism (supplied by the concept of figural representativeness); the embarrassing inadequacy of artistic tradition (compensated for by the teleological distinction between the Old World and the New); the problems in integrating successive waves of immigrants (obviated by the notion of exodus as spiritual rebirth); the question of territorial rights in the West (settled by the claims of manifest destiny). The list could easily be expanded. It should not exclude as too obvious the positive factors that sustained the myth: the coincidence, for example, that America actually turned out to be a land flowing with milk and honey, and that in an age of emergent nations it became something of a light to the world.

Above all, perhaps, the persistence in outlook reflects the steady growth of the major middle-class civilization of modern times. As the concept of "Americanus" absorbs the contradictions in Reformed Protestantism, it offers a striking instance of what anthropologists have found to be the primary function of myth, its capacity to reconcile antithetical cultural pressures. The colonial Puritan myth linked self- and social assertion in a way that lent special support to the American Way. From Mather through Emerson, auto-American-biography served rhetorically to resolve the conflicts inherent in the very meaning of "free-enterprise": spiritual versus material freedom, private versus corporate enterprise, the cultural "idea," expressed by the country's "purest minds," versus the cultural fact, embodied in a vast economic-political undertaking. The same Puritan myth, differently adapted, encouraged Edwards to equate conversion, national commerce, and the treasures of a renovated earth, Franklin to record his rise to wealth as a moral vindication of the new nation, Cooper to submerge the historical drama of the frontier in the heroics of *American* nature, Thoreau to declare self-reliance an economic model of "the only true America," Horatio Alger to extol conformity as an act of supreme individualism, and Melville, in *Moby-Dick*, to create an epic hero who represents in extremis both the claims of Romantic isolation and the thrust of industrial capitalism. And if that fusion of opposites could exacerbate the differences between history and the dream—if it could issue in the bleak deadpan of *Huckleberry Finn*, or the nihilism of *Pierre*, *The Education of Henry Adams*, and *The Great Gatsby*—it more broadly sustained the unbounded hope and omnivorous egoism of Emerson's "imperial self."

So conceived, the changing relations between myth and society in America require a separate study. My present purpose has been to consider the rhetorical continuities in their own right, as the legacy of seventeenth-century New England. For the rhetoric survived, finally, not by chance but by merit, because it was compelling enough in content and flexible enough in form to invite adaptation. Colonial Puritan hermeneutics, we have seen, evolved through an essentially symbolic interaction of perceiver and fact, thus allowing for different kinds of perceivers and a variety of historical contexts. The perceiver had to identify himself as a regenerate American, but since the meaning of America lay in an act of will and imagination, he could claim that his interpretation embodied the only true America. The desert-paradise *allegoria* remained constant, but since the source of meaning lay in the American landscape, the terms of signification could change with changing national needs. What for Mather had been the purifying wilderness, and for Edwards the theocratic garden of God, became for Emerson's generation the redemptive West, as frontier or agrarian settlement or virgin land. Every stage of this long development bespeaks the astonishing tenacity of the myth. For well over two centuries, under the most diverse conditions, the major spokesmen for a self-proclaimed people of God subsumed the facts of social pluralism (ethnic, economic, religious, even personal) in a comprehensive national ideal, transferred the terms of conflict normally inherent in that ideal from history to rhetoric, and secured the triumph of that rhetoric by identifying it with the assertion of a representative American self. The palpable social effects of this strategy argue the importance of ideology (in the Marxist sense) in the shaping of the United States. The persistence of the myth is a testament to the visionary and symbolic power of the American Puritan imagination.

Appendix

Cotton Mather's Life of John Winthrop

The text is from the second edition of Mather's *Magnalia Christi Americana;
or, The Ecclesiastical History of New England,* ed. Thomas Robbins, 2 vols.
(Hartford, 1853), I, 118–31 (book two). I have noted any significant
variations from the first edition (London, 1702). In modernizing the text, I
have (a) deleted the citations in Greek (noting where I did so), since
Mather himself generally translates these in the text into both Latin and
English; (b) changed punctuation and paragraphing in a few cases; and
(c) omitted Mather's frequent use of italics and capitalization, and his
numbering of paragraphs. I am aware that some of these devices reflect
seventeenth-century rules of logic and rhetoric as well as modes of pulpit
exhortation. But the fact remains that they now hinder comprehension,
and my aim is to offer a readable and readily accessible text. I am
indebted to the annotations to the Life of Winthrop in K. B. Murdock's
edition of *Selections from Cotton Mather* (New York, 1960), and in G. E.
McCandlish's Harvard dissertation, 1963; the annotations here, however,
are wholly my own.

Nehemias Americanus. The Life of John Winthrop, Esq., Governor of the
Massachusetts Colony

Quincunque venti erunt, ars nostra certe non aberit. CICERO[1]

Let Greece boast of her patient Lycurgus,[2] the lawgiver, by whom
diligence, temperance, fortitude and wit were made the fashions of a
therefore long-lasting and renowned commonwealth; let Rome tell of her
devout Numa,[3] the lawgiver, by whom the most famous commonwealth
saw peace triumphing over extinguished war, and cruel plunders and
murders giving place to the more mollifying exercises of his religion. Our

1. "Whatever winds may blow, our art will surely never pass away." Cicero *Epistulae ad
Familiares* 12.25.5.
2. According to tradition, the great reformer of the Spartan Constitution (7th century
B.C.). His "criminal disorders" may refer to the war machine Lycurgus is said to have built to
prevent trouble with the Helots; more likely the reference is to the uprisings of the wealthy
citizens deprived by Lycurgus of their wealth.
3. Numa Pompilius: legendary king of Rome after Romulus; supposedly authored the
Roman ceremonial law; his "heathenish madness" probably refers to his supposed adherence
to the doctrines of Pythagoras.

New England shall tell and boast of her Winthrop, a lawgiver as patient as Lycurgus, but not admitting any of his criminal disorders; as devout as Numa, but not liable to any of his heathenish madnesses; a governor in whom the excellencies of Christianity made a most improving addition unto the virtues, wherein even without those he would have made a parallel for the great men of Greece or of Rome, which the pen of a Plutarch has eternized.

A stock of heroes by right should afford nothing but what is heroical, and nothing but an extreme degeneracy would make anything less to be expected from a stock of Winthrops. Mr. Adam Winthrop, the son of a worthy gentleman wearing the same name, was himself a worthy, a discreet, and a learned gentleman, particularly eminent for skill in the law, nor without remark for love to the Gospel, under the reign of King Henry VIII; and brother to a memorable favorer of the Reformed religion in the days of Queen Mary, into whose hands the famous martyr Philpot[4] committed his papers, which afterwards made no inconsiderable part of our martyr-books. This Mr. Adam Winthrop had a son of the same name also, and of the same endowments and employments with his father; and this third Adam Winthrop was the father of that renowned John Winthrop who was the father of New England and the founder of a colony which, upon many accounts, like him that founded it, may challenge the first place among the English glories of America. Our John Winthrop, thus born at the mansion-house of his ancestors, at Groton in Suffolk, on June 12, 1587,[5] enjoyed afterwards an agreeable education. But though he would rather have devoted himself unto the study of Mr. John Calvin than of Sir Edward Cook,[6] nevertheless the accomplishments of a lawyer were those wherewith heaven made his chief opportunities to be serviceable.

Being made at the unusually early age of eighteen a Justice of Peace, his virtues began to fall under a more general observation; and he not only so bound himself to the behavior of a Christian as to become exemplary for a conformity to the laws of Christianity in his own conversation, but also discovered a more than ordinary measure of those qualities which adorn an officer of humane society. His justice was impartial, and used the balance to weigh not the cash but the case of those who were before him:

4. John Philpot (1516–1555), Archdeacon of Winchester; early Puritan martyr, burned at the stake; memorialized in John Foxe's *Book of Martyrs*. The references below to Winthrop's lineage are to Adam Winthrop, grandfather (1498–1562); Adam Winthrop, father (1548–1623); and William Winthrop, uncle (1529–82).

5. Should read January 12, 1583.

6. Or Coke (1552–1634); Lord-Chief-Justice and compiler of the authoritative *Institutes of English Law*; Mather's reference to Winthrop's early plans to enter the ministry implicitly juxtaposes Calvin's *Institutes* with Coke's.

prosopolatria he reckoned as bad as *idolatria*.[7] His wisdom did exquisitely temper things according to the art of governing, which is a business of more contrivance than the seven arts of the schools:[8] *oyer* still went before *terminer*[9] in all his administrations. His courage made him dare to do right, and fitted him to stand among the lions that have sometimes been the supporters of the throne.[10] All which virtues he rendered the more illustrious by emblazoning them with the constant liberality and hospitality of a gentleman. This made him the terror of the wicked and the delight of the sober, the envy of the many but the hope of those who had any hopeful design in hand for the common good of the nation and the interests of religion.

Accordingly, when the noble design of carrying a colony of chosen people into an American wilderness was by some eminent persons undertaken, this eminent person was, by the consent of all, chosen for the Moses who must be the leader of so great an undertaking. And indeed nothing but a Mosaic spirit could have carried him through the temptations to which either his farewell to his own land or his travel in a strange land must needs expose a gentleman of his education. Wherefore, having sold a fair estate of six or seven hundred a year, he transported himself with the effects of it into New England in the year 1630, where he spent it upon the service of a famous plantation founded and formed for the seat of the most reformed Christianity, and continued there conflicting with temptations of all sorts, as many years as the nodes of the moon take to dispatch a revolution.[11] Those persons were never concerned in a new plantation who know not that the unavoidable difficulties of such a thing will call for all the prudence and patience of a mortal man to encounter therewithal; and they must be very insensible of the influence which the just wrath of heaven has permitted the devils to have upon this world, if they do not think that the difficulties of a new plantation, devoted unto the evangelical worship of our Lord Jesus Christ, must be yet more than ordinary. How prudently, how patiently, and with how much resignation to our Lord Jesus Christ our brave Winthrop waded through these difficulties, let posterity consider with admiration. And know that as the

7. I.e., the worship of men is tantamount to idolatry; literally *prosopolatria* means "face-worship."

8. The trivium (grammar, rhetoric, logic) and the quadrivium (arithmetic, music, geometry, astronomy).

9. I.e., listened to all sides of the argument before judging the case; literally: "hearing" before "judging."

10. Solomon's throne was supported by lions on both sides (1 Kings 10 : 19–20, 2 Chron. 19 : 20–21); Daniel's faith saved him from the lions (Dan. 6 : 23).

11. I.e., 18.6 years.

picture of this their governor was, after his death, hung up with honor in the statehouse of his country, so the wisdom, courage, and holy zeal of his life were an example well worthy to be copied by all that shall succeed in government.

Were he now to be considered only as a Christian, we might therein propose him as greatly imitable. He was a very religious man; and as he strictly kept his heart, so he kept his house, under the laws of piety; there he was every day constant in holy duties, both morning and evening, and on the Lord's Days and lectures.[12] Though he wrote not after the preacher,[13] yet such was his attention, and such his retention in hearing, that he repeated unto his family the sermons which he had heard in the congregation. But it is chiefly as a governor that he is now to be considered. Being the governor over the considerablest part of New England, he maintained the figure and honor of his place with the spirit of a true gentleman, but yet with such obliging condescension to the circumstances of the colony that when a certain troublesome and malicious calumniator, well known in those times, printed his libellous nicknames upon the chief persons here, the worst nickname he could find for the governor was John Temperwell.[14] And when the calumnies of that ill man caused the Archbishop to summon one Mr. Cleaves[15] before the King, in hopes to get some accusation from him against the country, Mr. Cleaves gave such an account of the governor's laudable carriage in all respects, and the serious devotion wherewith prayers were both publicly and privately made for his Majesty, that the King expressed himself most highly pleased therewithal, only sorry that so worthy a person should be no better accommodated than with the hardships of America.

He was, indeed, a governor who had most exactly studied that book which, pretending to teach politics, did only contain three leaves, and but one word in each of those leaves, which word was "Moderation." Hence, though he were a zealous enemy to all vice, yet his practice was according to his judgment thus expressed: "In the infancy of plantations, justice should be administered with more lenity than in a settled state, because people are more apt then to transgress, partly out of ignorance of new laws

12. 1 Tim. 3 : 4–5, Prov. 4 : 23, Deut. 11 : 18–19. Lectures were informal sermons.

13. Listeners sometimes recorded the sermon verbatim in shorthand.

14. Thomas Morton, *New-English Canaan* (London, 1637), part 4, chapter 23. Morton (ca. 1579–1649) was an adventurer and an Anglican who came into conflict with the Puritans on several occasions; the most famous of these was in 1628 at the settlement Morton founded at Mount Wollaston, or "Merry Mount" (now Quincy, Mass.).

15. George Cleaves settled at Richmond Island, Maine, in 1630, and returned briefly to England in 1636. He continued his associations with Morton until at least 1643. William Laud (1573–1645) was made Archbishop of Canterbury by Charles I in 1633.

and orders, partly out of oppression of business and other straits. *Lento gradu*[16] was the old rule; and if the strings of a new instrument be wound up unto their height, they will quickly crack." But when some leading and learned men took offence at his conduct in this matter, and upon a conference gave it in as their opinion that a stricter discipline was to be used in the beginning of a plantation than after its being with more age established and confirmed, the governor, being readier to see his own errors than other men's, professed his purpose to endeavor their satisfaction with less of lenity in his administrations. At that conference there were drawn up several other articles to be observed between the governor and the rest of the magistrates, which were of this import: that the magistrates, as far as might be, should aforehand ripen their consultations, to produce that unanimity in their public votes which might make them liker to the voice of God; that if differences fell out among them in their public meetings, they should speak only to the case, without any reflection,[17] with all due modesty, and but by way of question, or desire the deferring of the cause to further time, and after sentence to intimate privately no dislike; that they should be more familiar, friendly, and open unto each other, and more frequent in their visitations, and not any way expose each others' infirmities, but seek the honor of each other and all the court; that one magistrate shall not cross the proceedings of another without first advising with him; and that they should in all their appearances abroad be so circumstanced as to prevent all contempt of authority; and that they should support and strengthen all under-officers; all of which articles were observed by no man more than by the governor himself.

But whilst he thus did as our New English Nehemiah the part of a ruler in managing the public affairs of our American Jerusalem, when there were Tobijahs and Sanballats[18] enough to vex him and give him the experiment of Luther's observation, "Omnis qui regit est tanquam signum, in quod omnia jacula Satan et mundus dirigunt," [19] he made himself still an exacter parallel unto that governor of Israel by doing the part of a neighbor among the distressed people of the new plantation. To teach them the frugality necessary for those times he abridged himself of a thousand comfortable things which he had allowed himself elsewhere. His habit was not that "soft raiment" which would have been disagreeable to a wilderness;[20] his table was not covered with the superfluities that would

16. "By slow degrees."

17. I.e., without "casting some imputation on a person" *(N.E.D.)*.

18. Sanballat, governor of Samaria, and Tobijah, a Persian official, opposed the rebuilding of the walls of Jerusalem and later tried to depose Nehemiah (Neh. 2, 4, 6).

19. "All who rule are targets at which Satan and the world hurl their darts." *(Loci Communes)*.

20. Matt. 11 : 8; Luke 7 : 25.

have invited unto sensualities: water was commonly his own drink, though he gave wine to others. But at the same time his liberality unto the needy was even beyond measure generous, and therein he was continually causing "the blessing of him that was ready to perish to come upon him, and the heart of the widow and the orphan to sing for joy" [21]—but none more than those of deceased ministers, whom he always treated with a very singular compassion, among the instances whereof we still enjoy with us the worthy and now aged son of that Reverend Higginson[22] whose death left his family in a wide world soon after his arrival here, publicly acknowledging the charitable Winthrop for his foster father. It was oftentimes no small trial unto his faith to think "how a table for the people should be furnished when they first came into the wilderness!" [23] And for very many of the people his own good works were needful, and accordingly employed for the answering of his faith. Indeed, for a while the governor was the Joseph unto whom the whole body of the people repaired when their corn failed them.[24] And he continued relieving of them with his open-handed bounties as long as he had any stock to do it with; and a lively faith to see the return of the "bread after many days," and not starve in the days that were to pass till that return should be seen, carried him cheerfully through those expenses. Once it was observable that on February 5, 1630, when he was distributing the last handful of the "meal in the barrel" unto a poor man distressed by the wolf at the door, at that instant they spied a ship arrived at the harbor's mouth laden with provisions for them all.

Yea, the governor sometimes made his own private purse to be the public, not by sucking into it but by squeezing out of it; for when the public treasury had nothing in it, he did himself defray the charges of the public. And having learned that lesson of our Lord, that "it is better to give than to receive," he did, at the General Court, when he was a third time chosen governor, make a speech unto this purpose: that he had received gratuities from diverse towns, which he accepted with much comfort and content; and he had likewise received civilities from particular persons, which he could not refuse without incivility in himself; nevertheless, he took them with a trembling heart in regard of God's word

21. Job 29 :13. Cf. Neh. 5 : 14–18, on Nehemiah's good deeds.

22. Francis Higginson (1587–1630), author of *New-Englands Plantation*, died a year after his arrival at Salem; his son, John (1616–1708), wrote a laudatory "Attestation" to Mather's *Magnalia*.

23. From David's psalm on the sins of the Exodus: "Yea, they spake against God; they said, Can God furnish a table in the wilderness?" (Ps. 78 : 19–20).

24. Gen. 41 : 56. The three following quotations are (respectively) from Eccles. 11 : 1, 1 Kings 17 : 2, and Acts 20 : 35 (altered).

and the conscience of his own infirmities, and therefore he desired them that they would not hereafter take it ill if he refused such presents for the time to come. 'Twas his custom also to send some of his family upon errands unto the houses of the poor about their mealtime, on purpose to spy whether they wanted; and if it were found that they wanted, he would make that the opportunity of sending supplies unto them. And there was one passage of his charity that was perhaps a little unusual. In an hard and long winter, when wood was very scarce at Boston, a man gave him a private information that a needy person in the neighborhood stole wood sometimes from his pile, whereupon the governor in a seeming anger did reply, "Does he so? I'll take a course with him; go, call that man to me, I'll warrant you I'll cure him of stealing!" When the man came, the governor, considering that if he had stolen it was more out of necessity than disposition, said unto him, "Friend, it is a severe winter, and I doubt you are but meanly provided for wood; wherefore I would have you supply yourself at my woodpile till this cold season be over." And he then merrily asked his friends whether he had not effectually cured this man of stealing his wood.

One would have imagined that so good a man could have had no enemies, if we had not had a daily and woeful experience to convince us that goodness itself will make enemies. It is a wonderful speech of Plato (in one of his books *de Republica*), "For the trial of true virtue, 'tis necessary that a good man, though he do no unjust thing, should suffer the infamy of the greatest injustice." [25] The governor had by his unspotted integrity procured himself a great reputation[26] among the people; and then the crime of popularity was laid unto his charge by such who were willing to deliver him from the danger of having "all men speak well of him." Yea, there were persons eminent both for figure and for number unto whom it was almost essential to dislike everything that came from him; and yet he always maintained an amicable correspondence with them, as believing that they acted according to their judgment and conscience, or that their eyes were held by some temptation in the worst of all their oppositions. Indeed, his right works were so many that they exposed him unto the envy of his neighbors; and of such power was that envy that sometimes he could not stand before it; but it was by not standing that he most effectually withstood it all.

Great attempts were sometimes made among the freemen[27] to get him left out from his place in the government upon little pretenses, lest by the

---

25. Plato *Republic* 361C. 4–5 (slightly altered). Citation in Greek deleted.
26. *Repntation* in first edition; possibly, an abbreviation or misspelling of "representation."
27. In early Puritan New England only the male church-members had the right to vote. The preceding lines refer to Luke 6 : 26, Eccles. 4 : 4, and Prov. 27 : 4.

too frequent choice of one man the government should cease to be by choice; and with a particular aim at him, sermons were preached at the Anniversary Court of Election, to dissuade the freemen from choosing one man twice together. This was the reward of his extraordinary serviceableness! But when these attempts did succeed, as they sometimes did, his profound humility appeared in that equality of mind wherewith he applied himself cheerfully to serve the country in whatever station their votes had allotted for him. And one year when the votes came to be numbered, there were found six less for Mr. Winthrop than for another gentleman who then stood in competition. But several other persons regularly tendering their votes before the election was published were, upon a very frivolous objection, refused by some of the magistrates that were afraid lest the election should at last fall upon Mr. Winthrop; which, though it was well perceived, yet such was the self-denial of this patriot that he would not permit any notice to be taken of the injury. But these trials were nothing in comparison of those harsher and harder treats which he sometimes had from the forwardness of not a few in the days of their paroxysms, and from the faction of some against him, not much unlike that of the Piazzi in Florence against the family of the Medici;[28] all of which he at last conquered by conforming to the famous judge's motto, *prudens qui patiens.*[29] The oracles of God have said "Envy is rottenness to the bones," [30] and Gulielmus Parisiensis[31] applies it unto rulers, who are as it were the bones of the societies which they belong unto: "Envy," says he, "is often found among them, and it is rottenness unto them." Our Winthrop encountered this envy from others, but conquered it by being free from it himself.

Were it not for the sake of introducing the exemplary skill of this wise man at giving soft answers, one would not choose to relate those instances of wrath which he had sometimes to encounter with; but he was for his gentleness, his forbearance, and his longanimity a pattern so worthy to be

28. In 1478 the Piazzi family assassinated a leading member of the Medici family; the war that resulted came to involve most of Italy.

29. "He who is patient is prudent"; attributed to Edward Coke.

30. From Proverbs 14 : 30. The context of this reference is clearly on Mather's mind through much of his description of Winthrop as magistrate: "In the fear of the Lord is strong confidence: and his children shall have a place of refuge. . . . In the multitude of people is the king's honor: but in the want of people is the destruction of the prince. He that is slow to wrath is of great understanding. . . . A sound heart is the life of the flesh: but envy the rottenness of the bones. He that oppresseth the poor reproacheth his Maker: but he that honoreth him hath mercy on the poor. The wicked is driven away in his wickedness. . . . Righteousness exalteth a nation" (Prov. 14 : 26–34).

31. William of St. Amour (d. 1272), opponent of the Dominican and Franciscan attempt to dictate the curriculum at the University of Paris, and well known as a satirist.

written after that something must here be written of it. He seemed indeed never to speak any other language than that of Theodosius:[32] "If any man speak evil of the governor, if it be through lightness, 'tis to be contemned; if it be through madness, 'tis to be pitied; if it be through injury, 'tis to be remitted." Behold, reader, the meekness of wisdom notably exemplified! There was a time when he received a very sharp letter from a gentleman who was a member of the court, but he delivered back the letter unto the messengers that brought it with such a Christian speech as this: "I am not willing to keep such a matter of provocation by me!" Afterwards the same gentleman was compelled by the scarcity of provisions to send unto him that he would sell him some of his cattle, whereupon the governor prayed him to accept what he had sent for as a token of his good will, but the gentleman returned him this answer, "Sir, your overcoming of yourself hath overcome me"; and afterwards gave demonstration of it.

The French have a saying that "Un honnête homme est un homme mêlé!" ("a good man is a mixed man"); and there hardly ever was a more sensible mixture of those two things, resolution and condescension,[33] than in this good man. There was a time when the Court of Election being for fear of tumult held at Cambridge, May 17, 1637, the sectarian part of the country, who had the year before gotten a governor more unto their mind, had a project now to have confounded the election, by demanding that the court would consider a petition then tendered before their proceeding thereunto. Mr. Winthrop saw that this was only a trick to throw all into confusion by putting off the choice of the governor and assistants until the day should be over; and therefore he did, with a strenuous resolution, procure a disappointment unto that mischievous and ruinous contrivance. Nevertheless, Mr. Winthrop himself being by the voice of the freemen in this exigency chosen the governor, and all of the other party left out, that ill-affected party discovered the dirt and mire which remained with them after the storm was over; particularly the sergeants, whose office 'twas to attend the governor, laid down their halberds. But such was the condescension of this governor as to take no present notice of this anger and contempt, but only order some of his own servants to take the halberds; and when the country manifested their deep resentments of the affront thus offered him, he prayed them to overlook it. But it was not long before a compensation was made for these things by the doubled respects which were from all parts paid unto him.

Again, there was a time when the suppression of an Antinomian and

32. Theodosius Flavius I (346–395), Christian emperor of Rome. The dispute discussed below concerned Thomas Dudley (1574–1653), a leader of the theocracy; the "messengers" were John Haynes and Thomas Hooker.
33. "Courteous disregard of difference of rank or position" (N.E.D.).

Familistical faction[34] which extremely threatened the ruin of the country was generally thought much owing unto this renowned man; and therefore when the friends of that faction could not wreak their displeasure on him with any political vexations, they set themselves to do it by ecclesiastical ones. Accordingly, when a sentence of banishment was passed on the ringleaders of those disturbances, who

> . . . maria et terras, caelumque profundum
> quippe ferant rapidi secum, vertantque per auras,[35]

many at the church of Boston, who were then that way too much inclined, most earnestly solicited the Elders of that church whereof the governor was a member to call him forth as an offender for passing of that sentence. The Elders were unwilling to do any such thing; but the governor, understanding the ferment among the people, took that occasion to make a speech in the congregation to this effect:

> Brethren, understanding that some of you have desired that I should answer for an offence lately taken among you: had I been called upon so to do, I would, first, have advised with the ministers of the country whether the church had power to call in question the civil court; and I would, secondly, have advised with the rest of the court whether I might discover their counsels unto the church. But though I know that the reverend Elders of this church, and some others, do very well apprehend that the church cannot enquire into the proceedings of the court, yet for the satisfaction of the weaker who do not apprehend it, I will declare my mind concerning it. If the church have any such power, they have it from the Lord Jesus Christ; but the Lord Jesus Christ hath disclaimed it, not only by practice, but also by precept, which we have in his Gospel, Matthew 20 : 25–26.[36] It is true indeed, that magistrates as they are church-members are accountable unto the church for their failings, but that is when they are out of their calling. When Uzziah would go offer incense in the temple, the

34. The faction was led by Anne Hutchinson (1591–1643). Antinomianism held that the elect stood beyond the moral law as set forth in the Old Testament; Familism, which takes its name from an English sect called the Family of Love (ca. 1570), adhered to a similar doctrine. The electoral dispute of 1637, to which Mather refers above, concerned the Antinomians' support of Sir Henry Vane for governor because of his sympathies for their doctrinal position. Vane returned to England in August, 1637; Anne Hutchinson was banished from Massachusetts the following year.

35. ". . . would, indeed, swiftly bear off with them the sea, the land, and the deep heaven, and turn them about through the air." (*Aeneid* 1. 59–60). Modern readings have *verrant* rather than the seventeenth-century reading *vertant* (i.e., "scour" rather than "turn").

36. "You know that the rulers of the Gentiles lord it over them, and their great men exercise authority over them. It shall not be so among you; but whoever would be great among you must be your servant."

officers of the church called him to an account and withstood him; but when Asa put the prophet in prison, the officers of the church did not call him to an account for that.[37] If the magistrate shall in a private way wrong any man, the church may call him to an account for it; but if he be in pursuance of a course of justice, though the thing that he does be unjust, yet he is not accountable for it before the church. As for myself, I did nothing in the causes of any of the brethren but by the advice of the Elders of the church. Moreover, in the oath which I have taken there is this clause: "In all causes wherein you are to give your vote, you shall do as in your judgment and conscience you shall see to be just and for the public good." And I am satisfied, it is most for the glory of God, and the public good, that there has been such a sentence passed; yea, those brethren are so divided from the rest of the country in their opinions and practices that it cannot stand with the public peace for them to continue with us; Abraham saw that Hagar and Ishmael must be sent away.[38]

By such a speech he marvelously convinced, satisfied, and mollified the uneasy brethren of the church; "sic cunctus pelagi cecidit fragor." [39] And after a little patient waiting, the differences all so wore away that the church, merely as a token of respect unto the governor, when he had newly met with some losses in his estate, sent him a present of several hundreds of pounds.

Once more, there was a time when some active spirits among the deputies of the colony, by their endeavors not only to make themselves a court of judicature, but also to take away the negative by which the magistrates might check their votes, had like by over-driving to have run the whole government into something too democratical. And if there were a town in Spain undermined by coneys,[40] another town in Thrace destroyed by moles, a third in Greece ranversed by frogs, a fourth in Germany subverted by rats, I must on this occasion add that there was a country in America like to be confounded by a swine. A certain stray sow, being found, was claimed by two several persons[41] with a claim so equally maintained on both sides that, after six or seven years hunting the business from one court unto another, it was brought at last into the General Court, where the final determination was that it was impossible to proceed unto any judgment in the case. However, in the debate of this matter, the

37. Uzziah, king of Judah, suffered his attack of leprosy, according to the priests, because of his hidden sins (2 Chron. 26); the incident with Asa and Hanani is in 2 Chron. 16 : 7–10.
38. Gen. 21 : 9–14.
39. "With that, the entire tumult of the sea subsided." (*Aeneid* 1. 154).
40. Rabbits.
41. Robert Keayne, the merchant (1595–1656), and the Boston widow Goody Sherman; the incident occurred in 1634.

negative of the upper house upon the lower in that court was brought upon the stage, and agitated with so hot a zeal that a little more and all had been in the fire. In these agitations the governor was informed that an offence had been taken by some eminent persons at certain passages in a discourse by him written thereabout; whereupon with his usual condescendency, when he next came into the General Court, he made a speech of this import:

> I understand that some have taken offence at something that I have lately written; which offence I desire to remove now, and begin this year in a reconciled state with you all. As for the matter of my writing, I had the concurrence of my brethren; it is a point of judgment which is not at my own disposing. I have examined it over and over again, by such light as God has given me from the rules of religion, reason, and custom, and I see no cause to retract any thing of it; wherefore I must enjoy my liberty in that as you do yourselves. But for the manner, this, and all that was blameworthy in it, was wholly my own, and whatsoever I might allege for my own justification therein before men, I waive it, as now setting myself before another Judgment Seat. However[42] what I wrote was upon great provocation, and to vindicate myself and others from great aspersion, yet that was no sufficient warrant for me to allow any distemper of spirit in myself; and I doubt I have been too prodigal of my brethrens' reputation. I might have maintained my cause without casting any blemish upon others when I made that my conclusion, "And now let religion and sound reason give judgment in the case"; it looked as if I arrogated too much unto myself and too little to others. And when I made that profession that I would maintain what I wrote before all the world, though such words might modestly be spoken, yet I perceive an unbeseeming pride of my own heart breathing in them. For these failings I ask pardon both of God and man.

> > Sic ait et dicto citius tumida aequora placat,
> > collectasque fugat nubes, solemque reducit.[43]

This acknowledging disposition in the governor made them all acknowledge that he was truly "a man of an excellent spirit." In fine, the victories of an Alexander, an Hannibal, or a Caesar, over other men, were not so glorious as the victories of this great man over himself, which also at last proved victories over other men.

42. I.e., "although."

43. "So he spoke, and even before he finished speaking he had calmed the swelling sea, put the gathered clouds to rout, and brought back the sun." (*Aeneid* 1. 142–43). The quotation that follows is from Prov. 17 : 27.

But the stormiest of all the trials that ever befell this gentleman was in the year 1645, when he was in title no more than deputy governor of the colony. If the famous Cato were forty-four times called into judgment, but as often acquitted,[44] let it not be wondered if[45] our famous Winthrop were one time so. There happening certain seditious and mutinous practices in the town of Hingham,[46] the deputy governor as legally as prudently interposed his authority for the checking of them. Whereupon there followed such an enchantment upon the minds of the deputies in the General Court that upon a scandalous petition of the delinquents unto them—wherein a pretended invasion made upon the liberties of the people was complained of—the deputy governor was most irregularly called forth unto an ignominious hearing before them in a vast assembly; whereto with a sagacious humility he consented, although he showed them how he might have refused it. The result of that hearing was that, notwithstanding the touchy jealousy of the people about their liberties lay at the bottom of all this, prosecution, yet Mr. Winthrop was publicly acquitted and the offenders were severally fined and censured. But Mr. Winthrop, then resuming the place of deputy governor on the bench, saw cause to speak unto "the root of the matter" after this manner:

I shall not now speak anything about the past proceedings of this court, or the persons therein concerned. Only I bless God that I see an issue of this troublesome affair. I am well satisfied that I was publicly accused and that I am now publicly acquitted. But though I am justified before men, yet it may be the Lord hath seen so much amiss in my administrations as calls me to be humbled; and indeed for me to have been thus charged by men is itself a matter of humiliation, whereof I desire to make a right use before the Lord. If Miriam's father spit in her face, she is to be ashamed.[47] But give me leave before you go to say something that may rectify the opinions of many people, from whence the distempers have risen that have lately prevailed upon the body of this people. The questions that have troubled the country have been about the authority of the magistracy, and the liberty of the people. It is you who have called us unto this office; but

44. Cato (234–149 B.C.) came into frequent conflict with Roman officials because of his attacks on the immorality of men in power.

45. First edition reads "and if."

46. Directed against the government-appointed captain of the town militia.

47. Num. 12 : 14. Miriam was punished by God for speaking against Moses, her brother; she was subsequently forgiven. The preceding allusion to "the root of the matter" is to Job 19 : 28.

being thus called, we have our authority from God; it is the ordinance of God, and it hath the image of God stamped upon it; and the contempt of it has been vindicated by God with terrible examples of his vengeance. I entreat you to consider that when you choose magistrates, you take them from among yourselves, men subject unto like passions with yourselves. If you see our infirmities, reflect on your own, and you will not be so severe censurers of ours. We count him a good servant who breaks not his covenant. The covenant between us and you is the oath you have taken of us, which is to this purpose: "that we shall govern you and judge your causes according to God's laws and our own, according to our best skill." As for our skill, you must run the hazard of it; and if there be an error, not in the will, but only in the skill, it becomes you to bear it. Nor would I have you to mistake in the point of your own liberty. There is a liberty of corrupt nature, which is affected both by men and beasts, to do what they list; and this liberty is inconsistent with authority, impatient of all restraint; by this liberty *sumus omnes deteriores*,[48] 'tis the grand enemy of truth and peace, and all the ordinances of God are bent against it. But there is a civil, a moral, a federal liberty, which is the proper end and object of authority; it is a liberty for that only which is just and good; for this liberty you are to stand with the hazard of your very lives; and whatsoever crosses it is not authority but a distemper thereof. This liberty is maintained in a way of subjection to authority; and the authority set over you will in all administrations for your good be quietly submitted unto by all but such as have a disposition to shake off the yoke and lose their true liberty by their murmuring at the honor and power of authority.

The spell that was upon the eyes of the people being thus dissolved, their distorted and enraged notions of things all vanished; and the people would not afterwards entrust the helm of the weather-beaten bark in any other hands but Mr. Winthrop's until he died. Indeed, such was the mixture of distant qualities in him as to make a most admirable temper; and his having a certain greatness of soul, which rendered him grave, generous, courageous, resolved, well-applied, and every way a gentleman in his demeanor, did not hinder him from taking sometimes the old Romans' way to avoid confusions, namely *cedendo*,[49] or from discouraging some things which are agreeable enough to most that wear the name of gentlemen. Hereof I will give no instances, but only oppose two passages of his life.

48. "We are all the worse." (Terence *Heaucton Timorumeuos* 3.1).
49. "By yielding [the point]." The reference is possibly to the Roman general Fabius (d.

In the year 1632, the governor, with his pastor Mr. Wilson[50] and some other gentlemen, to settle a good understanding between the two colonies, traveled as far as Plymouth, more than forty miles, through an howling wilderness, no better accommodated in those early days than the princes that in Solomon's time saw servants on horseback,[51] or than Genus and Species in the old epigram, "going on foot." [52] The difficulty of the walk was abundantly compensated by the honorable, first reception, and then dismission, which they found from the rulers of Plymouth, and by the good correspondence thus established between the new colonies, who were like the floating bottles wearing this motto, "Si colidimur, frangimur." [53] But there were at this time in Plymouth two ministers[54] leavened so far with the humors of the rigid separation that they insisted vehemently upon the unlawfulness of calling any unregenerate man by the name of "Goodman Such-an-One," [55] until by their indiscreet urging of this whimsy the place began to be disquieted. The wiser people being troubled at these trifles, they took the opportunity of Governor Winthrop's being there to have the thing publicly propounded in the congregation; who in answer thereunto distinguished between a theological and a moral goodness, adding, that when juries were first used in England, it was usual for the crier, after the names of persons fit for that service were called over, to bid them all, "Attend, good men and true"; whence it grew to be a civil custom in the English nation for neighbors living by one another to call one another "Goodman Such-an-One," and it was pity now to make a stir about a civil custom so innocently introduced. And that speech of Mr. Winthrop's put a lasting stop to the little, idle, whimsical conceits then beginning to grow obstreperous.

Nevertheless, there was one civil custom used in (and in few but) the

203 B.C.), known as "Cunctator," "the delayer" (from Enniu's eulogy: "cunctando restitit rem"); or else to Ovid *Ars Amatoria* 2.197.

50. John Wilson (ca. 1591–1667), a leading first-generation minister.

51. Eccles. 10 : 7. Throughout the Renaissance, the Book of Ecclesiastes was ascribed to Solomon; cf. Eccles. 1 : 1.

52. Apparently, a reference to the principles of rhetoric and logic; the proverb itself, a Renaissance commonplace, first appears in the medieval lyric poem, "De Clerico et Puella": "Bettere on fote gon, then wycked hors to ryde."

53. "If we collide, we are smashed." (Motto inscribed on Dutch coins of the period.)

54. Ralph Smith (1590–1661) and Roger Williams (1604?–83); both had come from Salem to Plymouth, where they felt they could more fully put their Separatist convictions into practice. Williams stayed only briefly; Smith remained as Plymouth's first settled minister from 1629 to 1636.

55. I.e., Goodman so-and-so (whatever the particular family name of the individual involved). The usual form of address at Plymouth was "Master" or "Sir." Williams and Smith seem to have attached the status of visible sainthood to the form of "Goodman"—i.e., attributed to it a theological (as distinct from a general legal or "moral") meaning.

English nation, which this gentleman did endeavor to abolish in this country; and that was the usage of drinking to one another. For although by drinking to one another no more is meant than an act of courtesy, when one going to drink does invite another to do so too for the same ends with himself, nevertheless the governor (not altogether unlike to Cleomenes, of whom 'tis reported by Plutarch—"nolenti poculum nunquam prae-buit" [56]) considered the impertinency and insignificancy of this usage, as to any of those ends that are usually pretended for it, and that indeed it ordinarily served for no ends at all, but only to provoke persons unto unseasonable and perhaps unreasonable drinking, and at last produce that abominable health-drinking which the Fathers of old so severely rebuked in the pagans, and which the Papists themselves do condemn when their casuists pronounce it "Peccatum mortale provocare ad aequales calices, et nefas respondere." [57] Wherefore in his own most hospitable house he left it off, not out of any silly or stingy fancy, but merely that by his example a greater temperance, with liberty of drinking, might be recommended, and sundry inconveniences in drinking avoided. And his example accordingly began to be much followed by the sober people in this country (as it now also begins to be among persons of the highest rank in the English nation itself) until an order of court came to be made against that ceremony in drinking, and then the old wont violently returned, with a *nitimur in vetitum.* [58]

Many were the afflictions of this righteous man! He lost much of his estate in a ship and in an house quickly after his coming to New England, besides the prodigious expense of it in the difficulties of his first coming hither. Afterwards his assiduous application unto the public affairs (wherein "Ispe se non habuit, postquam respublica eum gubernatorem habere capit")[59] made him so much to neglect his own private interests, that an unjust steward ran him £2,500 in debt before he was aware; for the payment whereof he was forced many years before his decease to sell the most of what he had left unto him in the country; albeit by the observable blessing of God upon the posterity of this liberal man his children all of them came to fair estates and lived in good fashion and credit. Moreover, he successively buried three wives, the first of which was the daughter and

56. "He never tempted the reluctant to drink." Citation in Greek deleted. Cleomenes III, who reigned 235–222 B.C., was the last great reformist king of Sparta.

57. "It is a deadly sin to challenge another person to a drinking contest, and impious to accept the challenge."

58. "We reach for that which is forbidden." (Ovid *Amores* 3.4.17).

59. "He could no longer attend to his own possessions after the state possessed him as its governor." The steward was James Luxford. The "afflictions" (above) refer to Ps. 34 : 19.

heiress of Mr. Forth, of Much Stambridge[60] in Essex, by whom he had "wisdom with an inheritance," and an excellent son. The second was the daughter of Mr. William Clopton, of London,[61] who died with her child within a very little while. The third was the daughter of the truly worshipful Sir John Tyndal, who made it her whole care to please, first God, and then her husband, and by whom he had four sons which survived and honored their father.[62] And unto all these, the addition of the distempers every now and then raised in the country procured unto him a very singular share of trouble. Yea, so hard was the measure which he found even among pious men, in the temptations of a wilderness, that when the thunder and lightning had smitten a windmill whereof he was owner, some had such things in their heads as publicity to reproach this charitablest of men, as if the voice of the Almighty had rebuked I know not what oppression which they judged him guilty of; which things I would not have mentioned but that the instances may fortify the expectations of my best readers for such afflictions.

He that had been for his attainments, as they said of the blessed Macarius,[63] "an old man while a young one," and that had in his young days met with many of those ill days whereof he could say he had little pleasure in them, now found old age in its infirmities advancing earlier upon him than it came upon his much longer-lived progenitors. While he was yet seven years off of that which we call the grand climacterical,[64] he felt the approaches of his dissolution; and finding he could say,

> non habitus, non ipse color non gressus euntis,
> non species eadem quae fuit ante manet,[65]

he then wrote this account of himself: "Age now comes upon me, and

60. Also Great Stambridge; Winthrop married Mary Forth (1583–1615) in 1606; of their six children only their son, John (b. 1606), survived the father.

61. Or of Castleine, near Groton; Winthrop married Thomasine Clopton (1583–1616) in 1615. The preceding quotation is from Eccles. 7 : 11.

62. Winthrop married Margaret Tyndal in 1618; their four sons were Steven (b. 1618), Adam (b. 1618), Deane (b. 1622), and Samuel (b. 1627).

63. From Palladius Historia Lausiaca 17, 2 (citation in Greek deleted), on the life of Macarius of Egypt, also called Macarius the Great (ca. 300–ca. 390). "Macarius" means blessed and so Mather probably intends the adjective as a pun. Palladius's meaning, which Mather adopts, is that Macarius had accomplished a great deal when he was still a young man.

64. I.e., he was 63 years old. The "grand climacterical" denotes the age of seventy; the number seven has figural significance (as a "holy number") here and throughout the Magnalia's seven books.

65. "Neither his bearing, nor even his complexion, nor his step as he walks, nor his overall appearance—nothing remains as it was before" (Maximianus Elegies 1.210–11). Regarding Winthrop's speech which follows, see: 2 Tim. 4 : 6, Ps. 31 : 15, 1 Cor. 4 : 2, Matt. 25 : 21–23.

infirmities therewithal, which makes me apprehend that the time of my departure out of this world is not far off. However, our times are all in the Lord's hand, so as we need not trouble our thoughts how long or short they may be, but how we may be found faithful when we are called for." But at last when that year came, he took a cold which turned into a fever whereof he lay sick about a month, and in that sickness—as it hath been observed, that there was allowed unto the serpent the bruising of the heel,[66] and accordingly at the heel or close of our lives the Old Serpent will be nibbling more than ever in our lives before, and when the Devil sees that we shall shortly be where the wicked cease from troubling,[67] that wicked one will trouble us more than ever—so this eminent saint now underwent sharp conflicts with the tempter, whose wrath grew great as the time to exert it grew short;[68] and he was buffeted with the disconsolate thoughts of black and sore desertions, wherein he could use that sad representation of his own condition:

> nuper eram judex, jam judicor; ante tribunal
> subsistens paveo, judicor ipse modo.[69]

But it was not long before those clouds were dispelled, and he enjoyed in his holy soul the great consolations of God! While he thus lay ripening for heaven, he did out of obedience unto the ordinance of our Lord send for the Elders of the church to pray with him: yea, they and the whole church fasted as well as prayed for him. And in that fast the venerable Cotton[70] preached on Psalms 35 : 13–14: "When they were sick, I humbled myself with fasting; I behaved myself as though he had been my friend or brother; I bowed down heavily, as one that mourned for his mother." From whence I find him raising that observation, "The sickness of one that is to us as a friend, a brother, a mother, is a just occasion of deep humbling our souls with fasting and prayer," and making this application:

> Upon this occasion we are now to attend this duty for a governor who
> has been to us as a friend in his counsel for all things, and help for our
> bodies by physic, for our estates by law, and of whom there was no
> fear of his becoming an enemy, like the friends of David;[71] a governor

66. Gen. 3 : 15, the *protevangelium*, where God tells the snake—Satan, "that old serpent" (Rev. 12 : 9, 20 : 2)—that man "shall bruise thy head and thou shalt bruise his heel."

67. Job 3 : 17.

68. Rev. 12 : 12.

69. "Recently I was a judge, now I am judged; I tremble as I stand before the tribunal, to be judged myself."

70. John Cotton (1584–1652), Cotton Mather's grandfather and namesake.

71. David's appointed counsellors and magistrates who joined with Absalom in his revolt against David (2 Sam. 16).

who has been unto us as a brother: not usurping authority over the church, often speaking his advice, and often contradicted, even by young men, and some of low degree; yet not replying, but offering satisfaction also when any supposed offences have arisen; a governor who has been unto us as a mother, parent-like distributing his goods to brethren and neighbors at his first coming, and gently bearing our infirmities without taking notice of them.

Such a governor, after he had been more than ten several times by the people chosen their governor, was New England now to lose; who, having like Jacob first left his council and blessing with his children gathered about his bedside,[72] and like David served his generation by the will of God,[73] he gave up the ghost and fell asleep on March 26, 1649, having, like the dying emperor Valentinian,[74] this above all his other victories for his triumphs, his overcoming of himself.

The words of Josephus about Nehemiah, the governor of Israel, we will now use upon this governor of New England, as his

Epitaph

Vir fuit indole bonus ac justus
et popularium gloriae amantissimus;
quibus eternum reliquit monumentum,
Novanglorum moenia.[75]

72. Gen. 49 : 1–33.
73. Acts 13 : 36.
74. Christian emperor of Rome, d. 375.
75. "By nature he was a man good and just, and most zealous for the glory of his countrymen; he left behind for them an eternal memorial—the walls of New England." The Latin substitutes "New England" for the original Greek "Jerusalem." The passage from Josephus (ca. 37–100) appears, in prose, in his *Antiquities of the Jews*, bk. 11, chap. 5. Citation in Greek deleted.

Notes

1 This pertains as well to his comments on adversaries—e.g., his description of Roger Williams as Don Quixote, or of the theocracy's conflation of Anne Hutchinson's biological and doctrinal "false conceptions" (Cotton Mather, *Magnalia Christi Americana; or, The Ecclesiastical History of New England*, ed. Thomas Robbins, 2 vols. [Hartford, 1853], II, 495, 519; vol. I is dated 1855, evidently a misprint for 1853). Critics have also overlooked Mather's sometimes surprising tolerance for dissenters, as in his commemoration of Hanserd Knollys, one of New England's "godly Anabaptists" (I, 43).

2 T. H. Breen's recent analysis of Puritan political ideas, for instance, follows Mather in considering the Keayne-Sherman case a landmark in Winthrop's career, and reiterates his emphasis on the antagonism between the colonial administrators, led by Winthrop, who demanded wide-ranging discretionary power for themselves, and the freemen who considered such power a usurpation of public trust (*The Character of the Good Ruler: A Study of Puritan Political Ideas in New England, 1630–1730* [New Haven, 1970], pp. 8–11, 36, 59, 61–62, 64–65, 79, 82).

3 This trend towards realism has been connected with both Reformed and humanist thought: with the resurgent interest in classical biography, which encouraged specificity in character analysis; with the rise of nationalism, which spurred the production of partisan local biographies; with the influence of Machiavelli's "reason of state," as adapted by Puritan casuists from Perkins to Winthrop; and with the Protestant polemic against Rome, which demanded a literalistic reinterpretation of the past. As Thomas Fuller put it, "a little skill in Antiquity inclines a man to Popery; but depth in that study brings him about again to our religion" (*The Holy and the Profane State* [1642], ed. Maximilian Graff Walten, 2 vols. [New York, 1938], II, 69). For these and similar reasons, Protestants and humanists joined forces in their assault on medieval hagiography. The Reformers' secular bias expressed itself in their concern with experience, utility, and psychology. So, too, the humanists regarded man in a wholly historical continuum. Renouncing scholastic allegory, as did the Reformers, they advocated direct rational access to cultural expression and experience. Scholars have accordingly located the origins of modern English biography in the Renaissance. Most begin with humanist works, the sixteenth-century Lives by Thomas More, Richard Roper, and George Cavendish; others, with the Reformed biographies of the next century: Francis Bacon's political study of Henry VII (1622), the incisive portraits of contemporaries by Izaak Walton (1640), or John Dryden's Life of Plutarch (1683), which sanctioned the use of informal biographical material.

Whatever their precise beginnings, clearly the methods of what we call modern biography inform Mather's Lives.

4 Mather, *Magnalia*, I, 27–30, 31 (quoting Queen Mary), 41, 228, 603.

5 When, for example, the Renaissance biographer turned to Suetonius, Tacitus, and Plutarch, he did so believing that they regarded their subjects less as individuals than as character types, intended to inspire us to a zealous imitation. If the humanists denounced homiletic and legendary patterns, they sought to inculcate proper standards of behavior. The Reformers' antipathy to the Saints' Lives did not prevent them from adapting the old methods to their own needs, and through the sixteenth and seventeenth centuries they issued innumerable ecclesiastical biographies, tales of Protestant martyrs, and popular renderings of biblical heroes, all of these genres relevant in some degree to the Life of Winthrop. The Augustans who proposed writing the Lives of private men did so in the conviction that men equal to ourselves more naturally serve as models for behavior; even as they complained of the mist of panegyric that clouded the former age, hiding the man in order to set forth a hero, they insisted that biographers ought to take strong ethical positions.

6 See Martin R. P. McGuire, Introduction to Saint Ambrose, *Theodosius* (395), in *Funeral Orations by St. Gregory Nazianzus and Saint Ambrose*, trans. Leo P. McCauley [and others] (New York, 1953), p. 305, and Saint Ambrose, *Valentinian* (392), in *Funeral Orations*, p. 273. For Mather's allusions to Gregory Nazianzus, see *Magnalia*, I, 528, and II, 36, 121, and Cotton Mather, *Manuductio Ad Ministerium: Directions for a Candidate of the Ministry* (Boston, 1726), p. 36. A number of the *Magnalia*'s biographies, like the Life of John Baily, are funeral orations adjusted to suit the work's overall design, and accordingly they have their place in a tradition that runs from the Church Fathers through Andreas Hyperius, whose *Practis of Preaching* (London, 1577) instructs the eulogist to make the departed an example of how a believer may work in his social calling for God's glory.

7 Job 29 : 13–14: "I put on righteousness and it clothed me: my judgment was as a robe and a diadem." The traditional application of this text to the Good Magistrate dates back to medieval times—e.g., John of Salisbury, *Policratus* (1159), ed. John Dickinson (New York, 1963), p. 86—but it was redefined after the Reformation to accommodate the tenets of Protestant theocracy.

8 Gerald R. Owst, *Literature and Pulpit in Medieval England* (Cambridge, 1933), pp. 123, 154–56.

9 Valentinian, for example, who Ambrose tells us was crucified precisely in the manner of Jesus (*Funeral Orations*, pp. 280, 291); or Polycarp, whose "every step" retraced the road to Golgotha (*The Golden Legend, or Lives of the Saints as Englished by William Caxton* [1493], ed. F. S. Ellis, 7 vols. [London, 1900], I, 146–49). For the miracles noted below, see for example: II, 131 (Ste. Agatha); VI, 22 (St. Landry); VI, 34 (St. Edward); II, 209 (St. Paul the Hermit); VI, 164 (St. Clair); V, 24–25 (St. Bernard); VI, 139 (St. Leonard); VI, 71 (Ste. Margaret); VI, 155 (St. Martin). There are of course many similar miracles, such as the blood transformed to milk (IV, 97), and the miracle worked with the swine (III, 28).

10 The impress of this form on Catholic hagiography reaches well beyond the

medieval period. For our present purpose it will suffice to mention Motolinía's Life of Martín de Valencia, first governor of San Gabriel. As a governor, Father Martín resembles Winthrop in his humility, justice, and charity; and like Mather, Motolinía expands the *exemplum* by scriptural allusion (the hero sets out with twelve disciples to convert the natives; near death, he exclaims "It is finished now"; and so on). But these parallels are not intrinsic to the structure of the Life; they are ornamental, presented as it were in passing, or at most auxiliary to the model of sainthood. Motolinía is not the best writer of his kind; other Catholic hagiographers are more artful in integrating broad scriptural themes. Still, his Life reveals an important fact about the genre. The basic element in the model of holiness, the actual proof of sainthood, consists in Martín's Christ-like miracles: he "raised to life a dead person who had been commended to him; . . . he cured a sick woman who had devoutly prayed to him; . . . he freed a friar from a serious temptation that afflicted him. Many other things of this kind are related . . . wherefore," Motolinía concludes, "I pray to him to invoke his aid and intercession." Toribio de Motolinía, "Life of Martín de Valencia," [ca. 1531], in *History of the Indians of New Spain*, ed. and trans. Francis Borgia Stock [Washington, D.C., 1951], pp. 241–42.

11 John M. Headley, *Luther's View of Church History* (New Haven, 1963), pp. 24, 47, 49–50.

12 John Norton, *Abel being Dead yet speaketh; or, the Life & Death of . . . John Cotton* (London, 1658), p. 5.

13 *The Ancient Bounds* (1645), quoted in Arthur S. P. Woodhouse, *Puritanism and Liberty: Being the Army Debates, 1647–9* (London, 1938), p. 40.

14 John Donne, *Sermons*, ed. George R. Potter and Evelyn Simpson, 10 vols. (Berkeley, 1953–62), VII, 403; IX, 64–66; II, 122.

15 Erasmus and Luther, quoted in Douglas Bush, *The Renaissance and English Humanism* (Toronto, 1939), pp. 67–68.

16 Montaigne, "Of Experience," in *Selected Essays*, ed. Blanchard Bates (New York, 1949), p. 602. Montaigne's essays in self-examination invert every tenet of the Reformed microchristus. His concern with experience follows from his aversion to absolutes. He concentrates on the inner life in order to separate heaven from earth: introspection, he writes, yields "matter of opinion, not matter of faith; what I reason out according to me, not what I believe according to God"; "I live but to my self: there end all my designs." Most important, he presents the self as microcosm in order to explode didactic abstractions. "Each man bears the entire form of man's estate" because each is partial, unpredictable, limited by variant social necessities, defined by particular and unrepeatable responses (Montaigne, quoted in Rosalie L. Colie, *Paradoxia Epidemica: The Renaissance Tradition of Paradox* [Princeton, 1966], p. 375, and in James Olney, *Metaphors of Self: The Meaning of Autobiography* [Princeton, 1972], pp. 64, 86). Needless to say, Montaigne has no intention of subverting faith. In fact, his concept of selfhood, whatever its effects on subsequent writers, seems by design to reflect the dichotomy between the common human life and the saint's life, as this is implicit in *The Golden Legend*

and manifested in the Catholics' dual biographical tradition of hagiography and secular memoir.

17 Charles Trinkaus, *In Our Image and Likeness: Humanity and Divinity in Italian Humanist Thought*, 2 vols. (Chicago, 1970), I, xiv, xx–xxiii, 37, 51, 63, 95, 105, 150, 175, 247, 252–53, 301, 320; II, 482, 489, 509.

18 Arthur Dent, *Plain Man's Pathway* (1601), in *English Puritanism from John Hooper to John Milton*, ed. Everett Emerson (Durham, N.C., 1968), p. 168; Charles Chauncy, *Plain Doctrine* . . . (London, 1659), p. 75; Henry Smith, *The Trumpet of the Soul* . . . (London, 1591), sigs. A2 recto–B2 verso. Perhaps the proper spokesman for this occasion is the Digger Gerrard Winstanley, whom scholars have acclaimed the Puritan champion of natural rights: "There are onely two roots from whence . . . [all] differences spring up, that is, either from the Spirit . . . or from humane flesh [which] . . . jeeres and ejects the spirit. . . . *Adam* hath beene very fruitfull; he hath filled the earth with himself, and covered all with his darknesse, . . . corrupting the creation more and more, . . . [and driving] mankinde . . . to wonder after the beast, which is no other but self, or . . . every thing whereupon self is stamped. . . . Who was it that put the Son of Man to Death? . . . Surely that . . . self-satisfying glory . . . [which] shall become your hell-torment" (*Works*, ed. George H. Sabine [Ithaca, 1941], pp. 99, 118, 158–59, 174, 223, 81–82, 95, 489).

19 Owen C. Watkins, *The Puritan Experience: Studies in Spiritual Autobiography* (New York, 1972), pp. 40, 164, 238.

20 The Catholic devotion exerted considerable influence (through both Luther and Calvin) upon a wide range of Protestant thought; and the Protestants in turn influenced Catholic devotion. The distinctive impress of the concepts of *exemplum fidei* and *sola fides* may be seen in the totalistic nature of Reformed biography and autobiography, in contrast to the dual tradition, sacred and secular, of Catholic personal literature. Roy Pascal has argued that life in the Middle Ages was too violent and unpredictable to yield a meaningful coherence (*Design and Truth in Autobiography* [London, 1960], pp. 25, 36). But surely life was just as chaotic in Reformation Europe or Renaissance England—or, for that matter, during the period that Augustine wrote his *Confessions*. Paul Lehmann and Arthur M. Clark, discussing the neglect of the *Confessions* as autobiography in medieval self-portraits (despite the general popularity of the work), note that these self-portraits are interesting as cultural and historical documents, but not as spiritual self-examinations ("Autobiographies of the Middle Ages," *Royal Historical Society Transactions*, 5th ser. 3 [1953], 43–51; *Autobiography: Its Genesis and Phases* [London, 1935], p. 30). Nonetheless, medieval autobiographies are generally more informative and far more individuated than their Reformed counterparts. The Catholic view, from (say) Abélard through Newman, regarded hagiography as official dogma and doctrine, and personal literature as a mode of secular expression, fusing *vita* and *gesta*. From this perspective, the humanist autobiographies of Petrarch, Cardano, and Montaigne have their precedents in medieval writings (St. Patrick, Guibert of Nogent, Ratherius of Liége, Otloh of St. Emmeram, Gerald of Wales, Margery Kempe); they lead forward to

Rousseau's *Confessions*, with its aggressive subjectivity ("If I am not better, at least I am different"), and its presumption of establishing identity through a "process of fragmentation" and self-conscious "antagonism to the reader" (Christie Vance, "Rousseau's Autobiographical Venture: A Process of Negation," *Genre* 6 [1973], 99, 102, 107–09, 112).

21 Gordon S. Wakefield, *Puritan Devotion: Its Place in the Development of Christian Piety* (London, 1957), p. 160; Richard Baxter, *Reliquiae Baxterianae* (London, 1696), p. 26; William Dell, *Christ's Spirit*, quoted in Leo F. Solt, *Saints in Arms: Puritanism and Democracy in Cromwell's Army* (Stanford, 1959), p. 50; Richard Mather, *The Summe of Certain Sermons Vpon Genes: 15.6* (Cambridge, Mass., 1652), p. 23 (referring to 2 Cor. 3 : 18).

22 Calvin, quoted in T. F. Torrance, *Kingdom and Church: A Study in the Theology of the Reformation* (London, 1956), p. 5; Donne, *Sermons*, V, 153–60; Joseph Bellamy, *True Religion Delineated* (1750), in *The Great Awakening: Documents on the Revival of Religion, 1740–1745*, ed. Richard L. Bushman (New York, 1970), pp. 153, 144–45; Gregory of Nyssa, quoted in J. T. Muckle, "The Doctrine of St. Gregory of Nyssa on Man as the Image of God," *Medieval Studies* 7 (1945), 75–76.

23 Edward Taylor, quoted in Norman S. Grabo, *Edward Taylor* (New Haven, 1961), p. 53; Thomas Goodwin, *The Glories of Christ* . . . (Plymouth, 1818), p. 239; William Perkins, *The Combat of Christ and the Devil* (Cambridge, 1605), pp. 569–70, and *A Garden of Spiritual Flowers* (London, 1609), pp. C–D; John Bunyan, *Doctrine of Law and Grace* (London, 1659), fols. A5 verso–A6 recto; Taylor, Med. I:45, II:18, I:47, in *The Poems of Edward Taylor*, ed. Donald E. Stanford (New Haven, 1960), pp. 73, 111, 76; Dell, *Right Reformation*, quoted in Solt, *Saints in Arms*, p. 33.

24 John Robinson, *Essays* . . . , in *Works*, ed. Robert Ashton, 3 vols. (London, 1851), I, 91.

25 Taylor, quoted in Bert C. Bach, "Self-Depreciation in Edward Taylor's Sacramental Meditations," *Cithara* 6 (1966), 53; Richard Hooker, *A Learned Discourse of Justification* . . . (Oxford, 1612), pp. 4–7; Taylor, Med. II:77, I:46, in *Poems*, pp. 223, 75.

26 M. van Beek, *An Enquiry into Puritan Vocabulary* (Gröningen, 1969), p. 8; Augustine, *City of God*, quoted in C. A. Patrides, *The Grand Design of God: The Literary Form of the Christian View of History* (London, 1972), p. 17; John Preston, *The New Covenant* . . . (London, 1630), pp. 181–82; Richard Sibbes, *The Bruised Reed* . . . (London, 1635), p. 10; Thomas Hooker, *The Application of Redemption* . . . (London, 1656), IX, 51–52; Thomas Hooker, *The Christians Two Chiefe Lessons, viz. Selfe-Deniall and Selfe-Tryall* (London, 1640); Richard Baxter, *The Mischiefs of Selfe-Ignorance and the Benefits of Selfe-Acquaintance*, and *Christian Directory*, in *Practical Works*, ed. William Orme, 23 vols. (London, 1830), XI, 80, 136, 226; VI, 422–26.

27 William Haller, *The Rise of Puritanism* (New York, 1957), pp. 4–5; Thomas Hooker, *Heautonaparnumenos: Or a Treatise of Self-Denyall* (London, 1646), p. 26; Martin Luther, *A Commentarie on St. Paul's Epistle to the Galathians* (London, 1603), fol. 82 recto; Richard Sibbes, *Yea and Amen* . . . (London, 1638), p. 92; John Prime, *A Fruitefull and Brief Discourse* . . . (London, 1583), p. 93.

28 Karl Waentig, *Die Self-Komposita der Puritanersprache* (Leipzig, 1932), pp. 14, 65, 81, 97, 107, 115; Hooker, *Christians Two Chiefe Lessons*, pp. 37, 47; Thomas Adams, *The Deuills Banket* . . . (London, 1614), p. 197; Bellamy, *True Religion Delineated*, in *Great Awakening*, p. 150; William Bradford, quoted in Jesper Rosenmeier, " 'With My Owne Eyes': William Bradford's *Of Plymouth Plantation*," in *Typology and Early American Literature*, ed. Sacvan Bercovitch (Amherst, 1972), p. 78; Hooker, *Heautonaparnumenos*, pp. 22, 24–25; Henry More, *The Life of the Soul*, in *Complete Poems*, ed. Alexander B. Grosart (Edinburgh, 1878), pp. xvi, 148; Thomas Shepard, *The Parable of the Ten Virgins* . . . (London, 1659), part II, p. 149; Jacob Boehme, *The Way to Christ Discovered* . . . (London, 1648), pp. 21, 57.

29 George Goodwin, *Auto-Machia*, trans. J[oshua] S[ylvester] (London, 1607), no pagination. The popularity of Goodwin's poem is attested to throughout the literature—e.g., in Roger Brearley's "Self Civil War": "Unto myself I do myself betray, . . . I cannot live, with nor without myself." (*A Bundle of Soul Convincing . . . and Comforting Truths* [London, 1677], p. 94).

30 Louis L. Martz, *The Poetry of Meditation: A Study in English Religious Literature of the Seventeenth Century* (New Haven, 1962), pp. 321, 330; Taylor, Med. II:13, I:22, in *Poems*, pp. 102, 37; Karl Keller, "The Example of Edward Taylor," in *The American Puritan Imagination: Essays in Revaluation*, ed. Sacvan Bercovitch (New York, 1974), pp. 134–35. The theme of poetic unfulfillment runs throughout Taylor's poetry—"ragged" metaphors (I:22), sins as black as ink (II:6), "jarring Pen" (II:132), "padlockt" lips (I:17), "Pensill . . . / Broke, marred, spoil'd, undone, Defild" (I:30).

31 Thomas Shepard, *The Sound Believer* . . . (1670), in *Works*, ed. Edward Albro, 3 vols. (1853; reprint ed., New York, 1967), I, 181, and *Parable of Ten Virgins*, part II, p. 65; William Ames, *Cases of Conscience*, quoted in Keith L. Sprunger, *The Learned Doctor William Ames: Dutch Backgrounds of English and American Puritanism* (Urbana, Ill., 1972), p. 169.

32 George Fox, *Journal*, ed. John L. Nickall (Cambridge, 1952), p. 25; John Winthrop, "Christian Experience," in *Winthrop Papers* . . . , 5 vols. (Boston, 1929–47), I, 157–60; Jonathan Edwards, "Diary," in *The Works of President Edwards*, Worcester edition, 4 vols. (New York, [1849]), I, 202; ellipses deleted in all three quotations.

33 Thomas Hooker, *The Poor Doubting Christian* . . . , 5th ed. (London, 1638), p. 34.

34 It may help illuminate this tortuous dialectic to consider a non-Christian mode of the conversion narrative. A convenient example is the story of Te-ch'ing, the seventeenth-century Buddhist monk who changed the form of Chinese spiritual autobiography, amidst conditions strikingly similar to those of Puritan England (political turmoil, disruptive economic mobility, and a growing sense of individualism). Previously, the standard Chinese Buddhist form of autobiography was a chronological succession of discrete facts, rather like medieval European personal literature; the autobiography of Te-ch'ing began a widespread effort to review one's life in terms of fixed doctrine and exemplary patterns. In Te-ch'ing's case, as in the Puritan's, the pattern sets

out the road to self-transcendence. The Buddhist hears of the monk's way of life and decides to dedicate himself to it; he then receives instructions, perceives the spiritual order in a dream vision, becomes confident of his calling, and undertakes a series of contemplations through which he gradually achieves perfection. But nowhere is there a sign of inner conflict; nowhere does Te-ch'ing record the struggle with an opposing self. He seems to dissolve into the All virtually without the aid of will. As an initiate, of course, he has his difficulties, but these concern the mastery of a discipline, not (to recall a favorite Puritan analogue) the grim encounter in the night between Jacob and the angel: not the battle to the death which issues in the believer's rebirth, only to remind him of the greater battles to come. For Te-ch'ing the transcendent and the private state exist peacefully side by side. Since they are mutually exclusive, they pose no threat to one another. Once he has transcended the private state, he can regard the present objectively, wistfully recall his past, bemusedly and even indulgently analyze his secular concerns and prospects. The Buddhist could enjoy both worlds—of the self and of eternity—because he could have them separately. The Puritan was held accountable for both worlds at once, and then instructed to despise the one and to feel inadequate for the other. (I am indebted here to two still unpublished essays by Pei-yi Wu, "The Spiritual Autobiography of Te-ch'ing," and "Self-Eulogy: An Autobiographical Mode in Traditional Chinese Literature".)

35 I do not mean, of course, to gloss over the differences between biography and autobiography, or between autobiography and journal. One clue to these differences lies in the relation between rhetoric and action. Bunyan's *Pilgrim's Progress* renders one a function of the other; his *Grace Abounding* works through a sustained tension between the two. In effect, the autobiography posits two modes of identity, corresponding to the flesh and to the promise. The way of the flesh pertains to Bunyan as microcosm. It circles from self to Satan, and issues in the spiritual paralysis of self-acceptance. Its action is not-striving, resigning oneself to what one is. The other mode of identity, the way of the promise, pertains to Bunyan as microchristus. Ascending from self-conscious-ness to self-denial, it opens a process of striving which recalls Bunyan all the more forcefully to what he *is*, by affirming, rhetorically, what he *may* become.

36 Norton, *Abel being Dead*, p. 5; Isaac Barrow, "Imitators of Christ" (Sermon XXXIV), in *Works*, ed. James Hamilton, 3 vols. (New York, 1830), II, 338–39.

37 Edward Taylor, *Christographia*, ed. Norman S. Grabo (New Haven, 1962), p. 34.

38 Abiezer Coppe, *A Fiery Flying Roll* . . . ([London], 1649), pp. 1–2; William Erbery, *Nor Truth nor Error* . . . (London, 1646), p. 2; Roger Williams, *Complete Writings*, 7 vols. (New York, 1963), V, 72.

39 John Cotton, *A Treatise of* . . . *Faith* . . . (London, 1713), p. 16; Isaac Barrow, "Imitators of Christ," in *Works*, I, 397; Gerd Birkner, *Heilsgewissheit und Literatur: Metaphor, Allegorie und Autobiographie im Puritanismus* (Munich, 1972), pp. 6, 11. In Puritan New England, the extremes are most amply expressed,

though always within orthodox boundaries, by Edward Taylor, who vacillates between utter self-deprecation and a "theantropism" that some critics have found nearly heretical. This vacillation remains part of the Puritan legacy to our literature, through *Moby-Dick*. Its roots may be seen in Baxter's warning (*Works*, XI, 58) that "To be a natural individual person distinct from God our Creator, is . . . the state, we were created in; and therefore no man must under pretence of self-denial either destroy himself or yet with some heretics aspire to be essentially and personally one with God, so that their individual personality should be drowned in him as a drop is in the ocean."

40   Birkner, *Heilsgewissheit*, p. 39; Barrow, "Imitators of Christ," in *Works*, I, 398; Cotton, *Treatise of Faith*, p. 16.

41   Norton, *Abel being Dead*, p. 4.

42   Samuel Fisher, *The Testimony of Truth* . . . (London, 1679), pp. 440–41; Perry Miller, *The New England Mind: The Seventeenth Century* (Boston, 1961), p. 475. To take the long view, the fruits of *sola scriptura* may be seen in the writings of those Romantics who, liberated from the restrictions of theology, felt free to judge the holiness of the Bible by the degree to which the Bible coincided with their beliefs, or *(mutatis mutandis)* to invert the Bible's meanings, proposing Cain as our model of identity, Ishmael as a figure of the redeemed. Indeed, it is revealing of this movement that Melville's concept of Ishmael in *Moby-Dick* echoes Luther's eccentric view of Ishmael as a type of the redeemed.

43   Richard Baxter, *The Saints Everlasting Rest* (London, 1650), part III, p. 137; Robert Barclay, quoted in Howard H. Brinton, "Stages in Spiritual Development as Recorded in Quaker Journals," in *Children of Light: In Honor of Rufus M. Jones*, ed. Brinton (New York, 1938), p. 389.

44   Thomas Shepard, *The Sincere Convert* . . . (London, 1669), p. 91; John Donne, *Devotions upon Emergent Occasions* . . . (London, 1624), pp. 479–81; Adams, *Deuills Banket*, pp. 214–16; Mather, *Magnalia*, I, 30. According to Thomas Hooker (*Application of Redemption*, IX, 205), "Words must be judged acceptable, not by the . . . humors of men, but from the warrant they have from the scripture." Yet scripture gave ample warrant for "figurate speech" and "metaphors, a form of speech [of] which the Holy Ghost makes frequent use" (John Bale, *The Image of Both Churches* . . . , in *Select Works*, ed. Henry Christmas [Cambridge, 1849], p. 261; Samuel Willard, *The Heart Garrisoned* . . . [Cambridge, Mass., 1676] pp. 8–9). Thus the *Magnalia* recommends Nathaniel Rogers as a " 'fisher of men' who came with a *silken line*, and a *golden hook;* . . . an Apollo, who had his *harp* and his *arrows;* and the arrows his charming and piercing eloquence" (I, 417); and John Sherman for his "easie fluencie bespangled with such glittering figures of oratory, as caused his ablest hearers to call him a second Isaiah, the *honey-dropping* and *golden-mouthed* preacher" (I, 516). The stylistic comments that introduce the Bay Psalm Book are not particularly Puritan; the Anglican Augustan Sir John Denham voices virtually the same strictures in his preface to *A Version of the Psalms of David* (London, 1714), p. xiv.

45   Hooker, *Application of Redemption*, X, 205–21; John Milton, *De Doctrina Christiana* in *Complete Poems and Major Prose*, ed. Merritt Y. Hughes (New York, 1957), p. 905.

46   John Bunyan, "The Author's Apology for his Book," in *The Pilgrim's Progress*,
     ed. James B. Wharey, 2nd ed. revised by Roger Sharrock (Oxford, 1960), pp.
     5–7. Baxter's *Saints Everlasting Rest* characterizes the Puritan view of the
     relationship between scripture and conscience: "Soliloquy is Preaching to
     one's self. . . . Therefore, the very same *Method* which a Minister should use in
     Preaching to others, should a *Christian* use in speaking to himself" (pp. 209,
     213). In William Ames's view, the answer to the question "How can I be
     faithful?" lay in the fact that the chasm between " 'I' and 'faithful' could be
     bridged by the arguments or middle terms of Scripture" (John D. Eusden,
     Introduction to Ames, *The Marrow of Theology*, trans. Eusden [Philadelphia,
     1968], p. 50).

47   Hooker, *Application of Redemption*, IX, 5–7.

48   Fuller, *Holy and Profane State*, II, 91; Theodore Beza, "Discours . . . sur la vie
     et la mort de Maitre Jean Calvin" (1549), in Jean Calvin, *Avertissement Contre
     l'Astrologie* . . . , ed. A. Angliviel (Paris, 1962), p. 101. In his biography of his
     grandfather, Richard, Mather tells us he is following the example of Beza's
     Life of Calvin (*Magnalia*, I, 456), and in effect he recapitulates the deathbed
     scene of "Nehemias Americanus" in his Life of his father, Increase (*Parenta-
     tor* . . . [Boston, 1724], pp. 207–08).

49   Cotton Mather, *Christianity to the Life: Our Imitation of Our Saviour* . . . (Boston,
     1702), p. 17; Cotton Mather, *Diary*, ed. Worthington C. Ford, *Massachusetts
     Historical Society Collections*, 7th ser. 7 (Boston, 1911), 515, 562, 582–83; Cotton
     Mather, Introduction to *Parentator*, p. ii. Mather may have had the edition of
     Kempis's *De Imitatio Christi* published in Antwerp, 1647. Its central postulate is
     a main theme of both Catholic and Reformed devotional literature: *"Qui
     antem vult plenè & sapidè Christi verbi intelligere; opartet, vt totam vitam suam ulii studeat
     conformare"* (p. 2). Kempis's work was published at Cambridge, Mass., in 1667.
     It was suppressed by the authorities, but its publication, and Mather's
     advocacy, remain significant facts. There were many translations and
     paraphrases of *De Imitatione Christi* in English by 1700: e.g., *The Following of
     Christ* . . . (1685 and 1686); *The Christian Pattern* . . . (1684 and 1697); *The
     Christian's Pattern* . . . (1699); and *Christ the Perfect Pattern* . . . (1658).

CHAPTER 2

1   Rosemond Tuve, *A Reading of George Herbert* (Chicago, 1952), p. 113. The
     scriptural warrant for the connection between *figura* or *typos* and *exemplum* may
     be found in many passages in the gospels (both in the Geneva and the King
     James Bible); e.g.: 1 Cor. 10 : 6, 11; 1 Pet. 5 : 3; Phil. 3 : 17; 1 Thess. 1 : 7; 2
     Thess. 3 : 9; 1 Tim. 4 : 12; Titus 2 : 7. Thomas Wilson's *Christian Directory* . . .
     (London, 1611), a representative Reformed work of the time, defines "type" as
     a primary meaning of "example" (p. 4). From this perspective, one aspect of
     Mather's use of typology is his frequent comparison of biography to the fine
     arts—painting, sculpture, sketching, etc.—as a way of suggesting his heroes'
     likeness to Christ. Such comparisons are traditionally figural, from the

Church Fathers to the Renaissance. Thus Athenagoras, Scalinger, and Melito liken the *figura* to the *modellum*, the architect's or sculptor's scale-models; Origen to a statue approximating the divine image; and Benjamin Keach to a charcoal sketch that "rudely adumbrates" the perfect portrait of Jesus (*Tropologia. A Key to Open Scripture Metaphors*, 2 vols. [London, 1682], I, 227). Mather cites all of these patristic and Renaissance sources. They lend special significance to what otherwise seems a Renaissance commonplace, his own favorite analogy to the sculptor's "lasting monument" to Christ's glory.

2   John Colgan, *Triadis Thaumaturgae Seu Diuorum Patricii, Columbae, et Brigidae* . . . *Acta* (Louvain, 1647), p. 168.

3   Donne, *Sermons*, II, 308, 74 (my italics); Thomas Browne, *Religio Medici* (1642), ed. Jean-Jacques Denonain (Cambridge, 1953), p. 86.

4   John Beadle, *Journal or Diary of a Thankful Christian* (London, 1656), pp. 59–60.

5   Augustine, *The City of God*, trans. Marcus Dods (New York, 1950), p. 151; Baldwin, *Mirror for Magistrates*, quoted in Henry Ansgar Kelly, *Divine Providence in the England of Shakespeare's Histories* (Cambridge, Mass., 1970), pp. 163–64.

6   Sidney, quoted in O. B. Hardison, Jr., *The Enduring Monument: A Study of the Idea of Praise in Renaissance Literary Theory and Practice* (Chapel Hill, N.C., 1962), p. 58; Luther and Ralegh, quoted in Patrides, *Grand Design*, pp. 48, 90.

7   John Calvin, *Commentaries on the Prophet Jeremiah* . . . ed. John Owen, 5 vols. (Grand Rapids, Mich., 1950), III, 141; Samuel Danforth, *An Exhortation to All* . . . (1714) in *The Wall and the Garden: Selected Massachusetts Election Sermons 1670–1775*, ed. A. William Plumstead (Minneapolis, 1968), p. 154 (reference is to Hos. 11 : 1); Milton, *Paradise Lost*, XII, 554–55, in *Complete Poems*, pp. 466–67.

8   William Ames, quoted in David D. Hall, *The Faithful Shepherd: A History of the New England Ministry in the Seventeenth Century* (Chapel Hill, N.C., 1972), p. 58; Bacon, quoted in Michael Fixler, *Milton and the Kingdoms of God* (Evanston, Ill., 1964), p. 65; Edwards, quoted in Patrides, *Grand Design*, p. 119; Samuel Torrey, *An Exhortation Unto Reformation* . . . (Cambridge, Mass., 1674), p. 1.

9   Augustine, *City of God*, pp. 10–11, 166.

10 William Bradford, *Of Plymouth Plantation, 1620–1647*, ed. Samuel Eliot Morison (New York, 1952), pp. 52, 61–62.

11 David Levin, "William Bradford: The Value of Puritan Historiography," in *Major Writers of Early American Literature*, ed. Everett Emerson (Madison, Wisc., 1972), pp. 11–30; Bradford, *Of Plymouth Plantation*, pp. 329, 334, 347, 351–52.

12 Jonathan Mitchel, *Nehemiah on the Wall* . . . (Cambridge, Mass., 1671), pp. 7–8, 31; Increase Mather, Preface to Samuel Torrey, *A Plea for the Life of Dying Religion* . . . (Boston, 1683), sig. A4 verso. Regarding the shield as figural emblem, see Richard Reinitz, "Symbolism and Freedom: The Use of Biblical Typology as an Argument for Religious Toleration in Seventeenth Century England and America" (Ph.D. diss., University of Rochester, 1967), p. 128 (citing Ainsworth).

13 Ernst H. Kantorowicz, *The King's Two Bodies: A Study in Mediaeval Political Theology* (Princeton, 1957), pp. 46–47. "Not all the water in the rough rude sea," says Shakespeare's Richard II, "Can wash the balm off from an anointed

king; / The breath of worldly men cannot depose / The deputy elected by the Lord" (III.ii.54–57). The eulogies to Elizabeth depict the Queen as a *figura Christi*—another Moses, Deborah, Judith, Samson, David—and post-Elizabethan England as desecrated Jerusalem, an Eden-Canaan turned wilderness (Barbara K. Lewalski, *Donne's "Anniversaries" and the Poetry of Praise: The Creation of a Symbolic Mode* [Princeton, 1973], p. 21).

14   Edward Taylor, in Donald E. Stanford, "Edward Taylor's Metrical History," *American Literature* 33 (1961–62), 290.

15   Mather, *Magnalia*, I, 46; John Higginson, "Attestation," in Mather, *Magnalia*, I, 13–16.

16   Edward Johnson, *Wonder-Working Providence* . . . , ed. J. Franklin Jameson (New York, 1910), pp. 145, 148, 238; Thomas Shepard and James Allin, Preface to *A Defence of the Answer* . . . (London, 1648); John Cotton, *A Brief Exposition of . . . Canticles* . . . (London, 1648), p. 9; George Moxon, in Leo M. Kaiser, "Three Hymns Attributed to George Moxon," *Early American Literature* 8 (1973), pp. 104–09.

17   Increase Mather, *The Day of Trouble is Near* . . . (Cambridge, Mass., 1674), p. 18; I. Mather, Preface to Torrey, *Exhortation*, sig. A2 recto; Increase Mather, *The Times of Men* . . . (Boston, 1675), p. 16; Increase Mather, *The Greatest Sinners Exhorted* . . . (Boston, 1686), p. 115; Urian Oakes, *New-England Pleaded With* . . . (Cambridge, Mass., 1673), pp. 21, 40.

18   Cotton Mather, *Things to be Look'd for* . . . (Cambridge, Mass., 1691), pp. 35, 38; Cotton Mather, *The Wonderful Works of God* . . . (Boston, 1690), pp. 40–41; Mather, *Magnalia*, I, 25.

19   Increase Mather, *The Doctrine of Divine Providence* . . . (Boston, 1684), pp. 43, 37; Samuel Willard, *Useful Instructions* . . . (Cambridge, Mass., 1673), p. 15; Oakes, *New-England Pleaded With*, pp. 20, 23; I. Mather, *Doctrine*, pp. 43, 58; Winthrop, *Winthrop Papers*, II, 10; Oakes, *New-England Pleaded With*, p. 23; Cotton Mather, *A Pillar of Gratitude* . . . (Boston, 1700), p. 6; I. Mather, *Doctrine*, p. 58; John Winthrop, "Conclusions For the Plantation in New England" in *Old South Leaflets*, II (Boston, n.d.), no. 50, p. 9.

20   Edward Taylor, in Thomas M. and Virginia L. Davis, "Edward Taylor on the Day of Judgment," *American Literature* 43 (1972), 540; Increase Mather, *The Righteous Man* . . . (Boston, 1702), p. 49; I. Mather, *Times of Men*, p. 20.

21   I. Mather, *Times of Men*, p. 7, and *Day of Trouble*, pp. 4, 12–13, 26–28. Cotton Mather explains in *Wonders of the Invisible World* . . . (Boston, 1693)—part of which he incorporated into the *Magnalia* (II, 446–79)—that because "the Errand of our Fathers into these Ends of the Earth" fulfilled "the Promise of old," therefore "the Devil is making one attempt more upon us," "a thing, prodigious, beyond the Wonders of former Ages," a war "so *Critical*, that if we get well through, we shall soon Enjoy *Halcyon Days* with all the Vultures of Hell *Trodden under our Feet*." The conditional tense is no more an obstacle here than it is in the Life of Winthrop. In both cases, the prophetic sense of the Old Testament parallel renders the halcyon days a foregone conclusion. As in the biography, an American Job invites our sympathy—*"Have pity upon me, for the Wrath of the Devil has been turned upon me"*—in such a way as to make the remedy

manifest in the hero's plight. For New England as for Winthrop, Job's "Afflictive Disturbances" shadow forth the "Wonderful Methods and Mercies" that ensure the future of the American Jerusalem (Bercovitch, "Cotton Mather," in *Major Writers*, pp. 107–11). Mather stressed this outcome in an election-day sermon he preached during the same time period, with a characteristic application of scriptural text: "A Contrary and a Terrible Appearance of Things . . . is no . . . Sign that our Blessed *State of Peace*, is far Distant from us. . . . It is foretold . . . in Dan. 12.1. *There shall be a Time of Trouble . . . and at that Time thy People shall be Delivered*. So, then, the Blacker you see the *Troubles* of the Age to grow, the sooner and the surer may be the *Peace* which we are hoping for. . . . Pray then, let it not fright you to be in such a *Mount!* The Almighty God . . . [will] descend from Heaven to put a New, Joyful, Pleasant Face upon it all . . . Consider, Isai. 66. 7, 8 and Rev. 18.8, 10 . . . ! ["Who hath heard such a thing? who hath seen such things? Shall the earth be made to bring forth in one day? or shall a nation be born at once? for as soon as Zion travailed, she brought forth her children. . . . Alas, alas, that great city Babylon, that mighty city! for in one hour is thy judgment come."] " (*Things to be Look'd for*, p. 25).

22   Mather, *Magnalia*, II, 114, 116 (Oakes); I, 454–56 (Richard Mather); I, 341–42 (Hooker and Cotton); I, 482 (Parker); I, 144 (Hopkins); I, 479 (Fiske); I, 325 (Davenport); II, 149 (Shepard); I, 115 (Prince); I, 134–35 (Anne Bradstreet); I, 168, 183–84, 187, 202–03, 216 (Phips); I, 273, 276–80, and II, 39–41, 166 (the Mathers); I, 355 (Higginson); I, 463–65 (Chauncy); I, 498–501 (Cobbet). A very slight sampling of some of the other heroes embodied (in higher form) in the fathers of New England: (a) from pagan mythology: Hercules, Odin, and Apollo; (b) from the Bible: Abel, Aaron, Gideon, Luke, and Barnabas; (c) from early Christianity: Ambrose, Chrysostom, Theodosius, Boniface, Origen, Benedict, St. George, and Irenaeus; (d) from the ancient Greeks and Romans: Solon, Miltiades, Brutus and Caesar, Fabius and Hannibal, Tully, Aristides, Cato, and Cicero; (e) from modern times: Farel, Vivet, Boyle, Bucholtzer, and Copernicus; (f) "all" the rabbis that "had ever yet been in Europe" (I, 428).

23   Mather, *Magnalia*, I, 166, 375 (Phips); I, 273 (Cotton); I, 434 (Hooker); I, 528 (Eliot); I, 166 (Phips); I, 273 (Cotton); II, 114 (Oakes); I, 399 (Bulkeley); I, 108 (Bradford); I, 332 (Hooker); I, 479 (Fiske); I, 286 (Norton). In other characteristic openings, Mather speaks of the birth of Christ, contrasts the fall of Adam with Christ's calling of his disciples, notes the major developments from the days of Joshua through ancient Greece and Lacedomia to the present, and reviews the history of ecclesiastical biography, from Palladius to Fabius. Mather introduces the magistrates as men superior to "the greatest kings in the world" (I, 141), and his Life of each of them as a more "real and . . . faithful History" than Xenophon's, Curtius's, Virgil's, or Pliny's (I, 107). His preface to his Lives of the divines details the "many great men [who] . . . have successfully . . . shaken the kingdom of Anti-Christ" (I, 584).

24   Mather, *Magnalia*, I, 235, 107, 31, 27, 317.

25   Mather, *Magnalia*, I, 194.

26 Richard Mather, *An Apologie of the Churches in New England* . . . (London, 1643), pp. 1–3, 27, 31.

27 Increase Mather, *The Mystery of Israel's Salvation* . . . (London, 1669), p. ix; Winthrop, "Conclusions," p. 6; John Eliot, quoted in Samuel Sewall, *Phaenomena Quaedam Apocalyptica* . . . *Or, Some Few Lines Towards a Description of the New Heaven As It Makes to Those Who Stand Upon the New Earth* (Boston, 1697), p. 2. It has often been argued that Anglicans differed in their use of the *imitatio*, that they appealed to Christ's *agon*, allegorizing the Christian "I" as the embodiment of all souls, types, and ceremonies, whereas Puritans—committed as they were to history—preferred to identify with the drama of redemption. If so, the distinction confirms the Puritans' more militant espousal of Reformed soteriology.

28 Samuel Wakeman, *Sound Repentance* . . . (Boston, 1685), p. 18; Mather, *Magnalia*, I, 33; Nicholas Noyes, *New Englands Duty* . . . (Boston, 1698), pp. 43–45.

29 Mather, *Things to be Look'd for*, pp. 3, 34; John Eliot, "Letter . . . , 1664," in *New England Historical and Genealogical Register* 9 (1855), 131, and *The Christian Commonwealth* . . . (London, [1659]), sig. C1 recto; Anne Bradstreet, "Dialogue Between Old England and New," in *Works*, ed. Jeannine Hensley (Cambridge, Mass., 1967), pp. 185–88; Mukhtar Ali Isani, "Edward Taylor and the 'Turks'," *Early American Literature* 7 (1972), 121.

30 Higginson, "Attestation," in Mather, *Magnalia*, I, 16–17.

31 J. S., Preface to Mitchel's *Nehemiah on the Wall*, sigs. A2 recto–A2 verso.

32 Clement of Alexandria, *Stromata*, in *The Ante-Nicene Fathers* . . . , eds. Alexander Roberts and James Donaldson (New York, 1913), II, 305; Samuel Mather, *The Figures or Types of the Old Testament* . . . (Dublin, 1685), pp. 33, 86–87, 90; Mather, *Magnalia*, II, 578–79. Mather's use of this technique is explicit or implicit throughout the *Magnalia*. One more example must suffice: "There was a famous person in the days of Joshua, known by the name of Cadmus; who carried not only a *people*, but *letters* also, from Phoenitia into Boeotia. The Grecian fable of a *serpent*, in the story of Cadmus, was only derived from the name of an Hivite, which . . . signifies a *serpent*. . . . This renouned Cadmus was indeed a Gibeonite, who [was] . . . by Joshua . . . employed in the service of the true God. . . . Yea, when after ages, in their songs, praised Apollo for his victory over the dragon Pytho, they uttered but the disguised songs of Canaan, wherein this Cadmus had celebrated the praises of Joshua for his victory over the King of Bashan. . . . [Let this serve] as an *introduction* unto . . . New-English history; . . . when some ecclesiastical oppressions drove a colony of the truest Israelites into the remoter parts of the world . . . and our [Charles] Chauncy was the Cadmus . . . by whose vast labour and learning the knowledge of Jesus Christ . . . hath been conveyed unto posterity" (I, 463–64). Since Apollo is a type of the Son of Man, and Pytho of Satan, the "songs of Canaan," undisguised here by Mather, signify the cosmic nuptials for the Second Coming.

33 John Robinson, quoted in Rosenmeier, "William Bradford's *Of Plymouth*

Plantation," in *Typology and Early American Literature*, p. 92; Nathaniel Morton, *New Englands Memoriall* . . . , ed. Howard J. Hall (New York, 1937), p. 151, and "To the Christian Reader" (preface); Richard Montague, *The Acts and Monuments of the Church* . . . (London, 1642), p. 21.

34 In addition to Virgil, Mather compares himself as epic writer to Du Bartas, Blackmore, Milton, and Homer. One example among many of Mather's use of Virgil is his reference in the Life of Winthrop to the *Aeneid* 1. 142–43, which had standard associations (through medieval and Renaissance treatises on government) with Christ in his kingly or magisterial office. There are many studies of the exegetical adaptations of Virgil. The most exhaustive commentaries available to Mather were Bernard Silvestris, *Commentum* . . . *Eneidos Virgilii*, ed. Guilielmus Riedel (Gryphiswaldae, 1624), and Alexander Ross, *Virgilius Evangelisans* . . . (London, 1634), and *Mystagogus Poeticus* . . . *Explaining the Historical Mysteries* . . . *of the Ancient Greek and Latin Poets*, 6th ed. (London, 1675).

35 Donne, *Sermons*, VII, 51; Mather, *Things to be Look'd for*, p. 9; Increase Mather, *An Earnest Exhortation* . . . (Boston, 1676), p. 26; Cotton Mather, *The Serviceable Man* . . . (Boston, 1690), pp. 45–46; Thomas Shepard, *Eye-Salve, Or A Watch Word* . . . (Cambridge, Mass., 1673), p. 14; Eliphalet Adams, *The Necessity of Judgment* . . . (New London, Conn., 1710), p. 37.

36 Samuel Danforth, *A Brief Recognition of New Englands Errand into the Wilderness* (Cambridge, Mass., 1671), pp. 4–7; Thomas Shepard, Preface to Danforth, *Errand into the Wilderness*, sig. A2 verso; Martin Luther, *Confession Concerning Christ's Supper*, ed. Helmut T. Lehmann, in *Works*, ed. Jaroslav Pelikan et al., 55 vols. (Saint Louis, 1955–73), XXXVII, 262.

37 I. Mather, *Mystery of Israel's Salvation*, p. 102; Increase Mather, *A Discourse Concerning* . . . *the Glorious Kingdom* . . . (Boston, 1710), p. 29; Johnson, *Wonder-Working Providence*, p. 191, and quoted in Cecelia Tichi, "The Puritan Historians and Their New Jerusalem," *Early American Literature* 6 (1971), 147. Johnson's conflation of John the Baptist and John the Divine is characteristic of the Puritan outlook. Sometimes this is explicit, as in Mitchel's *Nehemiah on the Wall*, p. 9; more often the conflation is implicit, as in John Cotton's Preface to John Norton, *The Answer To* . . . *Apollonius* (1648), trans. Douglas Horton (Cambridge, Mass., 1958), p. 14: "John . . . was carried into the wilderness that he might see more clearly not only the judgment of the great whore but also the coming down from heaven of . . . New Jerusalem." Cotton is replying here to the charge that the New Englanders are a people cast into the "outer darkness."

38 Bercovitch, "Cotton Mather," in *Major Writers*, ed. Emerson, pp. 90–103.

39 John Winthrop, *Christian Charity*, in *Puritan Political Ideas, 1558–1794*, ed. Edmund S. Morgan (Indianapolis, 1965), p. 86; Oakes, *New-England Pleaded With*, pp. 1–3; Samuel Danforth, *The Building Up of Sion*, in *Bridgewater's Monitor* . . . (Boston, 1717), p. 2; Peter Bulkeley, *The Gospel-Covenant* . . . , 2nd ed. (London, 1651), p. 17; Johnson, *Wonder-Working Providence*, p. 52.

40 Mather, *Magnalia*, I, 27; Mather, quoted in Robert Middlekauff, *The Mathers: Three Generations of Puritan Intellectuals, 1596–1728* (New York, 1971), p. 337; Mather, *Magnalia*, II, 115.

41 Increase Mather, *A Discovrse Concerning the Danger of Apostasy* . . . (Boston, 1685), pp. 55–56; Cotton Mather, *A Companion for Communicants* . . . (Boston, 1690), dedication.

CHAPTER 3

1   John Foxe, *The Acts and Monuments of These Latter and Perillous Dayes, Touching Matters of the Church* . . . *Speciallye in this Realme of England* (1570 ed.), ed. S. R. Cattley, 8 vols. (London, 1837–41), I, xxv.
2   Foxe, quoted in William Haller, *Foxe's Book of Martyrs and the Elect Nation* (London, 1963), p. 250.
3   Martin Luther, "To the Burgomasters and Counsellors" (1525), quoted in John M. Headley, *Luther's View of Church History* (New Haven, 1963), p. 242; Haller, *Foxe's Book of Martyrs*, p. 107.
4   Foxe, *Acts and Monuments*, II, 806, 791.
5   Foxe, *Acts and Monuments*, II, 795–96 (my italics), 790, 792; VII, 252–55.
6   Foxe, *Acts and Monuments*, II, 797; IV, 132; II, 806, 26, 21.
7   Fuller, *Holy Profane State*, II, 66, 149, 258, 264; Izaak Walton, "The Life of Mr. George Herbert" (1670), in *English Biography in the Seventeenth Century*, ed. Vivian de Sola Pinto (London, 1951), p. 96; Thomas Fuller, *The Church History of Britain* . . ., ed. J. S. Brewer, 6 vols. (Oxford, 1845), I, 2; II, 6, 281; V, 244; VI, 346. In accordance with this tradition, Fuller constantly juxtaposes complex figuralism with a skeptical, sometimes ribald antiquarianism (e.g., I, 51–52, 83, 106, 111; II, 18, 66, 133; III, 61, 68, 83, 168).
8   Bale, quoted in Haller, *Foxe's Book of Martyrs*, pp. 70, 68; Bale, *Select Works*, pp. 5–8, 55, 100, 144, 243. Bale's attack centered on Polydore Vergil, the Italian secular priest who at the request of Henry VII undertook what became the first large-scale formulation of the "Tudor myth" of English history.
9   John Knox, *The History of the Reformation in Scotland* (1586–87), ed. William Croft Dickinson, 2 vols. (New York, 1950), I, 6; II, 6.
10 John Aylmer's famous remark that "God is English" is a marginal gloss to a text which urges the British to "fight not only in the quarel of [their] country: but also and chieflye in defence of . . . true religion"; John Lyly's belief that "The lyuing God is onely the English God" pertains to the defeat of the papal powers in England, and the country's just reward of "blessed peace" and a "happy prince" (William Haller, "John Foxe and the Puritan Revolution," in *The Seventeenth Century: Studies in the History of English Thought and Literature from Bacon to Pope* [Stanford, 1951; festschrift for Richard Foster Jones], p. 209).
11 Edmund Calamy, *The Great Danger of Covenant-refusing* . . . (London, 1646), pp. 1, 8, 11, 18; Greenham, quoted in Jens G. Møller, "The Beginnings of Puritan Covenant Theology," *Journal of Ecclesiastical History* 13–14 (1962–63), 65; Perry Miller, "Solomon Stoddard, 1643–1729," *Harvard Theological Review* 34 (1941), 286–88; Middlekauff, *The Mathers*, pp. 107–08, 116; Owen, quoted in Richard L. Greaves, "John Bunyan and Covenant Thought in the Seventeenth Century," *Church History* 36 (1967), 158–59, 162.
12 Charles S. McCoy, "Johannes Cocceius: Federal Theologian," *Scottish Journal of Theology* 16 (1963), 362–63.

13 Edmund Calamy, *England's Looking-Glasse* . . . (London, [1642?]), Prefatory Epistle and p. 22.

14 George Petter, *A Learned . . . Commentary upon . . . St. Mark . . .* , 2 vols. (London, 1661), II, 1077.

15 John Frederick Wilson, *Pulpit in Parliament: Puritanism during the English Civil Wars, 1640–1648* (Princeton, 1969).

16 John Milton, *History of Britain*, in *Complete Prose Works*, vol. 5, ed. French R. Fogle (New Haven, 1971), p. 129; Milton, quoted in Fixler, *Milton and the Kingdoms of God*, p. 217.

17 Richard Overton, *An Arrow Against All Tyrants* . . . (London, 1646), pp. 3–4.

18 Edward Stillingfleet, *Origines Britannicae* . . . (1685), ed. Thomas P. Pantin, 2 vols. (Oxford, 1842), I, xxxiii–xxxiv.

19 Samuel Crossman, *The Young Man's Calling* . . . (London, 1685), pp. 63–64; Thomas Gouge, *The Young Man's Guide Through the Wilderness of this World, to the Heavenly Canaan* . . . (London, 1670); John Owen, *Works*, ed. William H. Goold, 16 vols. (London, 1850–53), IX, 510; Edmund Calamy, Preface to *An Account of the Ministers . . . Silenced after the Restoration . . .* , 2nd ed. (London, 1713) sig. A3 recto.

20 This is the argument of Stephen Zwicker's *Dryden's Political Poetry: The Typology of King and Nation* (Providence, R.I., 1972). If Professor Zwicker is correct, there would seem to be certain parallels between Milton's final position and Dryden's, at least with respect to their late autobiographical *personae*: blind Samson among the Philistines, self-mocking counterpart of the revolutionary who had envisioned his country as an aroused Samson; the disenchanted artist whose *Britannia Rediviva* satirizes his former chauvinism. But the parallels more strongly declare the constant dilution of the metaphor of national election, its entropic running down from the tremendous explosive force that transformed seventeenth-century England. Foxe spoke for the entire nation, Milton for a broad political-economic movement. Dryden's faith, even in his most confident period, rested less on the people than on the institutions of monarchy, in a self-consciously "new age" which was turning against all forms of figuralism, as Dryden himself makes plain. In its strict soteriological meaning, the concept of England's national calling was a short-lived anomaly.

21 Samuel Clarke, *A Generall Martyrologie* . . . (London, 1677), fol. A1 recto.

22 Thomas Prince, *A Chronological History of New-England* . . . (Boston, 1736); Thomas Robbins, Preface to Mather, *Magnalia*, I, 6.

23 Stowe, quoted in Edmund Wilson, *Patriotic Gore: Studies in the Literature of the American Civil War* (New York, 1962), pp. 8–9, 84–85.

24 Timothy Dwight, *A Discourse . . . on the National Fast* (New York, 1812), pp. 42, 54; Thomas Frink, *A King Reigning in Righteousness* . . . (Boston, 1758), pp. 4–7; Abraham Cummings, *A Dissertation on the . . . Millennium* (Boston, 1797), p. 33; John Adams, quoted in Ernest L. Tuveson, *Redeemer Nation: The Idea of America's Millennial Role* (Chicago, 1968), p. 102.

25 Mather, *Things to be Look'd for*, pp. 53, 60; Torrey, *Exhortation*, pp. 12–13, 41; I. Mather, *The Glorious Kingdom*, pp. 78–79; William Hubbard, *The Happiness of a People* . . . (Boston, 1676), p. 91; Richard Mather and William Thompson, *An Heart-Melting Exhortation* . . . (London, 1650), p. 68.

26   Stephen Foster, *Their Solitary Way: The Puritan Social Ethic in the First Century of Settlement in New England* (New Haven, 1971), pp. 44–45. The English Puritan attack on this position is epitomized on one extreme by the leading Separatist, John Robinson, and on the other extreme by the leading national covenant theologian, Edmund Calamy.

27   R. Mather and Thompson, *Heart-Melting Exhortation*, p. 6; John Davenport, *A Sermon Preach'd at the Election* . . . (Cambridge, 1669), p. 16; John Higginson, *The Cause of God and His People in New-England* . . . (Cambridge, Mass., 1663), pp. 18–19; Thomas Thacher, Preface to Shepard, *Eye-Salve*, sig. A2 recto; Danforth, *The Building up of Sion*, in *Bridgewater's Monitor*, p. 28.

28   Lord Saye and Sele, quoted in Larzer Ziff, *Puritanism in America: New Culture in a New World* (New York, 1973), p. 83; Anne Hutchinson, quoted in Perry Miller, *Nature's Nation* (Cambridge, Mass., 1967), p. 62; *The Antinomian Controversy, 1636–1638: A Documentary History*, ed. David D. Hall (Middletown, Conn., 1968), pp. 17–18, 220, 274.

29   John Cotton, *Christ the Fountaine of Life* . . . (London, 1651), p. 126; John Davenport, *A Sermon Preach'd*, p. 15.

30   I. Mather, *Apostasy*, p. 65.

31   Cotton Mather, *The Duty of Children* . . . (Boston, 1703), pp. 61, 22, 26; Increase Mather, *Pray for the Rising Generation* . . . (Cambridge, Mass., 1678), pp. 111, 15; Increase Mather, *The First Principles of New-England* . . . (Cambridge, Mass., 1675), pp. 15, 17, 31–33 (quoting Norton, Cotton, and others); Cotton Mather, *The Fisher-mans Calling* . . . (Boston, 1712), p. 67 (ellipses omitted).

32   Increase Mather, *Dissertation* . . . (Boston, 1708), p. 85; I. Mather, *Discovrse Concerning Apostasy*, pp. 56, 77; Hubbard, *Happiness*, p. 33; Higginson, *Cause of God*, p. 12; Middlekauff, *The Mathers*, p. 138.

33   Cotton Mather, *A Midnight Cry* . . . (Boston, 1692), p. 26; Cotton Mather, *The Present State of New-England* . . . (Boston, 1690), p. 25; Increase Mather, *A Sermon Shewing That* . . . *Wonderful Revolutions* . . . *are Near* . . . (Edinburgh, 1710), p. 13; Cotton Mather, *Blessed Unions* . . . (Boston, 1692), p. 80; Mather, *Things to be Look'd for*, pp. 44–45; Mather, *Serviceable Man*, p. 28; Cotton Mather, *Eleutheria* . . . (London, 1698), p. 3. The threat of eternal punishment for opposing the theocracy deserves emphasis; it is a remarkable extension of early New England soteriology, and a persistent theme of the jeremiads. Thus, to select two examples out of many, Samuel Wakeman promised his Connecticut election-sermon audience that their efforts on the colony's behalf would bring "not only God's gracious presence with you in this world, but your everlasting enjoyment of him in that other world" (*Sound Repentance* . . . [Hartford, 1685], p. 42); and Increase Mather warned "the world [to] beware, of doing any wrong to . . . *New-England*. . . . Wo to that man, whoever he be, upon whom the Prayers of *New-England* shall fall, it will be better for that man that a mill-stone were hanged about his neck, and he thrown into the midst of the Sea" (*An Historical Discourse* . . . [Boston, 1677], p. 19).

34   Luther, quoted in Headley, *Luther's View*, p. 242; Higginson, *Cause of God*, p. 13.

35 Timothy H. Breen, and Stephen Foster, "The Puritans' Greatest Achieve-
    ment: A Study of Social Cohesion in Seventeenth-Century Massachusetts,"
    Journal of American History 60 (1973), 6.
36 For example: Dedication to *Companion for Communicants*, sig. A2 recto; *Wonders
    of the Invisible World*, p. 9; and *Pillar of Gratitude*, pp. 13–14, 27.
37 Higginson, *Cause of God*, p. 13; Mather, *Things to be Look'd for*, pp. 56–57;
    William Stoughton, *New-Englands True Interest* . . . (Cambridge, Mass., 1670),
    p. 17.
38 Mather, *Magnalia*, I, 581, 78, 42–43; Cotton Mather, "The Joyful
    Sound . . . ," in *India Christiana* (Boston, 1721), pp. 3–4. Samuel Sewall
    sometimes called the country *Columbina*.
39 Sewall, "Dedicatory letter," *Phaenomena Quaedam Apocalyptica*, pp. 27, 1–2;
    Cotton Mather, *Psalterium Americanum* . . . (Boston, 1718), p. 39; Mather,
    Magnalia, I, 42; Cotton Mather, *Batteries upon the Kingdom of the Devil* . . .
    (London, 1695), p. 20.
40 Sewall, *Phaenomena Quaedam Apocalyptica*, p. 40, sig. A2 verso. Sewall's reference
    is to Columbus's naming the first island he found in the New World "San
    Salvador," so that Christ might "rejoice on earth as He does in heaven when
    He foresees that so many souls of peoples hitherto lost are to be saved. Let us
    too rejoice," Columbus continues, "for the increase in temporal goods in
    which not only Spain but all Christendom together are to share" (*The
    Columbus Letter of 1493*, ed. Frank E. Robbins [Ann Arbor, 1952], pp. 8, 18).
    The name of "New England" seems to derive from a topological description
    by Captain John Smith: "New England is . . . opposite to Nova Albion in the
    South Sea, discovered by . . . Sir Francis Drake . . . [It] is styled New
    England, being in the same latitude" (quoted in A. L. Rowse, *The Elizabethans
    and America* [New York, 1959], p. 89). I take up the implicit contrast between
    these views and those of the Puritans in chapter 5.
41 William Hooke, *New Englands Teares for Old Englands Feares* . . . (London,
    1641), p. 21; Sir Simonds D'Ewes, *Autobiography and Correspondence*, ed., James
    Orchard Halliwell, 2 vols. (London, 1845), II, 116.
42 Higginson, *Cause of God*, p. 12.
43 Hooker, quoted in Mather, *Magnalia*, I, 341; Thomas Hooker, *The Danger of
    Desertion* . . . (London, 1641), p. 15; Nathaniel Ward, *The Simple Cobler of
    Aggawam in America* (1647), ed. P. M. Zall (Lincoln, Neb., 1969), pp. 5, 77;
    Winthrop, *Winthrop Papers*, II, 91; Winthrop, "Conclusions for the Planta-
    tion," in *Old South Leaflets*, p. 4. Mather's portrayal of Europe in the *Magnalia*
    deserves special comment, since it establishes a pattern which has since
    persisted in the American imagination. Commentators have often pointed out,
    rightly, that he wrote *in part* for an English audience; it is all the more striking,
    then, that following the logic of his vision, he describes the Old World, and
    England specifically, in a figural conflation that combines heathendom, the
    lands of persecution, captivity, and superstition, and the doomed cities of
    corruption—all "ripe for final ruine" (II, 150). At the start of the work, he
    prepares for the "fearful signs of total desolation" (I, 448) by describing
    Anglican persecution as the "bloodiest Minister of Death and hell" (I, 65).

Later, he explains that "Satan wanted a Shibboleth" to destroy the "holy [Puritan] minority" (I, 465–66); that the latter found themselves amidst *"dens of lions, . . . mountains of leopards,"* and "the scalding fires of a *Gehennon* . . . 'where the wicked never . . . cease from troubling' " (I, 263, 511–12); and that they fled a nation imminently to "be abased and brought down to hell," upon "as plain a command of heaven . . . as ever their father Abraham had for leaving the Chaldean territories," or the Israelites for leaving Egypt, or the early Christians for abandoning "the kingdom of Antichrist" (I, 341, 48, 584).

44 Johnson, *Wonder-Working Providence*, pp. 248, 151, 210.

45 Johnson, *Wonder-Working Providence*, pp. 75–79, 66, 154, 51–52, 25, **203**; Joshua Scottow, *A Narrative of . . . Massachusetts . . .* (Boston, 1694), in *Massachusetts Historical Society Collections*, 4th ser. 4 (1858), 287–88, 292. Ellipses deleted.

46 George Herbert, "The Church Militant," ll. 70–73, 235–36, 259–63, in *Works*, ed. F. E. Hutchinson (Oxford, 1941), pp. 216–18.

47 We might further recall in this connection the cloud-capped walls of the American Jerusalem that Mather conjures up to vindicate the trials of Winthrop, "chosen for the Moses who must be the leader of so great an undertaking," since "nothing but a Mosaic spirit could have carried . . . a gentleman of his education . . . [and] fair estate" to America. To select one of many other similar examples, Mather summarizes the accomplishments of Thomas Shepard, the "action" of the *Magnalia*, and the complete history of *"my country,"* by citing Shepard's view of what it means to be a "New-England man": "Look from one end of the heaven unto another, whether the Lord hath assayed to do such a work as this in any nation; to carry out a people of his own, from so flourishing a state, to a wilderness so far distant, for such ends, and for such a work. . . . When we . . . consider [this] . . . we cannot but wonder at our selves that so *many,* and some so *weak* and *tender,* with such *cheerfulness* and constant *resolutions,* against so many *persuasions* of friends, and *discouragements* from the ill report of this country, the *straits, wants,* and *trials* of God's people in it, yet should leave our accommodations and comforts—forsake our dearest relations, parents, brethren, sisters, Christian friends and acquaintances—overlook all the dangers and difficulties of the *vast seas,* the thoughts whereof was a terror to many—and all this, to go into a wilderness. . . . Was this from a stupid *sencelessness,* or a desperate *carelessness,* of what became of us or ours? . . . No, surely. . . . What shall we say of the singular providence of God, bringing . . . his people through so many dangers, as upon eagles' wings . . . ? What shall we say of the work it self of the *kingdom of Christ?* and the form of *commonwealth* erected in . . . this America [?]" (I, 387–88).

48 Samuel Sewall, *Diary . . .* , in *Massachusetts Historical Society Collections*, 5th ser. 5 (1878–82), 58; Sewall, *Phaenomena Quaedam Apocalyptica*, pp. 1–3, 37, 59; Sewall, quoted in Samuel A. Green, "Verses by Chief Justice Sewall," *Massachusetts Historical Society Proceedings*, 2nd ser. 2 (Boston, 1885–86), 42–43. The reference to Rachel is from Jer. 31.

49 Cotton Mather, Dedication to *Right Thoughts in Sad Hours* . . . (Dunstable, 1811), p. iii; Cotton Mather, *Theopolis Americana. An Essay . . . of Better Things to be Yet Seen in the AMERICAN World* (Boston, 1710), p. 43; Mather, quoted in Miller, *The New England Mind*, p. 188, and in Thomas Foxcroft's Preface to Jonathan Dickinson's *The True Scripture-Doctrine* . . . (Boston, 1741), p. ii; Mather, *Midnight Cry*, p. 59; Mather, Dedication to *Theopolis Americana*; Mather, *Wonders*, pp. 36–37, 43–45.

CHAPTER 4

1 Williams, *Complete Writings*, VII, 159; I, 141; III, 250; VI, 278–79; VII, 37.
2 For example, Morton sarcastically describes the 1630 migration as "a more miraculous thing . . . than it was for the Israelites to goe over Iordan Drishod," and the arrival in America as "all the 12. Tribes of new Israell come" to "take full possession" of "the Land of Canaan" (*New England Canaan*, in *Tracts and Other Papers* . . . , ed. Peter Force [Washington, D.C., 1836–1846], II, 108). His reference is to the prophecy in Isa. 11 : 10–16, concerning the establishment of New Jerusalem.
3 Luther, quoted in Frederic W. Farrar, *History of Interpretation* (London, 1886), pp. 327–28, and in Patrides, *Grand Design*, p. 48; Keach, *Tropologia*, I, 232; William Tyndale, *Obediĕnce of a Christen Man* (1528) in *Doctrinal Treatises*, ed. Henry Walter (Cambridge, 1848), p. 304; Richard Sibbes, quoted in Geoffrey F. Nuttall, *The Holy Spirit in Puritan Faith and Experience* (Oxford, 1946), pp. 23–24; William Whitaker, *A Disputation on Holy Scripture* . . . , trans. Rev. William Fitzgerald (Cambridge, 1849), p. 407.
4 Thomas Tilliam, "Upon the First Sight of New-England . . . ," in *The First Century of New England Verse*, ed. Harold S. Jantz (Worcester, Mass., 1944), p. 115; Cotton Mather, *The Call of the Gospel* . . . (Boston, 1686), p. 4; I. Mather, Preface to Torrey, *Exhortation*, sig. A2 recto; Sewall, *Phaenomena Quaedam Apocalyptica*, p. 28.
5 Oakes, *New-England Pleaded With*, p. 20 (my italics); Higginson, *Cause of God*, p. 10; William Hooke, *New Englands Sence* . . . (London, 1645), p. 23; Oakes, *New-England Pleaded With*, p. 21; I. Mather, Preface to Torrey, *Exhortation*, sig. A2 recto. (Ellipses deleted in last three citations.)
6 As the European Reformers adapted the jeremiad from the medieval pulpit, it was a dirge over fallen humanity. The colonial clergy turned the lament into exultation by translating worldliness, and the affliction that justly followed in its wake, as part of the trials of a saintly New England. All of God's people, Calvin stressed, had a *need* for punishment, "lest they should perish with the wicked, . . . lest they should be damned forever." But he hastened to add that such warnings of utter calamity were hyperboles: God needed some ultimate dramatic effect, a special terror-device, to ensure the fulfillment of prophecy. "He was, no doubt, constrained by necessity to speak in this severe way; for the kind of exhortation which He had used availed nothing; and yet God shewed at the same time by His threatening how much He loved the people" (Calvin, *Commentaries on Jeremiah*, I, 87; III, 371, 436–37; IV, 78). Through this

dialectic of fear and love, New England's Jeremiahs transmuted the colonists
they denounced into an emblem of the errant latter-day saint. To return that
saint to his true calling, they elaborated upon the prospect of his total
annihilation. For his encouragement, they lamented that he had so long
frustrated the Lord by resisting grace. For his solace, finally, they emphasized
the *miracula apocalypsis* that awaited him when, in due time, he would be made
to repent.

7   Scottow, *Narrative of Massachusetts*, pp. 281–82, 285–86. Scottow begins by
    denouncing the degeneracy of the times. God is "searching our *Jerusalem*," he
    declares, as each of its inhabitants must search his soul. In the course of the
    examination, singular and plural merge, "legal" disobedience reveals itself as
    "the closest Tills, and Cachotes of a deceitful and desperately wicked heart,"
    and the road to reform changes into *"the way Everlasting."* In effect Scottow
    rescues the social covenant by spiritualizing it into a preparation for salvation.
    As though to emphasize this, he frames his work with a memorial to the
    sainted John Cotton, and recalls how when God chastised the infant
    church-state, then "this halting *Jacob*, upon his [thus] Wrastling with the
    Angel of the *Covenant*, found Grace with him, that his Name was then changed
    into *Israel*" (p. 300). For the present generation, too, the solution lies in the
    very terms of their affliction: "We have cause to weep . . . begging [to] . . .
    be washed in the Blood of the Lamb. . . . [May] this Heavenly Dove sent into
    our hearts, make us groan . . . [as we] wait for the . . . Redemption of our
    Souls and Bodies" (pp. 325–26, 329–30).

8   Mather, *Magnalia*, I, 565; II, 82; I, 46; II, 565, 637; II, 556; I, 447–48; I, 78,
    42. It may be well, in view of my subsequent analysis, to specify Mather's use
    of imagery to attain the effect of federal hagiography. In the previous chapter
    (note 43) I outlined his portrayal of Europe, and of England in particular, as
    the city of doom, from which the saint flees in beginning his *peregrinatio* to the
    heavenly city. The second stage of Mather's narrative details the trials of
    "that unparalleled *undertaking* . . . over the Atlantic" (I, 449), which he
    calls—with pointed reference to the conversion-experience—another "river of
    Lethe" (I, 529). The emigrants undergo a baptism "by fire . . . as well as
    water" (I, 146–47); and the "violent disturbances . . . afflictions . . .
    buffetings and horrible tempests" they encounter (I, 108–09) unmistakably
    echo the metaphorical descriptions of numerous conversion-narratives. The
    echoes multiply in Mather's descriptions of the American "wilderness-condi-
    tion": "The most *crooked way* that ever was gone, even that of Israel's
    peregrination through the wilderness, may be called a *right way* . . . such was
    the *trial of the faith* in these holy men, who followed the call of God into *desarts*
    full of dismal circumstances. . . . When our Lord Jesus Christ underwent his
    humiliation for us . . . he was carried into the wilderness, and there he was
    exposed unto the buffetings and outrages of Azazel. The assaults that Satan
    then and afterwards made on our Lord . . . producing a most horrible
    anguish in his mind, made such a figure in his conflicts for us, that they were

well worthy of a most particular prefiguration. And one thing in the *prefiguration* must be, that the goat for Azazel must be sent into the desart." (I, 50, 52; II, 447).

These and many similar passages indicate that Mather is describing not only a series of individuals but, simultaneously, a tribal initiation ritual of the soul—or more accurately, perhaps, an initiation ritual of the tribal soul. He develops the ritual, as I note later in this chapter, through the metaphor of the garden of God. Finally, Mather's millennialism, though it expresses his expectations of the chiliad, *also* suggests the triumphant termination of the spiritual pilgrimage.

9   Everett Emerson, Introduction to Thomas Hooker, "A . . . Sermon of 1638," in *Resources for American Literary Study*, ed. Everett Emerson, vol. 2 (1972), p. 75; Hooker, "Sermon of 1638," pp. 84, 89; Thomas Hooker, Preface to *A Survey of the Summe of Church-Discipline* . . . (London, 1648), sig. A3 recto.

10 John Norton, *Three Choice and Profitable Sermons* . . . (Cambridge, Mass., 1664), pp. 19, 38; Bulkeley, *The Gospel-Covenant*, pp. 75, 105, 113, 276–78, 295–99, 425–26. It is true that the English Puritans also applied covenantal terms both to the nation and to the believer. Sometimes they went so far as to speak of salvation in their federal exhortations, particularly in their pleas for covenant renewal. Recalling the example of Nehemiah, they asked for a collective repentance that was analogous to personal piety, not only because it recommended contrition and belief, but because of the vocabulary of grace it employed: "Israel," "Temple-work," the "new world" opening before God's "faithful people," "the building up of Zion." But since they were analogies, as we have seen, rather than *figurae*, these phrases carried a double meaning for them. The English Puritans never forgot that their status as Israelites stopped short at the *foedus gratiae*. When they intoned the federal blessings of obedience, they "immediately qualified the proposition" by adding that theirs was a voluntary, legal compact (John F. Wilson, "Studies in Puritan Millenarianism under the Early Stuarts," [Ph.D. diss., Union Theological Seminary 1962], pp. 43, 113). When they claimed Nehemiah for their *exemplum*, they portrayed him as a patriot or a dutiful parliament-man. The Bay theocrats were sometimes compelled by the logic of experience to distinguish between figural and federal calling. But as a rule they assumed that their theocracy closed the gap between the two modes of identity. All those among us, said Samuel Torrey, in a characteristic summons to covenant renewal, "who are not yet savingly in Covenant with God"—who have not yet "actually, personally, and professedly" laid claim to election—have "a duty . . . to take hold upon the Covenant . . . unto the continuation of it, from generation to generation": upon that "eternal Choice . . . depends not only the Salvation of your own Souls, but even the deliverance and salvation of this people" (*Exhortation*, p. 13; *Dying Religion*, p. 41). In general, to see the difference between European Protestant and the New England Way we need simply compare sermon genres, or the use of scriptural imagery, and observe how often the colonial sermons violate traditional distinctions. "What came you into this wilderness to see . . . ?" asked Thomas Shepard in a sermon on grace; "will you now forget the end for which you came [to New England]?"

(*Parable of Ten Virgins*, part I, p. 112). We must "pass through a Wilderness of Miseries," cried Increase Mather, in a political sermon (*Day of Trouble*, p. 3), "e're we can arrive at the heavenly Canaan." The need to carry forward the "Temple-worke in our Hearts" (Danforth, *New Englands Errand*, p. 19) is a main theme of the election-day sermons. Bulkeley ends his great work on the covenant of grace with a recapitulation of the message of Winthrop's *Arbella* lay-sermon: "For our selves here, the people of New-England, we should in a speciall manner labour to shine forth in holiness above other people; . . . wee are as a City set upon an hill, in the open view of all the earth, the eyes of the world are upon us, because we professe our selves to be a people in Covenant" (*Gospel-Covenant*, p. 425).

11   David L. Minter, "By Dens of Lions: Notes on Stylization in Early Puritan Captivity Narratives," *American Literature* 45 (1973), 342–44; Mary Rowlandson, *Narrative of the Captivity* . . . (1682), in *Narratives of the Indian Wars, 1675–1699*, ed. Charles H. Lincoln (New York, 1913), pp. 134, 167.

12   Richard Mather, *Journal* . . . (1635) in *Dorchester Antiquarian and Historical Society Collections*, no. 3 (Boston, 1850), pp. 28–30, 33; John Winthrop, letter to his wife (March 10, 1629/30), in *Winthrop Papers*, II, 219; Johnson, *Wonder-Working Providence*, pp. 243, 62; Edward Johnson (?), "Good News from New-England," in *Seventeenth-Century American Poetry*, ed. Harrison T. Meserole (New York, 1968), pp. 156, 160–61; Increase Mather, *Remarkable Providences* . . . (Boston, 1684), p. 13; Shepard and James Allin, Preface to *Defense of the Answer*, pp. 7–8; Thomas Shepard, *Theses Sabbaticae* . . . , 2 vols. (London, 1649), I, 116; Mather, *Magnalia*, II, 674–75.

13   George A. Starr, *Defoe and Spiritual Autobiography* (Princeton, 1965), p. 40; J. Paul Hunter, *The Reluctant Pilgrim: Defoe's Emblematic Method and Quest for Form in Robinson Crusoe* (Baltimore, 1966), p. 86; Thomas Shepard, *Autobiography*, in *God's Plot: The Paradoxes of Puritan Piety; Being the Autobiography and Journal of Thomas Shepard*, ed. Michael McGiffert (Amherst, 1972), pp. 56, 60; Babette Levy, *Preaching in the First Half Century of New England History* (New York, 1967), p. 105; Hooker, *Application of Redemption*, pp. 160, 321; James Allin, *New-Englands Choicest Blessing* . . . (Boston, 1679), p. 13; Shepard, *The Sincere Convert*, p. 88.

14   Daniel B. Shea, Jr., *Spiritual Autobiography in Early America* (Princeton, 1968), pp. 119–22, 124–25; Roger Clap, *Memoirs*, ed. Thomas Prince, in *Dorchester Antiquarian and Historical Society Collections*, no. 1 (Boston, 1844), pp. 20–21, 17, 27–28, 31, 42; Shea, *Spiritual Autobiography*, p. 125.

15   John Hull, *The Diaries* . . . , in *American Antiquarian Society Transactions and Collections* 3 (1857), pp. 141, 145, 167–69, 171, 197.

16   Daniel Shea has observed that Anne Bradstreet's "Religious Experiences," John Dane's *Declaration*, and Edward Taylor's "Spiritual Relation" reveal "a public ritual inherent in the ecclesiology of the New England Puritan" (*Spiritual Autobiography*, p. 111). In every case, the process by which the private drama becomes public ritual follows the same pattern of inversion. Varieties of the pattern include the apocalypticism of Robert Keayne's "writing-book," the political focus of John Winthrop's journals, the spiritualizations of

Michael Wigglesworth's diaries, and, most amply, the figural strategy by which Increase Mather in his autobiography and Cotton Mather in his diary create themselves emblems of and spokesmen for the colonial errand.

17 Kenneth Silverman, *Colonial American Poetry* (New York, 1968), pp. 122, 127. So, too, Michael Colacurcio has pointed out that Taylor inverts the *sub specie aeternitatis* perspective of *Gods Determinations* in order to offer an epical defense of the New England Way ("Gods Determinations Touching Half-Way Membership: Occasion and Audience in Edward Taylor," *American Literature* 39 [1967–68], 298–314); Karl Keller finds that Taylor's meditative poetry is almost completely dominated by a theocratic concern with preparation ("The Example of Edward Taylor," in *American Puritan Imagination*, pp. 129–30); and Kenneth Requa suggests that Anne Bradstreet uses the conflict between Old England and New to resolve her own conflicting roles as "house-wife and public poet" ("Anne Bradstreet's Poetic Voices," *Early American Literature* 9 [1974], 8–9).

18 Jantz, *First Century*, p. 116 (on Chauncy's elegy to Winthrop); Benjamin Tompson, "New-Englands grand Eclips . . . ," in *First Century*, pp. 158–61; Samuel Sewall, in Samuel A. Green, "Verses by Chief Justice Sewall," *Massachusetts Historical Society Proceedings*, 2nd ser. 2 (1885–86), 42; John Fiske, "Upon the decease of . . . Nathaniel Rogers . . . ," and "Upon the decease of . . . John Cotton . . . ," in *First Century*, pp. 127–28, 121.

19 Benjamin Woodbridge, "Upon the TOMB of . . . Cotton," in *Colonial American Poetry*, p. 133. Woodbridge here fuses *exemplum fidei* with temporal progress ("Moses-Joshua" stands for both), links "Joshua" as *figura Christi* with "AMERICA," and justifies the theocracy ("happy Israel") by association with the glorified John Cotton. The complexity of the technique is remarkable because it is *not* the product of the author's "wit," but a cultural common-place: Simon Bradstreet, for example, uses the same image in his journal (*New England Historical and Genealogical Register* 9 [1855], 46), when recording the death of John Allin of Dedham.

20 Increase Mather, *The Life and Death of . . . Richard Mather* (1670) in *Dorchester Antiquarian and Historical Society Collections*, no. 3 (Boston, 1850), pp. 40, 39, 57; Norton, *Abel being Dead*, pp. 4–5, 7, 15, 17–19, 21, 34–35, 46. The Life of Richard Mather appears in Samuel Clarke, *The Lives of Sundry Eminent Persons . . .* (London, 1683), pp. 126–37; the Life of John Cotton appears in Samuel Clarke, *The Lives of Thirty-Two English Divines . . .* (London, 1677), pp. 217–29.

21 I. Mather, *Life of Richard Mather*, pp. 17, 48, 56–57, 59, 65, 69, 74, 76, 79, 81, 84. The conversion experience occupies only pp. 12–13. One example of the self-consciousness of Increase's technique is his Preface to *Johannes in Eremo*, a group of five Lives incorporated in book III of the *Magnalia*. Increase notes that his son's organizing theme is not John the Baptist but "Eremo," the New World landscape, scene of the mighty deeds of Christ in this closing act of sacred history. Or rather, it is the title as a whole, "Johns in the wilderness," illuminated by the idea of America: the Baptist serves as a christological analogue for the sainthood of each of the divines; his relationship to New

England is soteriological (a progression of wilderness errands); and what links the two functions is God's plan "that here might be seen a specimen of the new heavens and a new earth . . . which shall ere long be seen all the world over" (I, 245–49).

22 Johnson, *Wonder-Working Providence*, pp. 75, 270–71, 203 (ellipses deleted).

23 Cotton Mather, *Diary*, 358; Johnson, *Wonder-Working Providence*, pp. 235, 237.

24 Johnson, *Wonder-Working Providence*, pp. 235, 237, 268, 181, 268; Edward J. Gallagher, "An Overview of Edward Johnson's *Wonder-Working Providence*," *Early American Literature* 5 (1971), 31.

25 Johnson, *Wonder-Working Providence*, pp. 19, 147, 93, 98, 206, 101.

26 Johnson, *Wonder-Working Providence*, pp. 98, 102, 97, 196, 97, 93, 100–01, 147, 172.

27 Mather, *Magnalia*, I, 25. The comparison of history and biography with the drama is of course a standard device of the period (among Puritans as well as others), but Mather's use of it is pervasive, and often a means of fusing the two genres.

28 One reason for Mather's strategy in this respect is historiographical. Ever since Luther's despair over Germany, it had become something of a Reformed commonplace that "a bad generation always seems to follow a good," and Mather's emphasis on continuity amounts to a declaration that New England is impervious to the pitfalls of common providence. Elsewhere, he writes, history proves that "vinegar is the son of wine," and that "the sons of heroes are trespassers" (I, 157). Here, the sons are "the Seed of the blessed of the Lord": they have "happily *succeeded* (yea, and assisted) their *fathers* in the evangelical prophecies"; "the problem . . . 'whether a child may not confer *more* benefits on his father than he has received by him?' . . . hath been bravely answered in the affirmative among us" (II, 66–67, 146, 373; my italics). He supports his contention structurally and thematically by presenting the colony's ecclesiastical development as a peaceful flowering of the principles of the fathers, and by his persistent stress on filial succession.

29 Mather, *Magnalia*, II, 34; I, 326; II, 119, 107, 143; I, 62, 470, 296, 461, 398, 517, 411.

30 I. Mather, *Discovrse Concerning Apostasy*, p. 115; Mather, *Magnalia*, I, 528, 556, 579, 443; II, 115; I, 328, 144. Mather reinforces this connection between colony and colonist by his figural use of names: *not* christologically—in accordance with "the *figura* of the divine name" (Erich Auerbach, *"Figura,"* in *Scenes from the Drama of European Literature* [New York, 1959], p. 29)—but soteriologically, to extol the New England venture. His technique varies from a simplistic double meaning (on names like Stone, Newman, and Oakes) to the use of antonym, etymology, and anagram. The most complex variation is that of biographical parallel, as in "Nehemias Americanus," or (to select another example) "Janus Nov-Anglicanus," the title of his Life of Francis Higginson. Mather begins the biography by unveiling the true "figure" of Janus, as pagan mythographers had unwittingly "confessed" it. They gave "Janus the sir-name of *Pater*," as after the flood, a type of baptism, Noah was *pater omnium*. They made a ship the symbol of Janus, "doubtless with an eye to

the *ark* of Noah," a type of the church. They ascribed a *"double face"* to him "because of the view which he had of the *two* worlds, the *old* and the *new*," a type of the two covenants. Baptism, church, grace: the parallel makes for a generous compliment to any minister; but it is only preliminary to the comprehensive tribute of "Nov-Anglicanus." The real function of Janus-Noah is to place the hero, as saint and congregationalist, in the framework of the American theocracy: "in the reign of this Janus, all the dwellings of men were hedged in with *piety* and *sanctity*, in which tradition the exemplary *righteousness* of Noah seems to have been celebrated. . . . I will now lay before my reader, the story of that worthy man; who, when 'tis considered that he crossed the *sea* with a renowned *colony*, and that having seen an *old world* in Europe, where a flood of iniquity and calamity carried all before it, he also saw a *new world* in America; where he appears the first in a catalogue of heroes, and where he with his people were admitted into the covenant of God; whereupon an hedge of *piety* and *sanctity* continued about *that* people as long as *he* lived; may therefore be called the Noah or Janus of New-England. This was Mr. Francis Higginson" (*Magnalia*, I, 355).

The "flood of iniquity" serves: (a) historically, to underscore the connection between Janus's "hedged in" society and New England's "hedge of piety"; (b) biographically, to evoke the tradition of "exemplary righteousness" (Daniel Featley, *Clavis Mystica* . . . [London, 1636], p. 300; Robert Cawdray, *A Treasurie or Store-House of Similes* [London, 1600], pp. 90 ff.), that links Noah and Higginson; (c) historically and biographically, to recall the "old world" from which Aeneas, "first in a catalogue of heroes," led his "renowned colony" across the sea; (d) christologically, to emblemize the true believer fleeing from the iniquitous old Adam within and around him into the ark of the church (Hilaire de Poitiers, *Traité des Mystères*, ed. Jean-Paul Brisson [Paris, 1967], p. 103; John Weemse, *An Explanation of the Ceremoniall Lawes of Moses* . . . [London, 1632], sig. C3 recto); (e) soteriologically, to outline the progress from Noah's time to the final "fiery flood" (William Guild, *Moses Unveiled* . . . [London, 1658], sig. B7 recto; Obadiah Sedgwick, *An Arke Against A Deluge* . . . [London, 1644], p. 14). From the Church Fathers onwards, "Noah represented a new beginning of the cosmic week"; for Luther, "all the signs . . . had been fulfilled, and in 1530 one only awaited a Noah" (Headley, *Luther's View*, p. 253).

Mather clearly has all of these meanings in mind, and, indeed, he uses all of them explicitly in his *Work Upon the Ark: Meditations Upon the Ark as a Type of the Church* (Boston, 1689), esp. pp. 38, 47. Clearly, too, he unifies these various meanings in the Life of Higginson through the federal image, which he announces, climactically, in the epithet, "the Noah or Janus *of New-England.*" It is in this context we are to understand his allusion to the "flood of iniquity." Its immediate source is Peter's consolation to the elect; but the same text speaks directly to the motives for colonization: "there were false prophets [among the Israelites] . . . even as there shall be false teachers among you, who privily shall bring . . . swift destruction" upon their people (2 Pet. 2 : 1–3). The orthodoxy stressed the parallel with the Anglican "flood of

iniquity" over and again, as does Mather in the *Magnalia*; and characteristically they "opened" the parallel through further scriptural correspondences—
on the rising of the Redeemer "from the west" (Isa. 59 : 19–21); on the
promise of the "new heavens and a new earth" (2 Pet. 2 : 9–3 : 13); on the
flight from the land of captivity (Jer. 46 : 7–27) and the rebuilding of
Jerusalem (Dan. 9 : 25–27), and on "the woman fled into the wilderness,
where she hath a place prepared of God" (Rev. 12 : 6–17). Each of these texts
refers to Noah and the flood, and, as such, each became a major proof-text of
the colonial mission in the course of the century, from John Cotton's polemic
against Roger Williams—in which Cotton compares the settlement with the
construction of the ark, America with the land of promise, and the New
Englanders with the remnant rescued from captivity ("A Reply to . . .
Williams," in Williams, *Complete Writings*, II, 229)—to Joshua Scottow's vision
of the Great Migration as the saints' "Departure into another World"; the
progress of the first planters, after they "marched forth from their Floating
Arks," as "the setting up [of] the King of *Sions* Throne"; and "the true
New-England man" as a representative *"bifronted* Janus *who saw* the closure *of
the Old . . . World"* (*Narrative of Massachusetts*, pp. 287, 290, 292, and
"Dedication"). It seems no more than reasonable for Mather to have assumed
that his readers would understand his parallel in this context: that they would
see Noah-Janus as an image both of personal redemption and of sacred
history, and that their association would center on the meaning of the New
World.

31   Thomas Shepard, Preface to Bulkeley, *Gospel-Covenant*, sig. B2 verso; Mather,
     Magnalia, I, 326, 34 (I have slightly amended Robbins's translation of the
     Latin, a misquotation or altered quote from the *Aeneid* 9. 427).

32   Mather, *Magnalia*, I, 36, 27.

33   To some extent at least, this seems to have been recognized by members of the
     dwindling orthodoxy. Their "Attestations" to the *Magnalia*—acclaiming the
     "wonderful work of God in this *last age* . . . in these *ends of the earth*"—render
     Cotton Mather, anagramatically, as *"Tu tantúm Cohors es"* (Thou art alone a
     host), and predict that "Though here thou writest others' lives, yet thine /
     Shall glow resplendent in each living line" (*Magnalia*, I, 20–21).

34   Claude Lévi-Strauss, *The Savage Mind*, trans. George Weidenfeld (Chicago,
     1966), p. 261; Higginson, Preface to *Magnalia*, I, 16–17. Let me illustrate the
     tradition within which Higginson was writing by citing two fast-day sermons
     (urging covenant-renewal), published twenty years earlier: "though there be
     in special one grand accomplishment of Scripture Prophecies and promises;
     yet there are also many Specimens, beginnings of fulfilling them, partile
     accomplishments . . . wherein those prophecies and promises are fulfilled in
     their measure and degree. And so this Prophesy and promise of Gods pouring
     out his Spirit, however it may have its *full* and *compleat* accomplishments in
     some particular glorious time hereafter: yet there hath been a *glorious*
     accomplishment of it already" (Adams, *The Necessity of Judgment*, p. 35).

     "Concerning the fulfilment of this promise, this (as well as many other
     Scriptures which are prophetical, and promissary) doth admit of a Typical

and Partial, as also an Antitypical, and more plenary Accomplishment. . . . And there will be a more glorious accomplishment of this Prophecy and Promise, when God shall pour out . . . *his Spirit upon the . . . Posterity of his Servants*" (I. Mather, *The Rising Generation*, pp. 6, 71).

CHAPTER 5

1   Probably the major instance is New France, where the religious orders set out to convert Indians and the secular orders transplanted the seigneurial system of feudal France. To be sure, the two orders soon grew interdependent. Civic ordinances after 1650 often seem designed to uphold the religious hierarchy; church edicts often read like theocratic exhortations, urging social reform, decrying dances, plays, luxurious dress, and so on. But unlike the Bay saints, the Quebec colonists never claimed a unique status, either for themselves or for their locale. On the contrary, they bent church and state to enforce an Old World identity. Insofar as they adapted to America—to the extent, that is, that they were not merely missionaries or imperialists but French Canadians —they hoped "to make of a country that is crude, savage, and pagan, the commencements of a province . . . that is refined, happy, and Christian" (Jean-Baptiste Talon, "Memoir" [1673], in *The French Tradition in America*, ed. Yves F. Zoltvany [Columbia, S.C., 1969], p. 100).

2   Richard Hakluyt, Dedication to Pietro Martire d'Anghiera [Peter Martyr], *Decades of the New World . . .* , trans. R. Eden (1595; reprinted Ann Arbor, 1966); Andrew White, *A Declaration . . . of Mary-land . . .* (1633), ed. Lawrence C. Wroth (Baltimore, 1929), pp. 3–4; George Alsop, *Character of . . . Maryland* (London, 1666), p. 9; Robert Beverley, *History . . . of Virginia*, ed. Louis B. Wright (Chapel Hill, N.C., 1947), pp. 297–98, 233.

3   Beverley, *History of Virginia*, pp. 296–97.

4   J. Franklin Jameson, *The History of Historical Writing in America* (Boston, 1891), p. 6; Lewis, "Verses, . . . 1732," quoted in J. A. Leo Lemay, *Men of Letters in Colonial Maryland* (Knoxville, 1972), p. 162; John Hammond, *Leah and Rachel . . .* (London, 1656), p. 6.

5   John L. Stewart, *The Burden of Time: The Fugitives and Agrarians* (Princeton, 1965), pp. 113, 130; John Crowe Ransom, "Reconstructed But Unregenerate," in *I'll Take My Stand: The South and the Agrarian Tradition, By Twelve Southerners*, 2nd ed. (New York, 1962), p. 20.

6   Díaz, quoted in Lewis U. Hanke, *The Spanish Struggle for Justice in the Conquest of America* (Boston, 1965), p. 7.

7   John Phelan, *The Millennial Kingdom of the Franciscans in the New World* (Berkeley, 1970), pp. 11–13, 30, 41–42, 99–107.

8   Las Casas, quoted in Hanke, *Spanish Struggle*, p. 57.

9   Charles V, quoted in F. A. Kirkpatrick, *The Spanish Conquistadores* (Cleveland, 1968), pp. 345, 256; Arthur Scott Aiton, *Antonio de Mendoza, First Viceroy of New Spain* (New York, 1927), pp. 104, vii.

10 Simón Bolívar, *Carta de Jamaica*, reprinted by the Venezualan Ministry of Education (Caracas, 1965), pp. 62–64, 59, 22. The English translation here

234 NOTES TO PAGES 143-145

reads "a species midway . . ."; I have substituted for this the translation in Hugh B. Fox, "The Mainstream and Marginality: The Latin American Identity Crisis," *Western Humanities Review* 22 (1968), 3-4.

11 Octavio Paz, *The Labyrinth of Solitude* (New York, 1961), p. 87. "Our past has not yet become a real past," wrote Leopold Zea, "it is still a present which does not choose to become history"; according to Esteban Echevarría, "We are independent but we are not free; the arms of Spain no longer oppress us, but her traditions still weigh us down" (quoted in Stephen Clissold, *Latin America: A Cultural Outline* [London, 1965], pp. 7, 80).

12 Through all his provisional *personae,* Franklin, as even his first readers saw, assumes an identity representative of the rising nation. The link between the Franklins of the particular moments in his career and the "essential" Franklin is the *exemplum* of corporate selfhood, ascending from dependence to dominance. It was surely to hint at this soteriological *exemplum* that Franklin included in the work Benjamin Vaughan's letter hailing Franklin as the epitome "of *a rising* people" and assuring Franklin that his story would lead to the "bettering of the whole race of man" (*Autobiography,* ed. Leonard W. Larabee et al. [New Haven, 1964], pp. 135, 140). The representative stature of Natty Bumppo seems more problematic. It is as much the creation of Cooper's readers—a reflection of *their* response to the frontier—as it is the product of Cooper's imagination. We have come to see in Natty the positive values of transition as continuity: the promise of the New World landscape embodied in a sacrificial American hero. Cooper himself sometimes supports the Puritan vision of America—most forcefully, I think, in novels outside of the Leatherstocking Tales (e.g., *Wyandotté, The Heidenmauer,* and *Oak Openings*). But on the whole he appears to have adopted the tragic view of "the course of empire" (*Letters and Journals,* ed. James F. Beard, 6 vols. [Cambridge, Mass., 1960–68], V, 398), and in *The Crater,* his most explicit fable of America's development, he denounces the claims of manifest destiny.

13 Mather, "The Joyful Sound," in *India Christiana,* pp. 32–33; "The Great Nation of Futurity," *Democratic Review* 6 (1839), 427.

14 Samuel Sherwood, *The Church's Flight into the Wilderness* . . . (New York, 1776), p. 49; Thomas Bray, *A Dissertation of the Sixth Vial* . . . (Hartford, 1780), pp. 108–09 (ellipses deleted); Sherwood, *Church's Flight,* pp. 22–46 (ellipses deleted); Timothy Dwight, *A Discourse on Some Events* . . . (New Haven, 1801), pp. 39, 43, 54–56 (ellipses deleted); William G. McLoughlin, "Pietism and the American Character," *American Quarterly* 17 (1965), 167; Nathaniel Hawthorne, *Blithedale Romance* in vol. 3 of *Works,* 10 vols., ed. William Charvat et al. (Columbus, Ohio, 1962–74), pp. 62, 117, 25. According to the founder of Brook Farm, George Ripley, the "heavenly Jerusalem was in the clouds, waiting to descend. . . . The [American] disciples were gathered; the iniquity of the world was full; the angel had put the trumpet to his lips" (O. B. Frothingham, *George Ripley* [Boston, 1882], p. 111). The founders of Oneida similarly claimed to be on an errand intermediate "between the present time and the establishment of God's kingdom" (G. W. Noyes, *Religious Experience of John Humphrey Noyes* [New York, 1923], p. 308).

15   Smith, quoted in William D. Andrews, "William Smith and the Rising Glory
      of America," *Early American Literature* 8 (1973), 36–37, 41; David Avery, quoted
      in Alan Heimert, *Religion and the American Mind: From the Great Awakening to the
      Revolution* (Cambridge, Mass., 1966), p. 396; Cummings, *Dissertation on the
      Millennium*, p. 31; Philip Freneau and Hugh Henry Brackenridge, "A Poem,
      On the Rising Glory of America," in *Colonial American Poetry*, pp. 437–43. Some
      wavered in their faith, of course, like Bryant, Cole, and even William Smith.
      But significantly their wavering took an apocalyptic form. America's failure
      could not be considered with Herbert's detached irony, nor with the
      melancholy resignation of Luther and Milton after the failure of national
      election in their countries. Here the prospect of national collapse entailed the
      collapse of a federal covenant that signified the climactic unfolding of God's
      promise to His people. It could only mean a final and total betrayal by (or of)
      mankind.

16   Edward Bellamy, *Looking Backward: 2000–1887*, ed. Robert C. Elliot (Boston,
      1966), pp. 105, 201; Ralph Waldo Emerson, *Journals*, eds. E. W. Emerson and
      W. E. Forbes, 10 vols. (Boston, 1909–1914), II, 4–5, 72, 116; Cox, quoted in
      Tuveson, *Redeemer Nation*, p. 126.

17   David A. Moore, *The Age of Progress: or, A Panorama of Time. In Four Visions*
      (New York, 1856), pp. [3], 13, 45, 47, 58–60, 174–79; Arthur Bird, *Looking
      Forward: A Dream of the United States of the Americas in 1999* (Utica, N.Y., 1899),
      pp. 7–8, 234.

18   Daniel J. Boorstin, *The Genius of American Politics* (Chicago, 1953), p. 19; John
      William Ward, *Andrew Jackson: Symbol for an Age* (New York, 1955), p. 1; Roy
      Harvey Pearce, *Historicism Once More: Problems and Occasions for the American
      Scholar* (Princeton, 1969), pp. 166–67; Marshall W. Fishwick, *American Heroes:
      Myth and Reality* (Washington, D.C., 1954), p. 64; William Burlie Brown, *The
      People's Choice: The Presidential Image in the Campaign Biography* (Baton Rouge,
      La., 1960), pp. 145, 141; David Levin, *History as Romantic Art: Bancroft, Prescott,
      Motley, and Parkman* (Stanford, 1959), pp. 50–51, 62, 71.

19   Morris Golden, *The Self Observed: Swift, Johnson, and Wordsworth* (Baltimore,
      1972); Masao Miyoshi, *The Divided Self: A Perspective on the Literature of the
      Victorians* (New York, 1969). In discussing the evolution of novelistic character
      ("Penetration and Impenetrability in *Clarissa*," in *New Approaches to Eighteenth-
      Century Literature*, ed. Phillip Harth [New York, 1974], pp. 177–206), Leo
      Braudy shows how the work of Richardson and later writers builds upon an
      irreconcilable conflict between one's mundane needs and the spiritual
      imperative to keep one's identity intact—to make one's "true self" invulnera-
      ble to the demands of society, history, even biology. In this conflict, as in the
      auto-machia, self-denial becomes auxiliary to self-assertion, and selflessness
      the *summum bonum* of personal development. Braudy's analysis finds support in
      several comparable studies: on Defoe, for example, whose notion of "radical
      egocentricity" leads to a cleavage between realism and Christian symbolism
      (Homer O. Brown, "The Displaced Self in the Novels of Daniel Defoe,"
      English Literary History 38 [1971], 565–80), and on Rochester, who distinguishes
      his heroes according either to a worldly ideal of the self (aesthetic and ethical)

or to a religious ideal which rejects all social forms as "shams" (Vivian de Sola Pinto, *Enthusiast in Wit* [London, 1962], p. 146). I am aware that these ideals mark a departure from those of the microchristus. My point is merely that the persistent distinction between the individual's innate being and his outward, marketable, role-playing selves—or in modern terms, between the autonomous, "authentic" self and its imprisoning culture (Lionel Trilling, *The Opposing Self: Nine Essays in Criticism* [New York, 1955], pp. ix–xii)—has parallels in the earlier disjunction of christic from social selfhood.

20   Keats, quoted in Henry A. Murray, "Personality and Creative Imagination," in *English Institute Annual, 1942*, ed. Rudolf Kirk (New York, 1943), p. 142; Thomas Carlyle, "Biography," in *Works*, 30 vols. (London, 1896–1907), XXVIII, 52; Joseph W. Reed, Jr., *English Biography in the Early Nineteenth Century: 1801–1838* (New Haven, 1966), pp. 74, 30–31, 17, 67–68.

21   Oscar Handlin, "The History in Men's Lives," *Virginia Quarterly Review* 30 (1954), 534; William A. Bryan, *George Washington in American Literature, 1775–1865* (New York, 1952), p. 234; Reed, *English Biography*, pp. 87, 98–100.

22   Robert P. Hay, "George Washington: American Moses," *American Quarterly* 21 (1969), 784–91 (citing numerous eulogies of Washington); Theodore P. Greene, *America's Heroes: The Changing Models of Success in American Magazines* (New York, 1970), pp. 38–39; Lowell, quoted in Edmund Wilson, *Patriotic Gore: Studies in the Literature of the American Civil War* (New York, 1962), pp. 472–74.

23   Wilson, *Patriotic Gore*, pp. 85–86; Wesley Frank Craven, *The Legend of the Founding Fathers* (New York, 1956), p. 60; Nathaniel Hawthorne, "Main Street," in *Snow Image, and Other Twice Told Tales* (Boston, 1857), p. 85; Kenneth B. Murdock, Introduction to Miller, *Nature's Nation*, p. x; Michael D. Bell, *Hawthorne and the Historical Romance of New England* (Princeton, 1971), pp. 87, 21. Without discounting Hawthorne's ironic distance from the authorial *persona* in such statements, it seems safe to say that to some extent they express his own beliefs, among them his belief in the continuity between the Puritan errand and the Revolution.

24   Emerson, quoted in Edward Emerson's notes to Ralph Waldo Emerson, *Complete Works*, ed. E. W. Emerson, 12 vols. (Boston, 1903–04), XI, 614; Walt Whitman, *Specimen Days*, ed. David R. Godine (Boston, 1971), p. 90; William Gilpin, *The Central Gold Region*, in *The American Landscape, A Critical Anthology of Prose and Poetry*, ed. John Conron (New York, 1973), pp. 372, 377; Margaret Fuller, *Summer on the Lakes*, in *Writings*, ed. Mason Wade (New York, 1941), p. 22; Thomas Cole, "Essay on American Scenery," *American Monthly Magazine*, n.s. 1 (1836), 12; Elihu G. Holland, "American Scenery," *Essays . . .* (Boston, 1852), p. 30.

25   Miller, *Nature's Nation*, p. 159.

26   Sacvan Bercovitch, "Cotton Mather," in *Major Writers of Early American Literature*, ed. Everett Emerson (Madison, Wisc., 1972), pp. 124–34 (citing Mather); Cotton Mather, "Advertisement," in *Bonifacius: An Essay Upon the Good* (1710), ed. David Levin (Cambridge, Mass., 1966), p. 163.

27   Jonathan Edwards, *Thoughts on the Revival of Religion in New England, 1740*, in

Works, 4 vols. (reprint of Worcester ed., New York, n.d.), III, 314–15; Jonathan Edwards, *Images or Shadows of Divine Things*, ed. Perry Miller (New Haven, 1948), pp. 53–54. Edwards recounts in his *Personal Narrative* how the stirrings of grace prompted him to delight both in a newfound love of nature and in the end-time prophecies. His equivalent of Mather's "Biblia Americana" is the "great work" he projected (according to his letter to the Trustees of the College of New Jersey), called "the *Harmony of the Old and New Testaments*, in three parts. The first, considering the Prophecies . . . showing the . . . correspondence between prediction and events. The second part, considering . . . the agreement of type and antitype. The third and great part, considering . . . Doctrine and precept" (*Works*, I, 569–70).

28 Heimert, *Religion*, pp. 57–58, 144; Charles Chauncy, *Seasonable Thoughts on the State of Religion in New-England* (1743), in *The Great Awakening: Documents Illustrating the Crisis and its Consequences*, ed. Alan Heimert and Perry Miller (New York, 1967), pp. 302–303; Cotton Mather, *The Christian Philosopher* . . . (London, 1721), p. 303; Edwards, *Images*, p. 70; Edwards, Miscellany 479 ("WORK OF REDEMPTION: TYPES"), quoted in Mason I. Lowance, Jr., "Typology and Millennial Eschatology in Early American Writing," ms., p. 241. From this perspective, a useful index to the similarities and differences in Mather's and Edwards's attitude to the New Science, is their figural view of gravity and the telescope.

29 Edwards, *Images*, pp. 104–05, 86, 92, 116; Edwards, *Works*, III, 316; Heimert, *Religion*, p. 236. Roger Williams offers the traditional spiritual sense of the *figura*: "all sabbaths of seven days were figures, types and shadows, and forerunners of the Son of God. . . . The change is made from the remembrance of the first creation, and that (figurative) rest on the seventh day, to the remembrance of the second creation on the first, on which our Lord arose conqueror from the dead" (*Complete Writings*, VI, 361–62). Locke offers the traditional eighteenth-century naturalist view: "in the beginning all the world was America, and more so than it is now" (*Second Treatise of Government*, ed. T. P. Peardon [New York, 1952], p. 29). Edwards represents the continuity of American Puritan hermeneutics: "agreeably to many prophecies of Scripture . . . the most glorious renovation of the world shall originate from the new continent, and the church of God in that respect be from hence. . . . America was discovered about the time of the reformation . . . [as] the introduction of the church's latter day glory. . . . God caused the sun, to go from West to East, when Hezekiah was healed . . . which is often used by the prophet Isaiah, as a type of the . . . latter days" (*Thoughts on the Revival*, in *Works*, III, 314–16).

30 William Hubbard, *The Happiness of a People* . . . (Boston, 1676), p. 61; Edwards, *Works*, III, 316; Heimert, *Religion*, p. 68.

31 Edwards, *Works*, III, 314–16; Edwards, Miscellany 262, quoted in Douglas Ellwood, *The Philosophical Writings of Jonathan Edwards* (New York, 1961), p. 74; Edwards, *Images*, p. 102.

32 Emerson, "Young American," "Divinity School Address," and "Fortune of the Republic," in *Works*, I, 391, 364–70, 150; XI, 537, 540.

33   Bronson Alcott, *Journals*, ed. Odell Shepard (Boston, 1938), p. 112; Alcott, in *Selected Writings of the American Transcendentalists*, ed. George Hochfield (New York, 1966), pp. 252–53; Joel Porte, "The Problem of Emerson," *Harvard English Studies* 4 (1973), 97–98; Emerson, *English Traits*, in *Works*, V, 275.

34   Emerson, *Nature*, in *Works*, I, 25–35. Emerson's philology of nature recalls the Puritan belief, through Milton and Cotton Mather, that Hebrew is "*the most ancient and holy tongue*, . . . the tongue of Adam and of God," the divine original and parent language (Edward Leigh, *Critica Sacra* . . . [London, 1650], sig. A2 recto). For Puritan and Transcendentalist alike, etymology is a form of exegesis, a clue to sacred signs, self-discovery and higher laws. The literal yields the spiritual meaning by linked analogies that are inherent in the divine text. According to Emerson and Thoreau, to elaborate upon nature, stretch or pervert it to suit our fancy, is to debase the soul to the level of the discrete secular self; whereas to follow nature to its (verbal/botanical) "roots" is to show oneself an *exemplum* of faith.

35   Emerson, quoted in Edward Emerson's "Biographical Sketch" to Emerson, *Works*, I, xxviii; Emerson, *Journals*, VIII, 78; Emerson, *Nature*, in *Works*, I, 72; Michael H. Cowan, *City of the West: Emerson, America, and the Urban Metaphor* (New Haven, 1967), p. 101; Emerson, "Editors' Address" to *The Dial*, "History," "Fortune of the Republic," "Resources," "American Civilization," and "The Young American," in *Works*, XI, 392; II, 40; XI, 525–26, 530; VIII, 142; XI, 299; I, 371–75, 386–88. Cowan's commentary on Emerson's recurrent use of these images, especially those of Jerusalem and the wilderness, evokes the ghost of Roger Williams. Inverting "the metaphors traditionally connected with the [soul's] pilgrimage," Cowan explains with a note of wonder, Emerson "was attempting to suggest those elements of the City of God that might be found in America's City of Man" (*City*, p. 107). There is a still clearer echo of Williams in Carlyle, who " shuddered" at the "perilous altitudes" to which Emerson was summoning his countrymen. Carlyle also declared his astonishment at the popularity among "American audiences for such thoughts," considering "this cotton-spinning, dollar-hunting, canting and shrieking, very wretched generation of ours" (cited in John L. Thomas, "Romantic Reform in America, 1815–1865," *American Quarterly* 17 [1965], 672, and in Edward Emerson's "Biographical Sketch" to Emerson, *Works*, I, xxxvii).

36   Emerson, *Nature*, in *Works*, I, 70, 72, 76, 67; Thomas Carlyle, *Sartor Resartus*, ed. Charles Frederick Harrold (New York, 1937), p. 220.

37   Auerbach, *"Figura,"* in *European Literature*, p. 57; Ursula Brumm, *American Thought and Religious Typology* (1963), trans. John Hoaglund (New Brunswick, N.J., 1970), p. 107; John Lynen, *The Design of the Present: Essays on Time and Form in American Literature* (New Haven, 1969), p. 45. Another prominent critical term is "allegorical symbolism." The term is appropriate in the sense that the medieval and Renaissance allegorical poet seeks to reveal "the deeper truths of history," in contrast to the symbolic poet who makes "worlds out of his own brain" (Michael Murrin, *The Veil of Allegory: Some Notes Toward a Theory of Allegorical Rhetoric in the English Renaissance* [Chicago, 1969], pp. 168–69, 184–85).

38 Henry David Thoreau, *Journal*, ed. Bradford Torrey and Francis H. Allen, 14 vols. (Boston, 1949), XII, 389; II, 152; III, 268; XI, 402; II, 29, 229; Henry David Thoreau, "Walking," in *Walden and Other Writings*, ed. Brooks Atkinson (New York, 1950), p. 608. Thoreau admired the early New Englanders Wood and Josselyn, as well as Mather's "rich phrase," in opposition to what he termed Carlyle's artificial naturalism (*Journals*, VIII, 121; I, 336). Emerson notes (*Works*, IX, 479) that for Thoreau "the pond was a small ocean; the Atlantic, a large Walden Pond."

39 Horace Traubel, Foreword to Walt Whitman, *An American Primer*, ed. Horace Traubel (San Francisco, 1970)—my italics; Whitman, *An American Primer*, p. 2, and *Specimen Days*, p. 91; Nathaniel Hawthorne, *The Scarlet Letter*, ed. Harry Levin (Cambridge, Mass., 1961), p. 153.

40 C. S. Lewis, *Allegory of Love: A Study in Medieval Tradition* (New York, 1958), p. 233; Emerson, *Nature*, in *Works*, I, 76, 3.

41 Harold Bloom, *The Anxiety of Influence: A Theory of Poetry* (New York, 1973), pp. 152, 68; Augustine, *De Trinitate*, in *Patrologia Cursus Completus . . . Series Latirae*, ed. J. P. Migne, 221 vols. (1844–80), XLII, 1006; Coleridge, quoted in John O. McCormick, "Emerson's Theory of Human Greatness," *New England Quarterly* 26 (1953), 300–01.

42 Bloom, *Anxiety*, p. 101.

43 Blake, Schelling, and Wordsworth, quoted in M. H. Abrams, *Natural Supernaturalism: Tradition and Revolution in Romantic Literature* (New York, 1973), pp. 256, 284; Emerson, *Journals*, VIII, 251–52; II, 127; Ralph Waldo Emerson, *Journals and Miscellaneous Notebooks*, ed. William H. Gilman and others, 5 vols. (Cambridge, Mass., 1960–65), II, 83; Emerson, "Fortune of the Republic" and "Boston," in *Works*, XI, 536; XII, 199, 188. In this view, as in many others (including his view of American nature), George Bancroft's writings show many parallels with Emerson's.

44 Emerson, *Journals and Notebooks*, II, 72; Emerson, "Boston," in *Works*, XII, 201; Edward Emerson, notes to Emerson, *Works*, I, 437; Emerson, "Fortune of the Republic," "John Brown," "Historical Discourse at Concord," and "Lecture on the Times," in *Works*, XI, 515, 268, 85–86; I, 268–69; Emerson, *Journals*, VI, 52; Ralph Waldo Emerson, *Selections . . .* , ed. Stephen E. Whicher (Boston, 1960), p. 399; Emerson, "Boston," in *Works*, IX, 217; XII, 210.

45 Emerson, "Fortune of the Republic," and "Culture," in *Works*, XI, 535; VI, 145; Ralph Waldo Emerson, "The Genuine Man," in *Young Emerson Speaks: Unpublished Discourses on Many Subjects*, ed. Arthur C. McGiffert, Jr. (Boston, 1938), p. 180; Emerson, *Journals*, III, 185–86; Emerson, *Journals and Notebooks*, IV, 79; Edward Emerson, notes to Emerson, *Works*, I, 451; Pearce, *Historicism*, p. 210; Emerson, "Man the Reformer" and "The Poet," in *Works*, I, 228; III, 38.

46 Emerson, "The Poet," in *Works*, III, 37; Ralph Waldo Emerson, *Letters*, ed. Ralph L. Rusk, 6 vols. (New York, 1939), III, 413; Ralph Waldo Emerson, "Modern Aspects of Literature," in *Early Lectures*, ed. Robert E. Spiller et al. (Cambridge, Mass., 1961–72), I, 381, 383, 385; Emerson, "The Poet," in *Works*, III, 38; Henry B. Parkes, "Emerson," in *Emerson: A Collection of Critical*

Essays, eds. Milton R. Konvitz and Stephen E. Whicher (Englewood Cliffs, N.J., 1962), p. 132; Emerson, quoted in Cowan, *City*, p. 119, and in Loren Baritz, *City on a Hill: A History of Ideas and Myths in America* (New York, 1964), p. 259; Emerson, "The Fugitive Slave Law," "John Brown," and "Greatness," in *Works*, XI, 221, 268; VIII, 320; McCormick, "Emerson's Theory," p. 313; Emerson, "Young American," and "Fortune of the Republic," in *Works*, I, 370; XI, 537–40.

47 Emerson, *Nature* and "The American Scholar," in *Works*, I, 55, 81–82.

48 Lowell and Holmes, quoted in Edward Emerson's notes to Emerson, *Works*, I, 414–16; Emerson, "The American Scholar," in *Works*, I, 110, 114–15.

49 Henry Nash Smith, "Emerson's Problem of Vocation," in *Emerson*, p. 65; William Wordsworth, *The Prelude*, XII. 360–61, ed. E. de Selincourt and Helen Darbishire (Oxford, 1959); Walt Whitman, "Poets to Come," in *Complete Poetry and Selected Prose*, ed. James E. Miller, Jr. (Boston, 1959), p. 13; Emerson, "Uses of Great Men," in *Works*, IV, 34; Thoreau, "Walking," in *Walden and Other Writings*, pp. 608, 612; William Blake, *Jerusalem*, II, 38, in *Poetry and Prose*, ed. Geoffrey Keynes (New York, 1927), p. 620. The tradition behind Thoreau's spiritualization of Walden's "rebirth" goes back to Mather's *Christian Philosopher*—"the *Revival* of [nature] . . . in the *Spring* will carry us to the Faith of our own *Resurrection*" (p. 139)—and Edwards's *Images*, where the sun-rise and the spring often stand as types for the regeneration both of "the church of God and particular souls" (p. 104). The tradition behind the famous final image of *Walden* may be illustrated by two seventeenth-century sermons on the future of New England, one concerning the individual, the other concerning the entire church: "God causes Light to spring after darkness . . . [thus] raising up your spirits and expectations of good days. . . . This light that is promised is gradual, like the Light of Morning that shines more and more unto the perfect day. You must not say that there is no light because it is not noon at first, if it be but the dawning of the day, or the Light of the morning star, you have cause to acknowledge it. . . . It is as a Spring light [which heralds] . . . the rising of the Sun of Righteousness" (Thomas Thacher, *A Fast of Gods Chusing* . . . [Boston, 1678], p. 12).

"There is a day hastening, when it will be unspeakably more [wonderful] than ever yet has been. . . . Christ appear[ed] at the end of the Jewish world . . . *in the end of the world.* . . . [So, now] you may conclude that the Sun will quickly arise upon [us, and] . . . *New Jerusalem* shall come down from Heaven. . . . Christ is wont to appear first as a *Morning Star*, and then as the Sun . . . ; a blessed sign it is that all the glorious things spoken of . . . shall be fulfilled in this very Age" (Increase Mather, *The Morning Star* . . . , appended to *The Righteous Man*, pp. 71, 74–76, 80–81).

It is appropriate that Thoreau's naturalistic example of the process of his rebirth, which precedes his image of the morning star, should come from a New England legend. It is appropriate, too, that the redwood tree of which the legend tells should be made into the table which Melville tells us held his copy of Mather's *Magnalia*—and that "The Song of the Redwood Tree" should be Whitman's most euphoric celebration of the *translatio studii* theme (transmuted according to American tradition, into the movement of redemptive history).

50 Abrams, *Natural Supernaturalism*, pp. 361, 355, 256, 272, 187, 229–30, 52–53 (citing Hölderlin, Schelling, Coleridge, and Winstanley).

51 Emerson, "Divinity School Address," "Character," and "Sovereignty of Ethics," in *Works*, I, 132, 143–46, 149–51; IX, 117, 212. In a sense, too much has been made of Emerson's revolt against Unitarianism. Theologically, he did little more than apply certain tenets of Romanticism to what he rightly contrasted with Calvinism as a "pale, shallow religion" (*Journals*, IX, 408). What makes Emerson's view distinctive is his New World soteriology. *Nature* (1836) complains that Americans are still building on tradition, "the dry bones of the past," rather than on "a religion by revelation to us" (*Works*, I, 3); "The American Scholar" (1837) declares "that the natural philosophy that now is, is only the first gropings of [a] gigantic hand" (*Works*, I, 86). "The Divinity School Address" (1838) may be said to culminate the movement from past to future. Over two hundred years earlier, John Winthrop had invoked Ezekiel's vision of the dry bones to describe the colonists' relation to the coming Son of Man. Between 1836 and 1838, Emerson validated Winthrop's exegesis as an American Scholar of nature discovering the advent of God in the New World scripture. He prepared the Address in the conviction that "Whether or no there be a God, it is certain there will be" (quoted in Edward Emerson's notes to Emerson, *Works*, I, 417–18), so that the American prophet must "overturn, overturn . . . until he whose right it is to reign shall come into his kingdom" (*Journals*, III, 425, quoting Ripley).

52 Carl Woodring, *Politics in English Romantic Poetry* (Cambridge, Mass., 1970), pp. 30, 100, 317–18 (citing Wordsworth and Shelley). Essentially the same pattern applies to German Romantic literature. When Hölderlin's Hyperion (quoted in Abrams, *Natural Supernaturalism*, p. 30) calls out to "holy Nature,"

> Let all be changed from its foundations! Let the
> new world spring from the root of humanity! . . .
> They will come, Nature, thy men. A rejuvenated
> people will make thee young again too . . . ,

the prophecy pertains first and last to rejuvenation of the mind. The writer may have immediate political allegiances, he may even be urging a particular people to freedom, and probably he has humanity at large in view. But his concept of the self makes the reintegrated individual the primary referent, and so allows him to abandon politics, nation, even humanity if necessary, without abandoning his essential faith.

53 Emerson, *Journals*, IV, 241; Emerson, "Boston Hymn," *English Traits*, and "History," in *Works*, IX, 201; V, 286–87; II, 10; Emerson, quoted in Edward Emerson's notes to Emerson, *Works*, VIII, 387.

54 Henry David Thoreau, *A Week on the Concord and Merrimack Rivers* (London, n.d.), p. 289; Thoreau, *Journals*, I, 202; II, 29, 188, 229, 402; IV, 478; XIII, 17–18; XIX, 28; VII, 108–09; Carlyle, *Sartor Resartus*, p. 155; Thoreau, quoted in Edwin Fussell, *Frontier: American Literature and the American West* (Princeton, 1965), p. 180; Thoreau, *Walden*, pp. 187, 185.

55 Nietzsche, quoted in Stephen Donadio, "Emerson and the Christian Imagination," ms., p. 27; George Noël Gordon, Lord Byron, *Manfred*, III. iv. 127–32, in vol. 4 of *Works*, 13 vols., ed. E. H. Coleridge (New York, 1966; reprint of London 1898–1905 edition). The tradition is not, of course, distinctly Protestant. Among the Romantic Antinomians are (for example) the French Catholic poets—e.g., Mallarmé's seer, the martyr for an absolute outside the law, and Baudelaire's dandy, who justifies the abnormal by its aesthetic product.

56 Emerson, quoted in Edward Emerson's notes to *Works*, IX, 620; Emerson, *Journals*, IV, 449; Emerson, "Domestic Life," "Method of Nature," and "Self-Reliance," in *Works*, VII, 119; III, 187–88; II, 74, 59, 80, 59–60, 47. Emerson's reference to William Pitt, first Earl of Chatham, is surely meant to evoke Pitt's impassioned defense of the cause of the American colonists from 1766 through the Revolution.

57 Bell, *Hawthorne*, pp. 170–71; Hawthorne, "Mrs. Hutchinson," in *Works*, ed. George P. Lathrop, 15 vols. (Boston, 1882–96), XII, 217–26; *Enterlude of the Godly Queene Hester* (1560/61), quoted in Murray Roston, *Biblical Drama in England: From the Middle Ages to the Present Day* (Evanston, Ill., 1968), p. 72; Carol no. 194, in *The Early English Carols*, ed. Richard Leighton Green (Oxford, 1935), p. 144; Nicholas Baioun, "Prière à la Vierge," in Paul Meyer, "Notice et Extracts du Ms. 8336 de la Bibliothèque de Sir Thomas Philips," *Romania* 13 (1884), 509. A major source for Hawthorne, it seems probable, was Cotton Mather's *Ornaments for the Daughters of Sion* . . . (Cambridge, Mass., 1692), where Esther appears to instruct the reader that "a Comely Presence, an Handsome Carriage, . . . a Ready Wit . . . [must be] consistent with Vertue, . . . [lest the woman] *Deceive* her self into proud Imaginations, and into an Humour, *Conceited* of her self, or *Contemptuous* of others. . . . The virtuous woman does not *Deceive* Unwary men, *into* those Amours which bewitching looks . . . often betray [them]. . . . She sees *Vanity* in it, which is upon the quickly Withering Roses. . . . [She understands that] tho' a person were all over sparkling with peerless *Pearls*, yet there is a *Favour* and a *Beauty* before which, *No mention shall be made of Pearls*. . . . [Knowing] *Adultery* to be . . . *A Capital Crime*, . . . she affects to be [truly] an *Esther*, that is, *An Hidden One*. But if a foolish and froward Husband will wrong her . . . she will thence make a Devout Reflexion upon her Disloyalty to God; but at the same time very patiently vindicate her *Innocency* to man. . . . An *Esther*, a witty *Esther*, what can't she do with the most haughty Husband in the world?" (pp. 12–13, 36, 72, 74–75).

Hawthorne may also have been aware of the generally prominent role of women in millennial religious movements. There is some indication of this in his portrait of Hilda, the "daughter of the Puritans" who foresakes the Antinomian Miriam and in effect comes to represent the spirit of exodus from a depraved Old World. In any case, the contrast in these terms between Hester and the European tragic lover is unmistakable. A convenient illustration is Andrew Marvell's "The Unfortunate Lover" (in *Poems*, ed. Hugh MacDonald [Cambridge, Mass., 1963], pp. 23, 25):

ALAS, how pleasant are their dayes
With whom the Infant Love yet playes!
Sorted by pairs, they still are seen
By Fountains cool, and Shadows green.
But soon these Flames do lose their light,
Like Meteors of a Summers night:
Nor can they to that Region climb,
To make impression upon Time.
. . . .
This is the only *Banneret*
That ever Love created yet:
Who though, by the Malignant Starrs,
Forced to live in Storms and Warrs;
Yet dying leaves a Perfume here,
And Musick within every Ear:
And he in Story only rules,
In a Field *Sable* a Lover *Gules*.

58 Fussell, *Frontier*, pp. 107–08; Hawthorne, *Scarlet Letter*, p. 247; Hawthorne, "The Grey Champion," in *Works*, ed. Lathrop, I, 31.

59 F. O. Matthiessen, *American Renaissance: Art and Expression in the Age of Emerson and Whitman* (New York, 1941), p. 318; Emerson, *Journals*, V, 111; Geoffrey Hartman, *Beyond Formalism: Literary Essays 1958–1970* (New Haven, 1970), p. 301.

60 Emerson, *Journals and Notebooks*, VII, 200; Emerson, "Montaigne," in *Works*, IV, 183; Emerson, *Journals and Notebooks*, VIII, 10.

61 Emerson, *Journals and Notebooks*, II, 239–42; Emerson, *Journals*, VI, 200; Emerson, "Experience," "Compensation," and "Politics," in *Works*, III, 78; II, 97, 122; III, 216–17; Emerson, *Selections*, p. 209; Emerson, "Experience," in *Works*, III, 75, 72, 43; Emerson, *Journals and Notebooks*, II, 242; Emerson, "Progress of Culture," "Montaigne," and "Literary Ethics," in *Works*, VIII, 233–34; IV, 185; I, 160–61, 166–67.

62 Emerson, *Journals*, quoted in Edward Emerson's notes to Emerson, *Works*, VII, 417; Herman Melville, *Pierre; or, The Ambiguities*, ed. Henry A. Murray (New York, 1949), pp. 37, 8, 482. A later example of this outlook is Henry Adams's *Education*. Some seventy years before that auto-American-biography, George Bancroft had begun what was to become the most influential American history of his time by celebrating America's ascent to the pinnacle of human evolution (and predictably, he had concluded the first volume of *The History of the United States* with a long encomium to "The Place of Puritanism in History"). Like Bancroft and all the other great Romantic historians of the country, Adams had expected that America would "transmute . . . power into higher forms of thought . . . [and] produce . . . a higher variety of the human race. Nothing less than this was necessary for its complete success" (*History of the United States* . . . , ed. Ernest Samuels [Chicago, 1967], p. 184). And short of complete success, American society must be accounted a

complete failure, not only in itself but as an emblem of the entire course of history. The emblem comes to life in his autobiography as the betrayed "ideal American," that chimerical "type and model of what Adams would have liked to be, and of what the American . . . should have been, and was not." What should have been he had deduced from his inheritance, the country's Constitution, and its "pure New England stock." If, as he now felt, "the old Puritan nature [in him] rebelled *against* change" (my italics)—if the Puritans' standards were "better than those of [their] successors"—if, in short, the thing signified was worse than the thing—the logical figural conclusion was that history was spiraling *downward* towards doomsday (*Education*, ed. James Truslow Adams [New York, 1931], pp. 313, 312, 19, 26). The tradition continues through our own time, in such disparate works as Fitzgerald's *Great Gatsby*, Mailer's *Armies of the Night*, and Robert Penn Warren's *Brother to Dragons*.

63   Herman Melville, *Mardi, and A Voyage Thither*, ed. H. Bruce Franklin (New York, 1964), p. 412; Herman Melville, "Hawthorne and His Mosses," in *The Portable Hawthorne*, ed. Malcolm Cowley (New York, 1967), pp. 413, 419–20. *Typee* not only cites Spanish explorers but echoes their works: "enchanted gardens," "regions of gold" in "the primitive and summer garb of Eden," "strange and barbarous" inhabitants (*Portable Melville*, ed. Jay Leyda [New York, 1952], pp. 72, 122, 13–14). These phrases recur in *The Piazza Tales* (especially "The Encantadas") with significant ironic reversals.

64   One example is the controlling metaphor of *White-Jacket*, the ship-of-humanity become the westward-steering ark-of-America. The major Puritan precedent is Mather's concept of the christianographical Great Migration; the major Romantic precedent comes in Emerson's writings: "we drift, like white sail across the wild ocean . . . but from what port did we sail? Who knows? Or to what port are we bound? Who knows! There is no one to tell us . . . Where then [shall we find the answer] but in Ourselves. . . . Our helm is given up to a better guidance than our own; . . . and our little wherry is taken in tow by the ship of the great Admiral which knows the way. . . . In seeing this guidance of events, in seeing this felicity without example that has rested on the Union thus far, I find new confidence for the future. . . . Let us realize that this country, the last to be found, is the great charity of God to the human race" (*Works*, I, 287–88, 543–44).

So, too, Melville queries the direction of the *U.S.S. Neversink*, and criticizes its defections from the guide-lines of the Revolution, in order to announce, as compensation, that "Our Lord High Admiral will yet interpose": "The port we sail from is forever astern . . . yet our final haven was predestinated . . . at Creation. . . . The Future is, in all things, our friend. . . . Let us leave the Past, then, to . . . Europe. But for us, we will have another captain to rule over us—that captain who ever marches at the head of his troop . . . Come [therefore] and lie down under the shade of our ark. . . . The rest of the nations must soon be in our rear. We are sent on . . . to break a new path in the New World that is ours. . . . Long enough have we been sceptics with regard to ourselves, and doubted whether, indeed, the political Messiah had come. But he has come in *us*. . . . And let us always remember that with ourselves, . . . national selfishness is unbounded philanthropy; for we cannot do a good for America but we give alms to the world." (*White-Jacket, or the World in a Man-of-War*, ed. Hennig Cohen [New York, 1967], pp. 399, 149–50, 302).

Of course, Melville could never quite manage what he claimed Emerson did, to pull the veil over the shark's maw of reality. In *White-Jacket* he reminds us that "We have a Sick-Bay for the smitten and helpless, whither we hurry them out of sight. . . . Outwardly, our craft is a lie" (p. 399). In *Mardi*, he derides Vivenza for its pretensions in a world ruled by the "vicissitudes" of common providence: "each [age] thinks its own a novelty. . . . Throughout all eternity, the parts of the past are but parts of the future reversed" (p. 458).

65 Herman Melville, *Pierre*, p. 195; *Israel Potter: His Fifty Years of Exile* (New York, 1855), pp. 175, 72, 122, 13–14; *Clarel: A Poem and Pilgrimage in the Holy Land*, in *Works*, 16 vols. (reprint ed.; New York, 1963), XV, 250. The national exemplars in *Israel Potter* include Ben Franklin, master con-man, "the type and genius of his land"; Ethan Allen, the pseudo-Byronic ladies'-man, whose "western spirit is, or will yet be . . . the true American one"; John Paul Jones, who embodies the country's "boundless ambition," its "reckless, predatory" soul, and with whom "Israel, the American," once "a bondsman in English Egypt," sets sail for "the Promised land" in "the armed ship Ariel." Israel's "autobiographical story," Melville observes, though absent from "the volumes of [Jared] Sparks," has nonetheless received its due from "the Great Biographer: the national commemorator" of *Bunk*er Hill and Potter's Field—of which the biblical Potter's Field, Judas's resting place, may serve "at once [as] a parallel, a type, and a prophecy" (pp. 81, 244, 269, 256, 270, 216, 3–5, 197).

66 Emerson, "Terminus," in *Works*, IX, 251; Thoreau, "Walking," in *Walden and Other Writings*, p. 609; Thoreau, "Walden," copy 1120 of Huntington Library ms. 924; Thoreau, *Walden* (Boston, 1854), title page and p. 52; Whitman, "Song of Myself," in *Complete Poetry*, p. 27; Whitman, quoted in Roland Hagenbüchle, "Whitman's Unfinished Quest for an American Identity," *English Literary History* 40 (1973), 469, 450.

67 Whitman, *Democratic Vistas*, in *Complete Poetry and Selected Prose*, pp. 489, 544; Walt Whitman, "An English and an American Poet" (1856), in *Walt Whitman: The Critical Heritage*, Milton Hindus, ed. (New York, 1971), p. 45; John Burroughs, *Notes on Walt Whitman as Poet and Person* (New York, 1867), p. 32; Whitman, quoted in Pearce, *Historicism*, p. 218; Whitman, unsigned review (1855), in *Whitman*, ed. Hindus, pp. 34–35; Whitman, *Democratic Vistas*, pp. 491, 543, 459–60; Whitman, "Long, Too Long America," and "The Centenarian's Story," in *Complete Poetry*, pp. 223, 214.

68 Indeed, in many respects Whitman's strategy essentially follows that of "The American Scholar" and "Nehemias Americanus." Whitman begins, as do Emerson and Mather, with a survey of past cultures, all converging upon an America destined to embody "the moral political speculations of ages, long, long deferr'd." Like the American Scholar, his projected representative "poet

of the modern" comes from the "birthstock of a New World"; and like Mather, Whitman presents a Pisgah view of the Jerusalem to come, rising from the wilderness below to the promise beyond. Behind the poet, as behind Emerson's scholar and Mather's magistrate, loom the representatives of barbarism and feudalism—Homer, medieval troubadours, Shakespeare—all of them "hereditaments," all "specimens" or figural "models" of America's "unprecedented" achievement, "a new earth and a new man." (*Democratic Vistas*, pp. 458, 456, 474, 477, 461, 487, 513).

69 Emerson, *Journals and Notebooks*, V, 46; Whitman, *Democratic Vistas*, pp. 494, 475–76, 490, 499, 501.

70 I do not mean by this to denigrate Mather's efforts as a literary artist, but to reemphasize my approach to his achievement. Mather himself frequently compares the *Magnalia* to works of art, and, more revealingly, he repeatedly identifies himself as the isolated artist. His "hope in doing this work," he writes, is that he may be another "Orpheus, whose song might draw his disciples from perdition" (II, 116). Understanding, however, that the hope is a futile one, he generally turns for consolation to the nature of the song itself. Mockers dismay him less than they did Virgil when the Roman "read his *Bucolicks* reproached . . . and his *Aeneids* travestied"; like the sculptor Policletus he will proceed in despite of all criticism (I, 34, 31). "Let the . . . impotent cavils nibble at the *statues* which we have erected for our *worthies* . . . , the statues will out-live all their idle nibbles" (I, 603). He recalls the poets of other times who received rewards for their productions: Archimelius, Saleius, Ospian (I, 37)—even the outcast Antomachus Clavius. "Reciting to his assembled auditory from a large volume . . . all left him in the midst of his reading except Plato. 'I will still read on,' said the poet, 'for Plato alone is equal to them all' " (II, 124). Mather's audience contains no consoling Plato: "perhaps not *one* remains to hear *these* words" (I, 125). His "recompense" lies instead in the "prayer and expectation" that, as "David built a House of God in his psalms," so he will build a monument to the New English Jerusalem in his epic church history.

Index